PENGUIN BOOKS
The Other Side of the Dale

'A natural storyteller, he combines the timing of a professional comedian with the palpable warmth and the ability to deliver a message that is much more than just a series of jokes' *The Times Educational Supplement*

'Hilarious and touching' *Daily Mail*

'Gentle and warm, with a wry sense of humour, his style has been rightly compared to James Herriot. You cannot escape his enthusiasm for young people and the importance he places on good teachers' *Yorkshire Post*

'Gervase Phinn has a unique understanding and love of children, and a wonderful gift for storytelling . . . a real star' Esther Rantzen

'Gervase Phinn has become one of Britain's best-loved comic writers. Dubbed the James Herriot of schools, he writes with enormous warmth and wit about his romantic adventures, career struggles, and – above all – the children in the schools he visits, with uncanny ability to charm and embarrass him in equal measure . . . Uproarious and touching by turns, it is perfect Bank Holiday reading' *Daily Mail*

'Gervase Phinn writes warmly and with great wit, about the children and adults he meets in Yorkshire's schools. An enchanting montage of experiences. Colourful, funny, honest' *Express on Sunday*

'Gervase Phinn's memoirs have made him a hero in school staffrooms' *Daily Telegraph*

'Gervase Phinn is a natural storyteller . . . He has a marvellous ear for one-liners and a constant flow of anecdotes about the things children say' *Yorkshire Post*

Gervase Phinn is a teacher, freelance lecturer, author, poet, school inspector, educational consultant and visiting professor of education – but none of these is more important than his family.

For fourteen years he taught in a range of schools, then acted as General Adviser for Language Development in Rotherham before moving on to North Yorkshire, where he spent ten years as a school inspector. He holds five fellowships, honorary doctorates from Hull, Leicester and Sheffield Hallam universities, and is a patron of a number of children's charities and educational organizations.

Gervase lives with his family in Doncaster.

The Other Side of the Dale

GERVASE PHINN

PENGUIN BOOKS

PENGUIN BOOKS

Published by the Penguin Group
Penguin Books Ltd, 80 Strand, London WC2R ORL, England
Penguin Group (USA) Inc., 375 Hudson Street, New York, New York 10014, USA
Penguin Group (Canada), 90 Eglinton Avenue East, Suite 700, Toronto, Ontario, Canada M4P 2Y3
(a division of Pearson Penguin Canada Inc.)
Penguin Ireland, 25 St Stephen's Green, Dublin 2, Ireland (a division of Penguin Books Ltd)
Penguin Group (Australia), 250 Camberwell Road, Camberwell, Victoria 3124, Australia
(a division of Pearson Australia Group Pty Ltd)
Penguin Books India Pvt Ltd, 11 Community Centre, Panchsheel Park, New Delhi – 110 017, India
Penguin Group (NZ), 67 Apollo Drive, Rosedale, North Shore 0632, New Zealand
(a division of Pearson New Zealand Ltd)
Penguin Books (South Africa) (Pty) Ltd, 24 Sturdee Avenue, Rosebank,
Johannesburg 2196, South Africa

Penguin Books Ltd, Registered Offices: 80 Strand, London WC2R ORL, England

www.penguin.com

First published by Michael Joseph 1998
Published in Penguin Books 1999
Reissued in this edition 2010

059

Copyright © Gervase Phinn, 1998
Poems on pages vii and 277 © Gervase Phinn, 1996

The moral right of the author has been asserted

Printed in Great Britain by Clays Ltd, St Ives plc

A CIP catalogue record for this book is available from the British Library

ISBN: 978-0-140-27542-1

www.greenpenguin.co.uk

For Christine
and all other dedicated teachers who take on the most
important duty in society – the education of the young.

Acknowledgements

I am extremely grateful to Cynthia Welbourn, Director of Education, and Edna Sutton, Chief Education Adviser, North Yorkshire County Council, for their support in writing this book. I should like to thank Jenny Dereham, my editor, who has become an exceptionally wise and patient guide, and Esther Rantzen who invited me on to her television show 'Esther' and encouraged me to tell my stories in print.

A small child was splashing poster paint
On a great grey piece of paper.
'Do you paint a picture every week?'
Asked the school inspector.

The small child shook his little head.
'Hardly ever as a rule,
But Miss said we've got to paint today –
There's an important visitor in t'school!'

At long last, after a two-hour search up and down the Dale, along muddy twisting roads, across narrow stone bridges, up dirt tracks, past swirling rivers and dribbling streams, and through countless villages in an increasingly desperate search, I had eventually arrived at my destination. At the sight of the highly-polished brass plate on the door bearing the word BACKWATERSTHWAITE SCHOOL, I heaved a great sigh of relief and felt that sort of pioneering triumph which Christopher Columbus, Captain Cook and Scott of the Antarctic must have felt on arriving at their destinations after their difficult journeys.

I had seen no school sign, no traffic triangle warning of a school and children crossing, no playground, playing field, nothing that would identify the austere building as an educational institution. The tall, gaunt edifice deep in the dark valley looked like any other large, sturdy Yorkshire country house and I had passed it unknowingly several times during my vain attempt to discover the elusive school. Beneath the slate roof, greasy grey and edged with a pale purple lichen, tall leaded windows faced the ever-watchful fields. From the grey and white limestone walls gillyflowers and tiny ferns creviced. A little beck trickled alongside as I made my way to the heavy oak door. At long last I had arrived. I lifted the great grey iron knocker in the shape of a ram's head and let it fall with a heavy echoing thud.

I had arrived at Upperwatersthwaite much earlier in the

afternoon assuming, quite foolishly, that it was somewhere near Backwatersthwaite. As soon as I stepped through the door of the small village post office to ask for directions, all conversation ceased and every eye was directed my way. There were two sturdy, middle-aged women in thick brown woollen headscarves which were tied in enormous knots under their chins, a lean old farmer, clutching his pension book, who plucked the ancient pipe from his mouth at the sight of the stranger, and a young woman who jerked her toddler close to her when I made my entrance. I must have looked singularly out of place in the dark grey suit, formal college tie and white shirt. My black briefcase, with an official looking crest emblazoned on the front, was eyed suspiciously by the large, healthy-looking postmistress. She looked over the counter with a deadpan expression on her round red face. I joined what I took to be the end of the queue but was ushered forward by the pensioner.

'Nay, lad, thee carry on. Tha look as if tha're in an 'urry. We're not in any rush, are we ladies?' His companions, still viewing me like an exhibit in a museum, nodded and moved away from the counter.

'Thank you,' I replied smiling and stepping forward.

'Yes, young man?' asked the postmistress dourly.

'I wonder if you could direct me to Backwatersthwaite?' I asked cheerfully. 'I seem to have got myself well and truly lost.' The countenance of the large woman underwent a rapid transformation. She beamed widely and two great dimples appeared on her round rosy cheeks. She gave a long, audible sigh before she replied.

'Oh, is that all?' she said. 'I thowt for a minute you were here for summat else.' I suppose she had imagined me to be some sort of post office investigator, tax inspector or auditor and, hearing that I was not there to check the books, visibly relaxed. 'Ee, you're miles away from Back-watersthwaite, love,' she chuckled. 'You want t'other side of t'Dale.' Then followed a series of detailed instructions on how to get to Backwatersthwaite, punctuated periodically by the other customers in the post office. The journey, described in seemingly endless detail, involved a veritable expedition that took me via Brigg Rock and Hopton Crags to pass by Woppat's Farm, past the Bull and Heifer Inn at Lowerwatersthwaite, then through Bishopwatersthwaite, Chapelwatersthwaite, and along Stoneybrow Rise, and over Saddleside Edge.

'Then tha' best ask ageean,' the postmistress concluded. Her customers nodded in agreement. I thanked her, looked at my watch and made hastily for the door. 'And tha wants to slow down, love!' she shouted after me. 'It'll still be theer when thy arrives – it's not goin' anyweer.' Her words were accompanied by several grunts from the others.

Having negotiated Brigg Rock and passed by Hopton Crags at great speed with no sight of Woppat's Farm, I whizzed through a couple of small villages and arrived at Chapelwatersthwaite. The hamlet was a cluster of barns and cottages, a tall redbrick primitive Methodist Chapel and one small country inn: The Marrick Arms. In the centre of the village the road forked and I stopped the car at the side of the road for the umpteenth time that day to find my bearings. I cursed myself for forgetting to bring a map with me. I had been told at the office that the school was easy to find: just head down the Dale, follow the signs and you cannot miss it. As I sat there wondering in which direction to go, I noticed I had an observer. Standing in front of the hostelry and leaning on his walking stick, was an extremely old, wrinkled individual with a long gloomy face. He regarded me, as stern and motionless as a judge might observe a condemned prisoner in the dock. I was tempted to ask for further directions but dreaded another long, laborious set of instructions, so I decided on the wider of the two roads – the one named Old Stoneybrow Ridge that twisted north. I smiled genially at the ancient, and raised my hand in greeting. He stared back at me and nodded. The road twisted and turned for half a mile, then narrowed to a single track, then became a dirt track and finally came to a dead end at a gate on which was printed CRABTREE FARM – PRIVATE PROPERTY. I reversed angrily until I could find a gate to turn in, and made my way back to The Marrick Arms. The ancient was still standing and staring impassively. I wound down the car window to ask wearily for directions but before I could say a word he smiled, winked and shouted, 'I thowt tha'd be back!' He then pointed to a road sign partly concealed by the overgrown hedge which read: 'No Through Road'. Controlling my impatience, I asked him for directions.

'Backwatersthwaite!' he snapped as if I had said something blasphemous. 'What's tha' goin' up to Backwatersthwaite fer? There's nowt theer.' I explained that I had an appointment at the school. 'Scoil?' he repeated. 'Scoil! Nay, lad, they closed t'scoil in nineteen fotty!' I assured him that I had an appointment with the Headteacher of the school that very afternoon and that he would be expecting me about now.

The old man regarded me with a grave expression. 'Well I nivver did. They've gone an oppened it up ageean. There must be another family up t'Dale.' He peered up at the cold, grey sky and the scudding clouds. 'So tha' wants Backwatersthwaite, does tha'? Well, it's not a good day to go up theer, I can tell thee that. Not a good day at all.' He sighed. ''Tis bleak and treacherous over Saddleside Edge

4

this time o' year. Them gret, green marshes what border t'road ovver t'tops can be treacherous when t'mist comes down. Drive off t'road and tha'll end up, up to thee neck in peaty slime that'll drag thee to thy death inch by inch. Whole flocks o' sheep have disappeared up theer, tha knaws.' He shook his head and grimaced before adding, 'And t'shepherd were nivver seen ageean neither.' The Prophet of Doom paused and sucked his teeth thoughtfully. 'No, not a good time to go visitin' Backwatersthwaite.'

Hot and flustered and late for my appointment I persisted. 'I really must get there this afternoon so if you could . . .'

'Tha' wants to slow down, young man,' said the farmer. 'Not be in such a rush. Enjoy t'view. It's a grand sight ovver Saddleside Edge when t'mist clears. Backwatersthwaite's been theer since time o' Vikings. It'll still be theer when thee finds it – if tha' finds it! Anyroad, t'Headmaster won't be expecting thee on a day like this.'

I convinced him finally that I fully intended visiting Backwatersthwaite that very afternoon and drew from him a series of detailed instructions on how to get to the school. As I sped off in the direction of his bony finger I glanced in the rear view mirror to see the old man staring after me and shaking his head ruefully.

And so it was that an hour later I was standing outside the gaunt, grey building staring with relief at the highly-polished brass plate on the door bearing the words BACK-WATERSTHWAITE SCHOOL.

I lifted the great grey iron knocker in the shape of a ram's head and let it fall again with an equally heavy echoing thud. I heard slow footsteps and a few seconds later the door was opened by a lean, stooping man with grey frizzy hair like a mass of wire-wool and a most pallid complexion. The figure looked as if he had survived the Electric Chair.

'Yes?'

'Mr Lapping?'

'Yes.'

'I think you were expecting me.'

'Was I?'

'Yes, I wrote you a letter.'

'Did you?'

'Yes.'

'Oh.'

'Do you remember?'

'I might do.'

'I said I would be calling this afternoon.'

'Did you?'

'Yes I did!' I replied in an exasperated voice and getting rather tired of this verbal badinage. 'My name is Phinn.'

'Are you the man who does the guttering repairs?'

'No I am not!' I replied sharply. 'I am the man who does the school inspections.'

'Oh.'

'I'm the newly-appointed County Inspector of Schools for this area.'

'Are you indeed?'

'And I am making a number of initial visits to all the schools in this part of the county. Yours is one of the first schools I have on my list.'

'Is it indeed? I am most flattered.'

'Do you not remember, Mr Lapping? I wrote earlier last week saying I would be calling today?'

The tall figure scratched the growth of frizzy hair, but remained in the doorway, showing no sign of letting me enter the building. 'I do remember receiving a letter now I come to think of it,' he said. 'Official looking, in a brown envelope. Yes, I believe I did receive something of the sort.

Actually I've been so very busy that I have not got round to dealing with all the mail. I'm a teaching headteacher you see and I have to deal with letters and such when I can.' Then he glanced at his watch. 'But you are a little late for visiting, Mr Flynn. The children go home at three thirty and it's getting on for half past four.'

'Yes, I am sorry about the delay. I had some difficulty finding the school.'

'Most people do,' replied the Headteacher, smiling and nodding sagely.

'Never mind,' I shrugged. 'It was you I wished to speak to, Mr Lapping. Perhaps now that I know how to get here, I could arrange a further visit to see the children at work?' He made no move to welcome me inside. 'Do you think I might come in?'

'Yes, yes, of course,' he said with sudden eagerness. 'How very remiss of me, keeping you standing on the doorstep. Do, do come in, Mr Flynn.' I entered a large, bright classroom. Children's paintings, collages and beautifully-written poems covered the walls, while various savage-looking stuffed animals glared down from the shelves.

'We don't get many visitors up here once the summer holidays are over. I must admit I was quite surprised to see you at the door. And as for coming to see the children at work,' he continued amiably, 'that would be very nice, very nice indeed. We always enjoy visitors. Now I feel sure you would enjoy a cup of tea before you head off back down the Dale.'

'Yes, please, thank you,' I replied. 'But I don't intend to leave just yet. I would like to examine the school documentation to put me in the picture before I go.'

'School documentation?' He looked at me quizzically.

'Yes, reading test results, mathematics scores, school

7

prospectus, parents' brochure, curriculum policies, guide-lines and, of course, your School Development Plan.'

'My *what*?' he asked.

'Your School Development Plan. The document which sets out your aims, objectives, targets and forward planning initiatives.'

'I haven't got one.' He gave a wan smile.

'Oh, I see,' I murmured. 'Well, every school should have one.'

'I don't think I'd recognize one if it flew in through the window and that's the truth of it, Mr Flynn.'

'It's Phinn actually,' I said.

'You better tell me about this School Development Plan of yours over this cup of tea I promised to make.'

So we sat in the small schoolroom by a window through which we looked upon great dark hills which rose all around and I outlined what the writing of a School Development Plan involved.

When I had finished the schoolmaster sighed. 'You know, Mr Phinn, I've been a teacher in this school for near on forty years. I came here as a boy, taught all the children's parents and went to school with most of their grandparents. This school is a part of me. I live and breathe it. Look around. Outside is one of the most magnificent views in the world. Inside is a richness and a range and quality of work which speaks for itself. Every child in this school can read and write well, every child knows his or her tables, can paint and dance and sing and they all get on as you'll see on your next visit.' As I looked around me I knew these were no idle boasts. 'I would never leave this place,' he continued. 'When I visit the town I see all the people rushing about, with appointments to keep, no time to stop for a moment, to see the hills rising around them or the colours in the sky.' He paused. 'You town dwellers have a lot to learn about us country folk. It's a different way of life. It took fifty years for the Reformation to reach us up here in the Dale, Mr Phinn. I'll do my best, of course, but I reckon it'll be a while before you get your School Development Plan.'

I returned a month later. The drive along the cold grey roads was more leisurely and thoughtful. I skirted Brigg Rock and Hopton Crags, sheer and black and surrounded by tall ancient trees, through a deserted Chapelwatersthwaite and along Stoneybrow Rise where the banks were peppered with a dusting of hoarfrost, over the grim and silent Saddleside Edge to discover again the small school. It stood grim and secure in the deep grey valley where a wide unhurried river, brown with recent rain, flowed gently beneath the arches of the slender bridge.

The morning I spent with the children was memorable. They sat open-mouthed as their teacher read a story in a soft and captivating voice, they answered questions with enthusiasm and unusual perception, and they wrote the most moving and vivid poetry. Before I left, Daniel, a small nine-year-old with wide, unblinking eyes and hair as thick and bright as the bracken that covered the distant hills, approached me.

'Are thar t'scoil inspector?' he asked, his small face creasing into a serious expression.

'Yes,' I replied, 'I am.'

'Well, can I tell thee summat?'

'Of course.'

'I just wanted to tell you thee he's all reight is Mester Lapping. He's a reight good teacher, tha knaws.' I looked into the innocent eyes and smiled. 'Aren't tha' goin' to write it down in tha' big black book?' he continued. 'It's just that tha' might forget.'

'No,' I replied gently, watching the tall, stooping, rather eccentric figure who moved amongst his pupils with his calm, patient and gentle manner. 'I won't forget.'

County Hall was a large, grey, stone mansion of an edifice built to last. It stood like many a Yorkshire town hall, sturdy and imposing, and dominating the centre of the market town of Fettlesham. Surrounding it were formal gardens with well-tended lawns and neat footpaths. The interior was like a museum, hushed and cool, with long echoey, oak-panelled corridors, high ornate ceilings, marble figures and walls full of gilt-framed portraits of former councillors, mayors, aldermen, leaders of the Council, high sheriffs, lord lieutenants, members of parliament and other dignitaries. It was really quite a daunting place.

'Just be yourself, answer the questions honestly – and remember to smile,' I thought to myself as I waited with the four other candidates in the small anteroom to the Council Chamber. It was the good, sound, sensible advice I always gave to my students when, the term before they left school, I helped them to prepare for their job or college interviews. 'And if I'm not successful,' I thought, 'well, it's not the end of the world, is it? I enjoy my present job and have done pretty well to get a senior master's post in a large and flourishing comprehensive school before the age of thirty. In a few more years I could very well be a headteacher with all the challenges and demands that would bring.' But I was not convincing myself. I really wanted this job. The post of County Inspector of Schools with the responsibility for organizing courses, running workshops, working in the classrooms alongside teachers and students, meeting governors and parents, advising, influencing, encouraging and challenging others in the profession, held infinitely more appeal than the post of headteacher. I was so keen I was becoming increasingly tense and edgy. 'Just be yourself, answer the questions honestly and *smile*,' I reminded myself again but I was too nervous to listen to the small, reassuring voice in my head and fidgeted and fretted, adjusted my tie for the umpteenth time, tapped my fingers on my chin and smiled nervously at the other candidates on interview with me for the post.

I had heard about the position of County Inspector of Schools a couple of months before when I had entered the staffroom of Elmwood Comprehensive School at morning break, arriving in the middle of a lively discussion between Cyril, the Head of the History Department and Harry, the Head of English.

'It's just not you, Harry,' the Head of History had been saying. 'I'm sorry but it's not! For a start you've only taught in a couple of schools, you have no experience of English in primary or special education, you've never taught drama and, quite frankly, you're too old. They'll be looking for one of these sedate young Oxbridge sorts – cut-glass accent and more degrees than a thermometer. I mean, just think about the inspectors we've had in this school. Dry, dusty, poker-faced, mean-minded little men who spend their time watching points and nit-picking. Do you seriously think that sort of work would suit you? It must be an awful job, inspecting schools, sitting at the back of lessons, bored out of your mind, ticking little boxes and writing endless reports. You'll never see your family, you'll have to deal with awkward teachers all the time and you'll be travelling hither and yonder. And you don't even like driving – you're always complaining about the few miles you drive to school. Think of the miles you'd clock up touring the county along those narrow twisting roads in all weather. And what about all those late nights, all those weekends? And I mean, you're not getting any younger. You can hardly be described as "energetic" and "dynamic", now can you? It takes you all your time to get up the stairs in E Block and you need two cups of coffee and a cigarette to face 4C on Friday afternoon. Now be honest, Harry, it's just not the sort of job for you.'

'Well, if you've quite finished, thank you very much, Cyril. I am very appreciative of all your encouragement and support,' the Head of English had replied quite peeved by the advice his colleague had so freely and publicly given. 'With friends like you I don't need enemies. For your information, I merely *mentioned* that the post held some slight interest, that's all. I didn't request a lecture on why I would be singularly unsuitable. You make me sound like some broken-down old carthorse ready for the knackers' yard.'

'What are you two on about?' I had asked.

The Head of History, undaunted by his colleague's out-burst, had continued in a casual voice.

'You asked for an honest opinion, Harry, and that is what I gave. It would not suit me either, if it comes to that.' He had then turned in my direction. 'There's a post in this week's education supplement for a school inspector – English and drama. Harry was considering it and asked for my honest opinion. He is now sulking because I gave my honest opinion. I am nothing if not blunt.'

'I asked for an opinion not a character assassination –' Harry had begun but further discussion was curtailed by the sound of the bell. Both men, still arguing, had headed for the door. When they had gone, I had picked up the education supplement which Harry had left behind, and glanced at the advertisement which had been circled in red biro: 'Wanted for September, a County Inspector of Schools for English and Drama. We are looking to appoint a well-qualified, energetic, experienced and creative honours graduate, with senior management experience in a school or college. He or she would join a well-established, successful and dynamic team, responsible for the advice to, and for the inspection of schools in the North of England.' It seemed to jump off the page. Surely, all inspectors were not 'dry, dusty, poker-faced, mean-minded little men'. I had met some really lively and enthusiastic inspectors and the job is what you made it.

That evening I had thought hard and long about the post and decided to apply. I sent off for details and returned the completed application form within the week. A reply arrived three weeks later inviting me for interview at 9.00 am at County Hall in Fettlesham. So here I was waiting to be called into the Council Chamber to convince the Panel that I was the best candidate for the job. I was reasonably confident that I was well qualified and therefore in with a chance until I met the other four applicants for the post. Three of them seemed infinitely more self-assured and experienced and much better qualified than I. They sat in the anteroom calm and composed, chatting amiably – mostly about themselves.

'I completed my Ph.D. in early literacy problems,' a tall, confident young woman was telling an urbane distinguished-looking man. 'I feel certain I have read one of your books about qualitative and quantitative methods in the teaching of aphasic pupils, when I was undertaking my research into the specific learning difficulties of early years, itinerant inner-city children.'

'Quite possibly,' he replied in a cultured and confident voice, stretching back casually in his chair and staring at the ceiling. 'I've written extensively and lectured widely on the topic of aphasia. My doctorate was in dyslexia.'

'Yes,' added the third candidate, an equally suave and self-confident man in an immaculate blue suit and sporting a carefully trimmed beard. 'I remember you gave the keynote address on that very topic at the university where I lecture. It went down very well, I recall.'

'You are too kind,' drawled the object of the praise. 'I just hope that they are as receptive in the States this summer. I'm out there for a lecture tour, you know.'

The fourth candidate, a small, dark-haired, softly-spoken woman, smiled nervously in my direction. I guess she thought, looking at me, that we had much in common compared to the others. We had arrived at the same time and had spoken briefly as we had made our way along the dark corridor of the anteroom. She was the Headteacher of a large inner-city primary school and clearly loved her job. When she spoke about the children, the challenges, successes and the demands, her dark eyes lit up and her nervousness disappeared. She confided that she was not entirely certain that the post was right for her.

'At which university do you lecture?' asked the self-assured young woman suddenly, looking in my direction.

'I don't lecture,' I replied. 'I'm a schoolteacher.'

'Really?' pronounced the urbane man and his bearded companion in unison. Three sets of eyes stared at me curiously. I felt way out of my league here. Cyril had probably been right – 'cut-glass accents and more degrees than a thermometer'.

'Have you published?' asked the bearded Blue Suit.

'Nothing of any importance,' I replied. 'Just a few poems

and stories for children, and an occasional article for an academic journal.'

'No, I didn't recognize the name,' remarked the expert in dyslexia, staring at his watch. 'I do wish they would get a move on. I really cannot abide waiting about.'

That was the end of any further dialogue for the door opened and a tall, stooping, quietly spoken man entered and introduced himself. 'I am the Chief Education Officer of the county, Dr Brian Gore,' he said. 'I am so pleased you have all been able to attend for interview today.' He shook our hands warmly and chatted for a while, asking us if we had had a good journey and if we needed anything. He then glanced at his watch. 'I know how nerve-racking these interviews can be, but just be yourselves and try to enjoy the day. We have studied your applications thoroughly and have received very fulsome references and feel we have a particularly strong field for this post. The interview will be a pretty informal affair – about half an hour to forty minutes each and we will see candidates in alphabetical order, if you have no objections. The Interview Panel is composed of two councillors, an education officer, two headteacher representatives and myself. We hope to arrive at our decision today so you may wish to wait for the outcome. Alternatively, you may wish to leave after your interviews and I will contact you at home this evening. Now, if there is nothing else, I look forward to seeing each of you in the course of the morning.' He gave a reassuring smile and was gone.

I was the last candidate for interview so had a tedious yet apprehensive two-hour wait before I was called. For the first half hour or so I walked slowly down the long echoey, oak-panelled corridors, going over possible questions in my head. Feeling a tight knot of fear growing in the pit of my stomach, however, I made for the gardens where I could get a breath of fresh air. An old man in an ancient suit, and pushing a barrow-load of hedge clippings before him, smiled as I approached.

'Champion day,' he said.

'Yes, indeed,' I replied. 'Lovely and bright. The gardens look magnificent.'

'Well, I do try my best and you can't do more than that, can you?' he said, chuckling, and resting his barrow for a moment. 'Are you one of the new councillors then?'

'No, no! I'm here for an interview. School inspector's post.'

'School inspector, eh? I shall have to watch my p's and q's, won't I?' he laughed. 'Have you come far?'

'Just from Doncaster.'

'Not a town I know, Doncaster, but my father used to go to the races there. Do they still run the St Leger?'

'Yes, indeed, every year.' For a while we chatted about the weather and the countryside and the crowded roads and other commonplace topics which thankfully took my mind off the dreaded and fast-approaching interview.

'Well, I shall have to get on,' announced the gardener looking at the old chrome fob-watch which he had extracted from his waistcoat. 'I wish you well, young man. It's a lovely part of the country to work in and I hope you come in first and beat the other runners in your own St Leger this morning.'

'That's kind of you,' I replied, 'but having seen the other runners I have a feeling I'm the rank outsider in this particular race.'

'The favourite doesn't always win, just remember that.'

'Well, I shall certainly try my best,' I said smiling, 'and you can't do more than that, can you?'

'You can't, young man, you can't.'

For the next half-hour I walked around Fettlesham. It was a prosperous market town with a long main street full of smart dress shops, one or two expensive jewellers, various craft and antique shops, coffee shops, wine bars and banks. The estate agent's window displayed a selection of large, expensive farmhouses and modern detached 'executive' residences which were way above the price range I could afford.

As I arrived back at the small anteroom, I paused outside the heavy mahogany door for a moment and listened to raised, animated voices, inside: the young woman and the expert on dyslexia were comparing details of their interviews.

'Quite tough questions, I thought,' the urbane individual was saying. 'The vicar's very astute and the old councillor at the end knew his stuff. That Dr Gore's sharp, isn't he? I think I did myself justice, though, all things considered. I knew of all the reports to which they referred and they seemed most impressed with my portfolio of papers and articles.'

'Did they ask you about dyspraxia?' asked the woman. 'I thought it was going to come up. I was pretty well prepared for the question but they never asked anything about –' She immediately stopped talking as I entered. Then she changed the subject with consummate skill and began to talk about her recent research into learning difficulties.

'Not long to wait now,' said the primary school headteacher smiling in my direction. 'The interview wasn't too bad. Those on the panel were very pleasant and there were no trick questions. Actually I quite enjoyed it.'

'I shall be glad when it's over,' I replied quietly.

'I always think the last one in is at such a disadvantage,'

began the expert on dyslexia. 'The panel members are tired and probably quite restless by now, and they've heard answer after answer. I certainly don't envy you having to follow the rest of us.' He smiled condescendingly before adding, 'Still, someone's got to be last, haven't they?'

'Yes, someone's always got to be last,' I replied. The word 'last' seemed to have been mentioned a few too many times for my liking, I thought, just as the bearded candidate came back from his interview. He was somewhat red-faced and breathless.

'Phew, what a grilling,' he sighed heavily, and then turning to me said, 'Last man in!'

The Council Chamber was a magnificent circular room with a high domed roof. Ranks of highly-polished wooden desks and carved benches flanked a large central mahogany table at which was sitting Dr Gore and other members of the Interview Panel. Above their heads great gold letters shone down: 'Labor improbus omnia vincit – with work you achieve everything.'

'Do take a seat Mr Phinn,' said a solid, ruddy-faced individual in a thick tweed suit, 'and we will begin.'

The questions from the Panel members were wide ranging but straightforward enough – about my qualifications, experience and expertise, my views on changes in the education system and recently-published reports. Dr Gore sat listening intently to the answers, gazing fixedly at me with his long fingers steepled before him. When it came to his turn, the questions became quite specific and very probing: 'What are the characteristics of a good school? How can you tell whether a teacher is effective or not? How should reading be taught? Should children be taught the rules of spelling? What are the qualities of a good headteacher? How should a teacher stretch and challenge a gifted pupil? What is the most appropriate education for a child with special educational needs? How do you help the dyslexic child? What do you think are the roles and responsibilities of a school inspector?'

It was this last question which got me into such a tangle. Instead of answering the question directly as I had done with the others, on the spur of the moment I tried to be clever and drew an analogy. It was clearly lost on most of the Panel.

'I think a school inspector is rather like Janus,' I replied.

'Who?' asked the affable-looking cleric who had been smiling passively until this point.

'Janus,' I repeated.

'Jesus?'

'No, Janus the Roman god. He is depicted as looking in different directions at the same time.'

'I don't follow this line of thought,' said the cleric, his brow furrowing. 'Are you saying a school inspector needs eyes in the back of his head?'

'Well, I suppose sometimes he does,' I replied giving him a weak smile, 'but what I really mean is that the role of school inspector is, to my mind, a rather contradictory one.' I stared across at the bewildered faces.

'Janus,' Dr Gore interrupted with a wry smile, 'is the Roman god of doorways after whom January is named – is that not so, Mr Phinn? He is represented as two-faced, looking both forward and backward.'

'So a school inspector should be two-faced?' asked the confused cleric, looking quite alarmed. 'Is that what you are saying, Mr Phinn?'

'No, no,' I stammered. 'I mean he should look in one direction, to the schools and the teachers to help, support and advise, and at the same time he should look to the

Education Committee to act as its monitor of standards and quality in the county schools. In a sense, he is both adviser and inspector rolled into one. What I mean to say is, it is quite a complex and demanding role.'

'Sounds as if he needs to have a split personality,' commented a generously-shaped councillor, chuckling.

'Or hindsight,' remarked another, getting in on the act.

As I returned to the room where the other candidates were waiting, I felt pretty certain that I had trailed in last of the five runners. It had been a dire performance. I had tried to be clever at the last fence and had come a cropper. I had done what I always advised my pupils to do at interviews: been myself, attempted to answer the questions honestly, admitting when I did not know the answer rather than trying to bluff my way through and, at the outset of the interview at least, I had smiled a great deal. But I should not have tried to be clever.

We did not have to wait long for the Panel to reach its decision. Barely twenty minutes had elapsed when the door opened and Dr Gore entered. I felt a sinking feeling in my chest and a tightness in my throat. I had so much wanted this job. I knew I could have made a success of it. The small reassuring voice in my head could be heard again, 'Well, it's not the end of the world, is it?'

'Mr Phinn,' said Dr Gore quietly, 'could you return to the Council Chamber, please?'

'Me?' I replied, startled.

'If you would be so kind.'

I was walking on clouds as I followed Dr Gore back down the long corridor to the interview room.

'We would like to offer you the position of County Inspector of Schools,' said the solid, ruddy-faced individual in the thick tweed suit. I was speechless. 'We liked your answers and thought they were very sensible and honest and to-the-point. We think you'll get on with the children and the teachers and be a real asset to the county. We're a plain-speaking people in this part of the country, Mr Phinn, and we can't be doing with folk who think they are God's own gift to education. No disrespect to some of the other candidates but we don't put people on pedestals in Yorkshire – they nobbut want dustin'.' I was still unable to say a word so surprised was I at being offered the post. 'Well, young man, has the cat got your tongue? Have you got an answer for us or do we take it that your silence is a "no"?'

'Y . . . yes,' I stuttered, 'I mean n . . . no, I mean I would very much like to accept the position,' and I shook the large hand that was extended in my direction heartily.

When I returned to the anteroom after a brief conversation with Dr Gore, all but one of the candidates had departed. The primary school headteacher was waiting to congratulate me and she shook my hand warmly.

'Well done,' she said. 'I am sure they made the right choice. You're a bit of a dark horse, aren't you? You didn't give very much away about yourself. I must say it's a bit of a relief, to be honest, that I wasn't successful. I wasn't too sure whether I wanted the post or whether I could actually do it. I'm sure you will be a great success.'

'Thank you,' I replied, 'that's very kind of you.'

'And it may be that you'll be inspecting my school one of these days,' she added smiling.

As I made my way down the neat gravel path to the car park with a definite jaunty spring in my step, I met the gardener who was wheeling his bicycle towards the front gate, his trouser bottoms neatly encased in shining clips.

'How did you get on?' he asked.

'I got the job,' I replied laughing. 'I actually got the job.'

'I thought you would,' he said. 'I'm a pretty good judge of character. I had my money on you from the start.'

3

'Hello!' I called hesitantly through the open door. There was no reply. 'Hello!' I called again, a little louder. 'Hello! Is there anyone there?' There was still no answer so I popped my head around the door and peered into a small cluttered office.

There were five heavy oak desks with brass-handled drawers, five ancient wooden swivel chairs, five tall grey metal filing cabinets and a wall-length of dark heavy bookcases crammed with books and journals, magazines and files. In the corner a computer hummed away on a small table. There was a half-drunk mug of tea on one desk, a half-eaten biscuit on a plate, a shopping basket, handbag, a woman's scarf and a set of keys. It looked as if someone had left in a hurry. Four of the desks were piled high with papers and folders so I assumed the fifth with just two empty wire 'IN' and 'OUT' trays would be mine and sat on the chair behind it, wondering what to do next. I had written to the Office saying I would be calling in that morning and, since I had received no reply, assumed it would be convenient. However, it was clear that no one seemed to be expecting me. The computer hummed and the clock on the wall ticked and the room looked like a cabin in the *Marie Celeste*. Perhaps they hadn't received my letter. I was just about to do a little exploration when the shrill ringing of the telephone made me jump up from the chair. I waited a few moments before lifting the receiver.

'Hello?' I asked charily.

'Is that free school meals?' The voice was angry and strident.

'Pardon?'

'Free school meals. I want free school meals!'

'You have the wrong department,' I replied.

'I've got this letter saying that my Kimberley can't have free school meals!' I tried to interrupt but to no avail. 'Well, Cherise, Mrs Simmonite's daughter, she's got them. Now, I can't see for the life of me why my Kimberley can't have free school meals when Mrs Simmonite's daughter can. It's just not fair.'

'If I could –'

'Well, do you think it's fair?' There was an expectant pause at the other end of the line.

'Well, it doesn't seem fair on the face of it, but I'm not really in a position to –'

'And don't you tell me it's because Mrs Simmonite's worse off than me because if you tell me that, then how come she can afford double glazing – upstairs *and* down I might add – if she's worse off than me? And how come she flits off on them foreign holidays if she's so badly off as well, because –'

'Hang on!' I snapped. 'I'm sure that –'

'So what I want to know,' the caller continued blithely, quite oblivious to the sharpness in my reply, 'is what are you going to do about it?'

'I'm afraid I can't do anything about it,' I replied.

'As I said, I want to – *What?*' The torrent momentarily faltered. 'Why can't you do anything about it?'

'Because you are through to the wrong department,' I answered when, thankfully, I could finally get a word in.

'Well, why didn't you tell me? Letting me ramble on.'

'I have been attempting to,' I replied, trying to remain calm.

'Don't take that tone with me, young man. I'm only trying to get what's right for my Kimberley.'

'I am sure that you are but I can't help you because I do not deal with free school meals. You need another department.'

'Well, who am I through to then?'

'The Inspectors' Division.'

'I don't want the police! Why did they put me through to the police? I asked for the education! I mean, I'm not made of money, feeding this telephone like an 'ungry piggy bank. I wanted the education –'

'This is the education,' I attempted another explanation, 'but –'

'Well, why did you tell me it was the police?'

'I didn't say it was the police!'

'Yes, you did.'

'Now, look, madam, this is getting us nowhere.'

'That's the first sensible thing I've heard you say, young man!'

'If you would just listen to me for a moment –'

'You said I was through to the inspectors.'

'It's the inspectorate, the *education* inspectorate.' This was getting out of hand.

'And you don't deal with free school meals?'

'No, I don't deal with free school meals,' I sighed. 'I deal with school inspections!'

'Well, who does then?'

'What?'

'Deal with free school meals?'

'I don't know. I'm new.'

'Oh, isn't that just typical.' The verbal badminton ceased

for a moment and the caller's voice took on a slow and sarcastic tone. 'Typical that is! Nobody ever knows. Everybody's new. Just passed on from pillow to post while my Kimberley has to do without her free school meals.'

'If you would like to leave your name and number –'

'I'm in a telephone box!'

'Well if you could just hold the line for one moment –'

'There's a queue.'

'. . . I will find out who may be able to help you.'

'Huh! Hang about in a drafty telephone booth that smells like a public lavatory while you traipse off to find someone who will probably be about as much help as you. And you're about as useful as a chocolate teapot! My brains aren't made of porridge, you know!'

'Well, if you leave your name and address, I promise that I will –' The telephone went dead. 'Oh dear,' I sighed, 'I hope this is not a flavour of things to come.'

'Mr Phinn?' I turned to find a young woman with bubbly blonde hair, long metal earrings and a bright open smile, framed in the doorway. 'Is it Mr Phinn?'

'That's right,' I replied.

'I'm Julie,' she said. 'The inspectors' clerk. I've been looking all over the office for you. I thought you might have come and gone. I was late because the traffic in Fettlesham was dreadful this morning. Being market day, the roads are a nightmare. You must have come up the back stairs.'

I rose and shook a long, red-nailed hand. 'I'm very pleased to meet you, Julie,' I said. 'I'm sorry, I assumed the entrance was around the side.'

'That's all right. It's a bit of a maze in this building. Anyway, the important thing is that you have found us.' She looked down at her hand and sighed dramatically.

'Gone and snagged a nail. Here, let me move all my things out of the way.' She collected the shopping basket, handbag, scarf and keys and dumped them on a chair, continuing her chatter as she did so. 'I've been working in this office this week. It's got more space than my room down the corridor. Well, I say "room", but it's got about as much space as a cubicle in a ladies' lav. There's no one in the office today except me since it's still the school holidays. The other inspectors are all on leave, I'm afraid, so you won't see them until next week at the beginning of term. Most usually take off the last two weeks of the summer holidays just before the schools start but they'll be back bright-eyed and bushy-tailed next Monday and then you can get to know everybody. The first week of term is pretty quiet on the whole. There's no visits for a few days.' She dug into her handbag, extracted a long nail-file and proceeded to saw away at the broken nail. 'It gives the children a chance to settle in.' Julie waved in the direction of the desks. 'That's when all these mountains of paper are cleared.'

'I see. I just thought I'd spend a few days up here before the school term starts, find some digs, settle in and see if there is anything urgent I need to do or any documents to read.' I turned in the direction of the empty desk. 'But I see there is nothing for me.'

'Oh, but there is,' replied Julie laughing, and pointed with the long nail-file to a large desk in the corner piled high with papers. 'That's your desk over there. The mountain started to grow as soon as everyone heard you'd been appointed. Mrs Young, the last English inspector, used to sit there. She's sunning herself in Spain at this moment, happily retired. She's sent you a postcard from the Costa somewhere-or-other, wishing you all the best, by the way. It's buried beneath that mound of paper.' Before I could reply and say how kind it was of Mrs Young, Julie chattered on blithely. 'Now, let me show you where everyone else sits. Mr Clamp, the creative and visual arts inspector is by the window next to Mr Pritchard who covers mathematics, PE and games. Dr Yeats, he's the Senior Inspector, looks after history, geography and modern foreign languages and that's his large desk in the middle.'

'I see,' I replied, not sure I'd remember any of this.

'Now, if you want to make a start on the paper mountain, I'll make us a cup of tea. I've prepared you a folder with some information about this and that, which you'll find in the top drawer. It has your travel claim forms and engagement sheets which have to be filled in on Fridays so I know where you are during the following week. That's in case I need to contact you urgently. You can leave those for the time being. There's also a full school list, education personnel handbook and your diary – all the things you need. Dr Yeats has organized a programme for the second week to take you around some schools with him and introduce you to various people. He also wants you to join him at some meetings and see how things work. You'll find details of that as well. He's really nice is Dr Yeats. In fact, they all are in this office. Now is that everything? Oh, yes, there's also a message for you from Mrs Savage.' Julie's voice took on a harder edge, her mouth twisted slightly and I saw a sudden glint in her eyes. 'She's Dr Gore's personal assistant. Not a person I warm to, Mrs Savage. I thought it wouldn't be long before Mrs High-and-Mighty got in touch.'

Before I could ask what Mrs Savage might want, Julie headed for the door. 'Well, I'll let you get on with things. Give me a shout if you need anything. My cubby-hole is down the corridor, by the way. I'll be through with the tea in a minute.' Then she was gone.

I looked around the cluttered office in something of a daze wondering where to start. The computer hummed and the clock on the wall ticked. A moment later Julie popped her head back around the door. 'I forgot to say – it's nice having you with us.'

I spent the entire day wading through letters, reports, questionnaires, publishers' catalogues, requests for references, conference papers, county documents, minutes of meetings, agendas and details of teachers' courses. I just did not know where it was going to end.

'And it gets worse,' said Julie bringing me the fourth mug of tea that day.

'I've never seen so much paper in one place in all my life,' I groaned, stretching my arms in the air.

'You haven't seen anything yet! Wait until the inspection reports come in. Piles and piles of paper, reams and reams of records, heaps of files, mounds of mail, stacks of documents. Sometimes I think that you inspectors ought to take saplings around in the boots of your cars.'

'Saplings?'

'You know, little trees – to plant in place of all the trees cut down to produce the tons of paper you go through. Somebody once told Mr Clamp on one of his art courses that every time he spoke a forest fell.' She smiled and continued to chatter on. 'Don't worry, it's not that bad. It's just that a lot of things have piled up over the weeks. It's always like this after the summer holidays. You'll soon have it cleared.'

'Do you think I should give Mrs Savage a ring?' I asked. 'It might be important.'

'If it was that important she'd have been over in person. No, it'll just be to fix a time to see Dr Gore to talk over a few things.' Julie paused and stared at me for a moment before adding, 'I didn't imagine that you'd look as you do. Your name sort of conjures up a very different picture. I imagined you'd be sort of French looking — dark and swarthy with an accent.'

'I'm sorry to disappoint you.' I laughed.

'Mr Clamp thought you would be a huge, red-headed Irishman and Mr Pritchard, a little, shy, bearded person. They had a bet on what you would look like.'

'And who won?' I asked.

'Dr Yeats. He said you would be just an ordinary, pleasant, agreeable chap.'

'Damned with faint praise, eh?'

'Actually, I reckon he'd seen you at the interview and had inside information. Anyway I'm sure you will settle in here. It's a very happy office. If there is anything else, Mr Phinn, anything at all, just ask.'

'You've been really helpful, Julie,' I replied. 'Thank you. I think you must have covered just about everything.'

'Did you find some digs, by the way?'

'Yes, on Richmond Road. I'll stay there until I find a flat to rent. I'm not in any hurry to buy at the moment. I want to look around a bit before buying a place up here.'

'And is there a Mrs Phinn and lots of little Phinns?' she asked.

'No, there's no Mrs Phinn and no little Phinns,' I replied.

'Foot loose and fancy free, eh? "The world's your lobster", as my mother would say. Well, I'll let you get on.' With that, Julie disappeared.

There nearly had been a Mrs Phinn. I had met Carol at the Rotherwood General Hospital when I took a pupil to the casualty department after his collision with a large opponent on the rugby field. I had been helping out teaching games at the time, coaching the under-thirteens. This particular game had been fast and furious and there had been quite a few knocks, grazes, cuts and collisions during the course of the match. The ground had been rock-like that Saturday and, had I been refereeing the match, I would have cancelled the game or, at the very least, abandoned it when the hailstones began to fall like bullets from the sky. Added to the bitter cold of the day, the icy wind and the hail, the opposing team had been much better than ours and arrogant with it and had thrashed us sixty points to nine.

I was not in the best of moods, therefore, as I sat impatiently with 'Little John', as we called him, on an uncomfortable, plastic-covered seat in the casualty department waiting for attention. John was very big for his age: a large, solid, amiable, easy-going boy and rugby was his life. In lessons he was quiet, amenable and slow in his work but when he was on the rugby pitch he transformed into a raging bull. He threw himself unrestrained into the game, metaphorically and literally, and often ended up concussed or cut, bruised or bloody, but always finished the match with a great friendly smile on his wide open face. It was his hard luck that he met an even larger and tougher opponent that Saturday. The hospital was crowded, noisy and smelly, and we were sandwiched between a groaning nosebleed on one side and a garrulous industrial burn on the other. As we waited, John, cradling his suspected broken arm in his lap, and looking around with fascination at the collection of casualties in bandages and splints, on crutches and stretchers, remarked cheerfully, 'It's quite interesting here, sir, isn't it?' Before I could respond, however, a young, bright-eyed female doctor appeared through the mayhem and racket, like some vision in white, and motioned us through to an examination room.

'You men want locking up,' she said in a not-too-serious tone of voice when she had heard it was a rugby accident. 'Big silly boys, the lot of you, chasing a ball up and down a field and ending up with broken bones in the process.'

'Is it broken then, miss?' asked John, with a doleful expression.

'No, I don't think it is, but we'll send you for an X-ray to be on the safe side.' Then she turned to me. 'And who are you?'

'His teacher,' I replied.

That was Carol – Dr Carol Christian. She had long, shoulder-length auburn hair and the most beautiful aquiline face and I fell in love with her on sight.

'She's a bit of all right, that doctor, sir, isn't she?' John remarked as I drove him home.

'Yes, John,' I replied. 'I have to agree with you there, she is.'

I was not too bothered about spending another afternoon in casualty when, a couple of Saturdays later, 'Little John' was carried off the pitch again and we made a return visit to the hospital. This time it was a suspected broken toe. I hoped that the radiant Dr Christian would be on duty and sure enough she was. John's face, like mine, lit up at the sight of her heading in our direction.

'It's that doctor again,' he whispered excitely. 'I wonder if she's married. Shall I ask her if she's married, sir? You could be in with a chance, sir.'

'Do not do anything of the sort,' I managed to splutter out before the doctor reached us. Dr Christian examined the toe, pronounced it definitely broken and then explained that there was nothing else she could do. It was not medical practice to put a plaster cast on a toe. It would mend in its own good time.

'Provided,' she said firmly, 'that you rest it and avoid rugby for a few weeks.' John's disappointment was obvious from the expression which clouded his round face.

'But what will I do without my rugby, miss?' he moaned.

'Couldn't you take up knitting?' she asked flippantly.

'No, miss,' John replied laconically, 'I'm allergic to wool. It brings me out in a terrible rash.' He looked bemused when we both began to laugh. As we left the examination room I turned to the boy.

'Haven't you forgotten to say something to the doctor, John?'

'Forgotten something, sir?' he asked.

'Yes, forgotten to say something to the doctor.' I wanted him to realize himself that he had not thanked the doctor for her time and trouble. Recognition suddenly illuminated his face.

'Oh, yes, sir,' he cried, beaming widely. Then he gave a very theatrical wink. With that he had hobbled back into the examination room and I heard him say brightly, and loudly enough for all those on the plastic-covered seats to hear, 'My teacher thinks you're a bit of all right, doctor.'

I had met Carol again at a charity dinner in aid of the children's hospital and plucked up the courage to ask her out. We suited each other and enjoyed the theatre, music, walking, reading, travelling. But neither of us seemed to want the relationship to get any more serious. We had been going out for a couple of years when new job prospects had come up for both of us at the same time. I was keen to move further north and into the inspectorate, Carol to accept a promotion to a registrar's position in Chester. So – decisions had to be made. Should we get married? If so, who would do the moving? Which one of us would sacrifice job and career? Our relationship had been a strange one in that we were both so busy in our respective careers that we did not see a great deal of each other. Carol frequently only had one night off a week from the hospital and I was usually occupied at weekends either playing rugby, refereeing, marking books, planning lessons, taking school trips or rehearsing the school play. When we did go to dinner parties together they were not greatly enjoyable occasions. I would meet her colleagues from the hospital and be bored by the constant discussion over the dinner table of ailments and operations, hospital politics and difficult patients. When she met my colleagues from school, Carol was similarly wearied by our endless conversations about the curriculum and examinations, standards of education, and difficult children. I think we both realized that our relationship would never survive the test of time. On our last evening together, we talked about things honestly and without recriminations before each deciding to go our separate ways. So we parted, on very amicable terms, to pursue our own careers.

The shrill ringing of the telephone made me jump and I snatched up the receiver. This would be the call I was expecting from Mrs Savage.

'Hello?' I said cheerily.

'Is that free school meals?' The voice was angry and strident.

'What?'

'Is that free school meals?'

I cupped my hand over the receiver. 'Julie!' I yelled. 'Julie!'

4

Dr Harold J. Yeats, Senior County Inspector, stood six feet three inches in height. With his great broad shoulders, arched chest, heavy bulldog jaw and large pale eyes set wide apart, he looked more like an all-in wrestler than a school inspector. I found him waiting for me in the office the following Monday morning. I had imagined him to be a diminutive, academic, retiring man so it came as something of a surprise to be greeted by this giant with the great tombstone teeth and hands the size of spades. He smiled warmly and shook my hand vigorously.

'Welcome, welcome!' he cried. 'I must say when I saw the name Gervase Phinn on your application form, I imagined a rather lean, sophisticated, Oscar Wilde-like figure.'

'And Julie told me you thought I would be just an ordinary-looking sort of chap,' I replied, looking up into the large pale eyes.

He roared with laughter. 'Ah, but that was after I had seen you. You see, Gervase, I had the advantage of having you pointed out to me by the Chief Education Officer just after the interview. I went to see him about the outcome and observed you from his room which overlooks the front of the building. You were talking to the gardener at the time, I recall. I had to admit to Dr Gore that it was something of a relief to find that – even with that name – you were just an ordinary, pleasant-looking chap. We could do with an injection of common sense and sanity in the office. Of course, you haven't met the other inspectors yet, have you? Sidney Clamp and David Pritchard are wonderful colleagues to work with, immensely generous and talented individuals, but are, like many clever and creative people, far from the ordinary – as you will find out.' Before I could respond he continued with good humour. 'Now you must tell me all about yourself. Gervase Phinn is such an unusual and literary sort of name, isn't it? I could see a Gervase Phinn in a Dickens or Trollope novel – the darkly-handsome but fiercely-ambitious young politician on his way to the top, or the brooding, calculating cleric who has his eye on the bishop's see. Now that the schools have heard about your appointment via the county newsletter, I should imagine there will be a fair bit of speculation as to what you look like. I know when I was appointed, way back in the Dark Ages, the teachers never imagined that I would look like this.' He smiled widely, showing a strong set of overlapping teeth. 'In fact, most people, when they meet me, don't believe I'm a school inspector so I wouldn't worry too much. In fact, if I had a penny for every time someone says when they meet me, "You don't look like a school inspector", I'd be a millionaire by now.'

Harold spent the morning going through the duties of a school inspector. I had joined a small team of inspectors responsible for different subjects in the curriculum. The main part of the job was to visit schools to check on standards and on the quality of the education and to give advice on how things might be improved. Sometimes the entire team would descend on a school for a week to carry out a full inspection. On other occasions it might be a single or paired visit to examine a subject or aspect. In addition to reporting to the Education Committee on the teaching and learning, accommodation and resources, management and finance, the inspectors had an advisory role which involved running courses, carrying out surveys, speaking at conferences, attending headship interviews, supervising young teachers in their first year of teaching and disseminating information from the Ministry of Education.

'My job this week and the next,' explained Harold cheerfully as we headed for lunch in the County Hall canteen, 'is to help you settle in and get to know the ropes. You'll meet a whole range of colleagues and support staff this week and learn about procedures and so forth. Next week I'll take you with me to some meetings and we'll visit a few schools. Then, dear boy, you are on your own. But if there is anything you need to know, anything at all, do please ask.' I felt as I looked into those large pale eyes that there would be many, many questions I would be asking in the first few weeks. 'And, of course, there's Julie,' he added. 'That young woman should not be underestimated. There is nothing Julie does not know about the workings of the school inspectorate. She's an absolute treasure.'

I must have looked very serious for Harold continued, 'You look rather pensive, Gervase, there's nothing wrong is there?'

'It's just the enormity of the job, Harold,' I said. 'There seems so much to do. I just hope I'm up to it.'

'Of course you're up to it, dear boy, you will fit in wonderfully well and be a great success. I have no doubts, no doubts at all about that.'

I just hope I prove him right, I thought to myself.

The first school we visited on the following Tuesday morning was a small, grey, stone primary school, high on the moors. It was in a folded hollow beneath tall sheltering oak trees and set high above a vast panorama dotted with isolated farms and hillside barns.

'And we get paid for this, Gervase,' sighed Harold with a great in-drawing of breath. 'It's like being on top of the world up here, isn't it? Beautiful, beautiful.'

When we arrived, Harold informed the secretary that he was a school inspector with a colleague and that we were expected. The secretary, a fussy, frail-looking woman with thick round glasses which made her eyes look unusually large and staring, peered up at the towering figure with the great broad shoulders and arched chest, the heavy bulldog jaw and round boxer's nose, with an expression of some incredulity.

'An inspector?' she asked blinking nervously behind the great spherical frames. 'A school inspector, did you say?'

'That is correct,' Harold replied, showing his set of great tombstone teeth. The secretary asked us to wait, and then scurried off down the corridor in search of the Headteacher. Harold explained that it was usual to have a word with the Headteacher at the beginning of any visit.

'She only started at the beginning of last term so I've not actually met her but I've heard very good reports that she has settled in well and is making some necessary changes. After our discussion with her, we'll then look at the policies and other documents, observe some lessons, share our observations and write a joint report.'

Harold was holding forth about good primary education when the Headteacher, a tall woman with a round red face and tiny, very dark eyes appeared. She was closely followed by the secretary. As they came closer, I noticed the dubious looks on both their faces.

'I wonder if I might see some means of identification?'

began the Headteacher, gazing fixedly up at Harold. 'You can't be too sure these days,' she said. 'I mean, you could be anybody!'

'Anybody!' echoed the secretary, peeping apprehensively from behind the taller woman.

Harold gave me a long, lugubrious look before sighing and reaching in his pocket to produce a visiting card.

'Do you see what I mean, Gervase?' he said, as we walked to the car. 'People have a picture in their minds of the typical school inspector, and it's not someone like me.'

The reception at the next school we visited could not have been more different. We were greeted by a beaming caretaker.

'You're from the Education Office, are you?' he asked with a bright and expectant look in the small eyes.

'Yes, yes,' replied Harold. 'From the Education Office. I think the Headteacher is expecting us.'

'Oh, oh, come this way, come this way,' said the overalled figure, dwarfed by Harold's great frame. 'We've *all* been expecting you. It's so good to see you.' The caretaker, poking his head around the school office door, announced with great enthusiasm to the school secretary, 'They're here, Mrs Higginbottom! The men from the Education. They're here! They've arrived!'

The secretary jumped up excitedly. 'Oh, good morning,' she beamed. 'It's so good to see you. The Headteacher will be over the moon.'

We were overwhelmed by such a warm welcome. Harold wore the face of the Prodigal Son.

'It's another recently-appointed headteacher here,' he whispered confidentially. 'The new ones always tend to be very keen for inspectors to visit early on, to offer advice and tell them a little about the county. Our reception at the last school was far from typical.'

'It's so good to see you,' enthused the secretary.

'Well, we're very pleased to be here,' Harold replied.

'I'll just tell the Headteacher you've arrived.' She paused and patted Harold affectionately on the arm. 'I can't tell you how delighted we all are to see you.' The caretaker nodded enthusiastically in agreement. I smiled, Harold beamed and everything seemed right with the world.

The Headteacher, a tall, horsy-faced woman, strode into the room a moment later and greeted Harold with a vigorous handshake.

'At last!' she cried. 'We've all been expecting you. I cannot tell you how pleased we are to see you here! You will have a cup of tea and a biscuit before you start, won't you – that's if you have the time.'

'Yes, yes,' replied Harold, 'that would be very acceptable.'

The Headteacher nodded to the secretary who departed to get the tea. 'It's just that I appreciate that your time is very precious and you may wish to make a start at once. The sooner the better as far as I'm concerned.'

'Well, we're here for the remainder of the afternoon,' replied Harold. 'May I introduce my colleague, Mr Phinn.'

The Headteacher shook my hand. 'I'm very pleased to meet you, Mr Phinn,' she said quickly before returning her attention to Harold. 'Won't it take longer than the afternoon?'

'I shouldn't think so,' replied Harold, smiling. 'It really depends on what we find.'

'Well, I think you'll find quite a lot needs doing,' she said, her words accompanied by grunts of agreement from the caretaker and the secretary who appeared at the door with two cups of tea. 'They are just not working and try as we might we can't get them to work. We've had such a lot of trouble this week.'

'I've tried my best to get them to work but it's no good,' added the caretaker shaking his head. 'They just won't work!'

'This does sound serious,' said Harold lifting the small china cup between large thumb and finger and sipping. 'From the look of the school as we entered, it appeared to be a very bright and welcoming place, and the quality of the children's work on the walls seemed to me to be of a high standard. And you say they just won't work. Why is that?'

'Well, the weather might have had something to do with it, of course. They were frozen solid last winter.'

Harold replaced his cup on the saucer with a tinkle of china. 'Frozen solid?' he repeated. 'They were frozen solid?'

'We thawed them out but they just froze again,' replied the Headteacher. 'Anyway, that's what you are here for, Mr Davies, to tell us why they won't work. And I must say this school will be a lot brighter and more welcoming when you've finished.'

'Yeats,' said Harold.

'I beg your pardon?'

'It's Yeats, Harold Yeats.'

'Aren't you Mr Davies from the Education Office – Premises and Maintenance – to see to the problem of the boys' lavatories?' asked the Headteacher with a rather alarmed look on her face. 'We are going out of our minds with the smell.'

'No, no,' replied Harold. 'I'm Dr Harold Yeats, Senior School Inspector, to see about the curriculum. I wrote saying I would be calling with a colleague.' The Headteacher looked crestfallen. Her face took on the long, gloomy expression of a saint who is approaching certain martyrdom.

The eyes of the school secretary looked pebble-hard behind the heavy frames of her spectacles and the caretaker looked singularly menacing.

The Headteacher cheered up a little when Harold delivered a glowing report at the end of the afternoon and she became positively jaunty and light-headed when he promised to take up the cause of the boys' lavatories back at County Hall, as a matter of urgency.

'You will find in education, Gervase,' he observed as we headed for the car, 'that sometimes lavatories take precedence over learning.'

On the Thursday of that week, Harold asked me to accompany him on a junior school class visit to the local sewage works. 'It appears that we cannot get away from lavatories this week, Gervase,' he said, chuckling. 'The one thing about this job is that you keep on learning. When you finish today you'll be a veritable expert in the process of sanitation.'

Harold then explained that the purpose of the visit out of school was for the children to use the environment as the focus for their work. They would be making notes, asking questions, and later be writing a report – as well as a letter of thanks. 'It can be a most productive and valuable experience for the children,' he said. 'All manner of talk and writing is stimulated by such visits.'

We arranged to meet the teacher with her class at the sewage works at 9.30 am, join them for the tour and observe the follow-up work the children undertook. On the morning of the visit we arrived rather early, met the engineer in charge and waited for the teacher and children at the entrance. The class arrived and the teacher ushered her charges off the bus and, seeing Harold standing near the entrance, asked the children to wait with the tall gentleman at the gates. Harold was immediately drawn into animated conversation with the children.

'What's all that water for?' asked one child. Harold did his best to explain that the water cleansed and purified the waste products.

'Where do those pipes go?' asked another. Harold attempted to explain. Then the questions came fast and furious:

'What do those wheels do?'

'Where does all the sewage come from?'

'What happens to it when it's been treated?'

'How much sewage is there?'

Harold had the enviable ability of seeming to know a great deal about almost any subject, display an amazing knowledge and carry the listener with him. The teacher arrived to find the children in an excited semi-circle around Harold.

'Miss! Miss!' exclaimed one of the children. 'It's fantastic, Miss!' He pointed to Harold. 'The man who runs the sewage works has been telling us all about it!'

Despite his somewhat frightening appearance, Harold was one of the gentlest, most modest and unassuming people it had been my pleasure to meet. During that second intriguing week I watched a real master at work: sensitive, intelligent, good-humoured, one who delighted in the company of children. Even the shyest, most nervous child soon felt confident and easy in his presence.

The final visit that day was to an infant school just outside Fettlesham. Harold said very little in the classrooms but watched somewhat bemused as I hurried from desk to desk – interrogating, commenting, examining, writing, inspecting all I saw. Leaving the school he said to me, 'You know, Gervase, you really enjoy the company of children, I can see that, and they obviously like you but – and I hope you won't mind my saying this – you don't listen to them enough. Give them a bit of breathing space.' He was right. I think, along with many adults, I could be a better listener when it comes to children and have tried hard over the years to follow that early advice.

Harold himself was a wonderful listener. He had a sensitive ear that encouraged even the most reticent child to open up and confide in him. He once related the story about how, when he had started as a school inspector in the early 1960s, he had visited a large infant school in the heart of an inner city. It had been a rather shabby, redbrick building with little displayed on the walls and a strong, musty smell pervading the atmosphere.

'Most of the children come here from very deprived homes,' the severe-looking Headteacher had explained to him. 'Their parents never really talk to them about life. I'm afraid we have to start from scratch, Dr Yeats. Most of the children arrive with a very limited command of the English language.'

Harold had then joined a class of seven-year-olds. In a corner of the classroom there had been a grubby but bright-eyed little boy splashing paint onto a large piece of sugar paper.

'Hullo, what are you doing?' Harold had asked.

'Paintin'!' had come the blunt reply.

'It looks very good.'

'We dunt paint much,' the child had said. 'Only we are today. We've got an important visitor coming.' There had been no thought in the boy's mind that the important visitor might be the gentle giant sitting next to him.

'And what are you painting?' Harold had asked.

'It's a jungle,' had come the reply. 'Prehistoric.'

'What's that creature?'

'Brontosaurus.'

'And that?'

'Triceratops. They 'ad three 'orns on their 'eads, tha' knows. Did tha' know that?'

'Yes.'

'This one's a pterodactyl and over 'ere's a pteranadon. A lot of people don't know t'difference, tha' knows. Do you?'

'Yes.'

'Well, a lot of people don't.'

'What's this one?' Harold had asked pointing to a round, fat, smiling creature.

'Stegosaurus. They had three brains, tha' knows.'

'Really?'

'One in their 'ead, one in their tail and one in their bum. It din't do 'em any good though.' The boy had pointed to a vicious looking monster with spikes along its back and great sharp teeth like tank traps. 'He ate 'em all – tyrannosaurus rex. He were reyt nasty, he was.'

'You know a lot about these creatures,' Harold had said.

'I know.' The little boy had put down his brush. 'I luv 'em. They're great. I draw 'em all t'time.'

'And are there any around today?'

'Course not! They're all dead. They're hextinct.'

'What does that mean?'

'Dead. Wiped aaht.'

'And why do you think that is?' the Inspector had asked.

The little boy had thought for a moment. 'Well, mister,' he had said, 'that's one of life's gret mysteries, in't it?'

On the Friday Harold and I compared notes. 'And do you think you will like this line of work, Gervase?' he asked, staring at me with those large pale eyes.

'I'm sure I will,' I answered. 'I feel a lot more optimistic and confident than I did last week. Thank you for looking after me. It's been so useful and quite fascinating.'

'It's been a pleasure. Well, it's getting late. We must be away. But if there is anything, anything at all I can be of help with, do please ask. Next week you are on your own. You've contacted all the schools we discussed, informing them of your intended visits, have you?'

'Yes. I'm very much looking forward to getting out and about.'

'We'll meet each Friday for the next few weeks, at about this time, to see how things are going. All right?' I nodded. 'And don't be afraid of asking for advice. Goodnight, Gervase. I think you'll fit in really well.'

'Goodnight, Harold, and thank you again,' I replied. I watched the great frame disappear through the door and heard the heavy footfalls as he descended the narrow stairs. I was tired but happy and knew in my heart that this was the job for me. I smiled, thinking of the little boy with the bright eyes and grubby face who Harold had described, and what he had said: 'Well, mister, that's one of life's gret mysteries, in't it?'

I was startled out of my reverie by the shrill ringing of the telephone.

'Hello?' I said cheerily.

'Is that free school meals?'

'I do not believe it!' I said in a hushed voice. 'I just do not believe it!'

'Listen to me, I want free school meals for my daughter, Kimberley Jenkinson. Are you still there? Hello!'

'Harold!' I shouted. 'Harold!'

5

The small, square schoolhouse was enclosed by low, craggy, almost white limestone walls. Beyond lay an expanse of pale and dark greens, cropped close by lazy-looking sheep. Further off the cold, grey fells, thick bracken slopes and long belts of dark woodland stretched to distant heights capped in a blue mist. The colouring of the scene was unforgettable on such a day. I had driven to the school early, along twisting narrow roads, and through the open car window I could feel the warmth of the September sun and catch the tang of leaf and loam and wood smoke. I had passed ancient trees, tranquil rivers, towering fells, great shaggy hills, stark grey outcrops, seas of dusky heather and even the shell of a gaunt castle, and had been filled with a huge sense of awe.

It was Tuesday morning, the third week into my new job and my first visit to Hawksrill School, a tiny primary school deep in the heart of the Yorkshire Dales. Now, after many years as County Inspector and after countless visits to hundreds of schools just like Hawksrill, I still feel the magic and wonder of the Dales that I felt in those very first few weeks.

I stood at the gate to the small school, breathing in the cold, clear morning air and taking in the panorama around me when a small, wide-eyed little girl of about ten with round cheeks and closely-cropped red hair, legs like pestles and a coat slightly too large, joined me. She had that wonderfully fresh rosy complexion of a daughter of the Dales.

'It's a grand day, mester, in't it?'

'It certainly is,' I replied.

'Them's our yows,' she said proudly, pointing to the sheep on the expanse of green below us. "Cross-breed Leicesters. Reight hardy breed, them. We've 'ad a good year. They weather up on t'wolds better than other breeds, tha' knaws.'

'Really?'

'Grandad Braithwaite won t'blue ribbon at t'Fettlesham Show wi' one of them tups. He 'ad a fair good head on him, a reight good straight back, four solid legs, one at each corner, and were near on twenty stone.'

'*Really?*'

I must have sounded astonished because she expanded further. 'Sheep I'm talkin' abaat, not me Grandad Braithwaite!'

I laughed and shook my head. The little girl looked at me for a moment and then tapped me gently on the arm. 'Are tha' comin' in then, mester, or are tha' stoppin' out theer all day admirin' view?'

I followed my little companion into a long room, bright and warm and full of colour, and introduced myself to Mrs Beighton, Headteacher of the school, and to Mrs Brown, her assistant. They were uncannily alike: broad and sturdy and ruddy complexioned with short steely-grey hair and wide, friendly faces. They were both dressed in brightly coloured floral dresses and cardigans and wore beads and matching earrings. As I discovered when I had spent a few years in the county, Mrs Beighton and Mrs Brown were the archetypal Yorkshire women: plain speaking, unflappable, hard working, generous to a fault and with a wry sense of humour. They both greeted me with warm smiles.

'Mr Phinn, I presume,' said the Headteacher. 'How very nice to meet you.'

'How very nice to meet you,' echoed Mrs Brown, 'and so early, too.'

'He is early, isn't he, Mrs Brown?'

'He is, Mrs Beighton.'

I explained that I wished to spend the first part of the morning with the juniors and the remainder with the infants, listening to the children read, looking through their exercise books and asking them a few questions about their work. I would also test them on their number work and spellings before I left.

'A pleasure,' replied the Headteacher.

'A pleasure,' echoed her assistant. 'We always enjoy having visitors here.'

'We do, don't we, Mrs Brown?'

'We do, indeed, Mrs Beighton.'

Mrs Brown and I went into the juniors' classroom, and soon the children started to arrive. They came in chattering excitedly, their keen, happy faces a pleasure to behold. They hung up their coats, changed into their indoor shoes, exchanged reading books and sat talking to each other quietly until Mrs Brown called for their attention. Then all eyes were on their teacher. The register was taken and the school day began.

There were sixteen bright-eyed children ranging between seven and eleven who listened attentively to Mrs Brown as she explained the first task of the day which was concerned with some number work. I sat in the small reading corner and, in the course of the first hour, heard one child after another read to me, first from their own reading book and then from some I had brought. I asked the younger pupils to read to me from *The Tales of Peter Rabbit*, the children's classic by Beatrix Potter. The selection of this book, I found, was singularly unfortunate and I came to appreciate just how shrewd, bluntly honest and witty the Dales child can be.

John, a serious little boy of about seven or eight with a tangled mop of straw-coloured hair, was clearly not very enamoured with the plot. He had arrived at that part of the story when poor Peter Rabbit, to escape the terrifying Mr McGregor who was searching for him in the vegetable garden, had become entangled in the gooseberry net. The frightened little rabbit had given himself up for lost and was shedding big tears. It was the climax to the story and when I had read this part to my little nephew Jamie and my niece Kirsten, their eyes had widened like saucers and their mouths had fallen open in expectation of the capture of the poor little rabbit by the cruel gardener. But John, having faltered in his reading, stared impassively at me with tight little lips and wide staring eyes.

'What a terrible thing it would be,' I said, hoping to encourage him on again, 'if poor Peter Rabbit should be caught.'

'Rabbits! Rabbits!' cried the angry-faced little lad, scratching the tangled mop of hair in irritation. 'They're a blasted nuisance, that's what my dad says! Have you seen what rabbits do to a rape crop?' I answered that I had not. 'Rabbits with little cotton-wool tails and pipe-cleaner whiskers,' he sneered, 'and fur as soft as velvet. Huh! We shoot 'em! They can eat their way through a rape crop in a week, can rabbits. Clear nine acres in a month! Millions of pounds' worth of damage when it's a mild winter. No amount of fencing will stop 'em.'

'We gas ours,' added the little girl of about ten with round cheeks and closely-cropped red hair who I had met earlier, and who was sitting nearby. 'That stops 'em, I can tell you.'

'Nay, Marianne,' retorted the boy curling a small lip, 'gassin' doesn't work.' Then, looking me straight in the eyes, he added, 'Never mind poor old Peter Rabbit. It's Mr McGregor I feel sorry for – trying to grow his vegetables with a lot of 'ungry rabbits all ovver t'place!'

'Perhaps we should look at another book,' I suggested feebly.

At morning break, Mrs Brown told me that John lived on a farm way out across the moors. It was a hard but happy life he led. He was expected, like most children from farming families, to help around the farm – feed the chickens, stack wood, muck out and undertake a host of other necessary jobs, and all that before he started his homework. He was a shrewd, good-natured, blunt-speaking little boy with a host of stories to tell about farm life. When he was little, Mrs Brown told me, he had been awakened by his father one night and taken into the byre to see the birth of a black Angus calf. The vet had suggested that it was about time the boy saw this miracle of nature. John had stood on a bale of hay in the cattle shed, staring in the half light as the great cow strained to deliver her calf. The small, wet, furry bundle soon arrived and the vet, wet with perspiration and with a triumphant look on his face, had gently wiped the calf's mouth and then held up the new-born creature for the little boy to see. John had stared wide-eyed.

'What do you think of that?' the vet had asked him. 'Isn't that a wonderful sight?'

John had thought for a moment before replying. 'How did it swallow the dog in the first place?' he had asked.

*

In the infants, I chose a bright picture book about a brave old ram who went off into the deep, snow-packed valley to look for a lost lamb. I decided that a story about sheep, which were clearly very popular in this part of the world, would be more appropriate and less risky than rabbits. Graham, a six-year-old, began reading the story with great gusto. 'Ronald was an old, old grey ram who lived in a wide, wide green valley near a big, big farm.' At this point he promptly stopped reading and stared intently at the picture of the ram for a moment. It had a great smiling mouth, short horns, a fat body and shining eyes like black marbles.

'What breed is that?' Graham asked.

'Breed?' I repeated.

'Aye,' said the child. 'What breed is he?'

'I don't know,' I answered in a rather pathetic tone of voice.

'Don't you know your sheep then?'

'No, I don't,' I replied.

'Miss,' shouted the child, 'could Tony come over here a minute? I want to know what breed of sheep this is.'

We were joined by Tony, another stocky little six-year-old with red cheeks and a runny nose. 'Let's have a look at t'picture then,' he said. I turned the picture book to face him. The large white sheep with black patches and a mouth full of shining teeth smiled from the page.

'Is it a Masham or a Swaledale?' he asked me.

'I don't know,' I answered in the same pathetic tone of voice.

Another child joined the discussion. 'It looks like a blue-faced Leicester to me. What do you reckon?'

'I have no idea,' I replied.

'Don't you know your sheep, then?' I was asked again

and once more replied that I did not. By this time a small crowd of interested onlookers had joined me in the reading corner.

'They're not Leicesters,' ventured Tony, 'because there's a low gate in t'picture.' There were grunts and nods of agreement from the other children.

Before I could ask about the significance of the low gate, Graham explained. 'Leicesters are a long-legged breed. They can get ovver low gates.'

'Is it a Texel?' ventured a plump girl, peering at the picture. Then she glanced in the direction of the ignoramus. 'That's a Dutch breed.'

'Texels have white faces, not black,' Graham commented.

Very soon the whole class was concentrating on the breed of the picture-book sheep.

'Well,' smiled Mrs Beighton, 'you are causing quite a stir in the reading corner, Mr Phinn. In order to solve the mystery, will you pop next door, Tony, ask Mrs Brown if we could borrow Marianne for a moment. Say we have a little problem she can help us solve.' Tony scampered off into the next room. 'Marianne has eight breeds on her farm,' explained the teacher, 'and her grandfather's prize ram won a blue ribbon at the Fettlesham Agricultural Show.'

'She knows her sheep does Marianne,' I was told by a serious-looking girl with dark plaits. The children nodded in agreement. Marianne strode confidently into the classroom from the juniors.

'Is it sheep?' she asked.

'What breed of sheep are these, do you reckon, Marianne?' asked Tony.

Marianne scrutinized the illustrations in the picture book, shook her head, sucked in her breath. All eyes were on her, everyone was waiting for the definitive answer.

'I reckon they're Bleu de Main or Rouge de l'Ouest,' she suggested. Then she turned to the dunce holding the book and looked me straight in the eyes. 'Them's French breeds.'

I was feeling mischievous and chanced my arm. 'Oh,' I said casually, 'I'm a Texel man myself.'

She looked at me intently for a moment. 'Are you?' she then asked suddenly.

'I don't think you can beat a good Texel.' I had only heard the word that morning.

'Well,' she said, 'they're a hardy breed, right enough. My Uncle Bob likes Texels.'

I was getting into my stride now. 'I wouldn't have any other breed,' I said smiling. 'You can keep your fancy French breeds, your Swaledales and your Mashams and your Leicesters with the low gates. You can't beat a good old Texel in my opinion.'

She thought for a while. 'Do you use OPs when you dip 'em?'

'Pardon?' I replied in that all too familiar feeble voice.

'Organo phosphates. Do you use 'em when you're dippin'?' I was lost for words. 'They get a deal of sheep scab Texels do, don't they? And of course you're not free o' blow fly at this time of year.'

Before I could answer, Tony, shaking his head like a little old man, remarked, 'He dunt know owt abaat sheep!'

'But I must admit,' I continued playfully, 'that I do like cross-breed Leicesters nearly as much. They're a very hardy breed and they weather very well up on the wolds. Good head, straight back, four solid legs.' This time it was Tony who was stuck for words. Marianne smiled knowingly.

'Well thank you for coming to see us,' said Mrs Beighton as we shook hands at the door of the school.

'Yes, thank you, Mr Phinn,' echoed Mrs Brown. 'And you must come again soon.'

'Yes, you must,' said Mrs Beighton. 'It's been a real pleasure, hasn't it, Mrs Brown?'

'It has indeed, Mrs Beighton.'

As I left the school that lunch-time, I paused at the school gate for a moment to take in the awesome view before me: the vast, white expanse of sky, the undulating green pastures dotted with sheep, the tall pine woods and distant sombre peaks. I thought for a moment of Marianne and Tony and John and all the other amazing children of the Dales I had met that morning. I thought of those two wonderful, dedicated, eccentric teachers who could have made a living on the stage as a double act. How very fortunate I was to meet such people. A shepherd, lean and hard, his bright-eyed collie beside him, waved as I made for my car. 'Grand day!' he shouted.

'Yes, indeed,' I replied. 'Yes, indeed.' I knew I was going to like my new job.

6

Harold Yeats was quite right. There was nothing Julie, the office clerk, did not know about the workings of the school inspectorate. I had only been in post for four weeks but was immensely impressed by this cheerful, clear-headed and highly efficient young woman who seemed to know every telephone extension number by heart, all the names of the headteachers and their schools and, of course, exactly who in the Education Office to contact for what. She could be very frank and forthright, as many a Yorkshire person can be, but she could also be charm and tact itself if she thought that approach was better. I had listened to a few calls she had taken from worried parents and anxious teachers and been full of admiration for the way she calmed down the caller, told them that the request or the complaint would be dealt with immediately and finished the conversation with a charming salutation of: 'Don't worry. It will all be sorted out. Thank you so much for calling.'

I arrived at the office one misty early October morning to find Julie sorting through the pile of letters with great gusto and with an expression on her face as if waiting for an unpleasant smell in the air to evaporate. She was clearly not in one of her charming or tactful moods.

'I've finally got to the bottom of the free school meals fiasco, you'll be pleased to hear,' she announced with almost manic intensity as she plonked my mail on the desk with a heavy thump.

'Thank goodness for that,' I replied. 'I'm tired of getting calls about free school meals. I was beginning to have dreams about Kimberley and Cherise.'

'It's that Mrs Savage!' exclaimed Julie. 'She's the one responsible for letting everyone know about staffing, new people, that sort of thing. In the new County Handbook with all the telephone contact numbers in, she only put you down for extension 5989 instead of 8989. Extension 5989 is discretionary grants.'

'It's an easy mistake to make,' I replied.

'It's a real pain in the neck, that's what it is,' countered Julie, 'because they don't go to print again until next term so it can't be changed until then. When you continue to get inundated with calls to sort out meals and clothes, you'll realize what a nuisance it is and then you'll not be saying, "It's an easy mistake to make." ' Julie was really getting into her stride now. 'And that's not all. She has you down as: the "English and Drama Inspector, Gervase Thinn"! You can imagine what confusion that will cause – and amusement because it makes you sound like something out of a fairy story. Now I call that sheer incompetence on a grand scale. I told Mrs Savage in no uncertain terms about the commotion, confusion, havoc and complete chaos she'd caused and how you'd been altogether disrupted, disturbed and disorganized. I must say, for once in her life, she was quite lost for words. Of course, there was no apology forthcoming. I just wonder how she would have reacted if her name had appeared in the new County Handbook as "Mrs Ravage" or "Miss Cabbage". She'd have gone up the wall! Have you met her yet by the way?' The flow ceased temporarily.

'No, not yet. She phoned to fix up the meeting with Dr Gore. She was quite formal but seemed pleasant enough.'

'Huh!' exclaimed Julie. 'Wait till you meet her.'

'Well, her error wasn't too bad, Julie,' I chuckled. 'We all get things wrong from time to time. Most people get my name wrong anyway. When I was invited for the interview for this job, the letter was addressed to Mr G. R. Pinn.'

'Well, that makes it even worse!' exclaimed Julie. 'Mrs Savage would have been responsible for sending out the letters so she got it wrong again.' Julie thought for a moment and then in a much quieter, tentative voice asked, 'I haven't spelled your name wrong, have I?'

'Well, now you come to mention it, Julie,' I replied, 'there's no letter "i" in Gervase.'

It is a fact that wherever I go I have to either repeat or explain this unusual name of mine. I have got quite accustomed to this by now and have come to expect that it will inevitably be misspelt or mis-pronounced. Over my years in teaching I collected a delightful range of inventive guesses which appeared on my letters. They ranged from 'Grievous Pain' to 'Gracious Dhin'. I have been called 'Germane', 'Germain', 'Germinal', 'Gercase', 'Gerund', 'Gervarse' and even 'Geraffe'. My surname has appeared as 'Flynn', 'Finn', 'Thin', 'Tinn', 'Pinn' and 'Chinn'. My favourite appeared when I was in my first year of teaching. A letter arrived addressed to 'Mr Phunn, Master-in-Charge of Games'.

'All Phunn and Games, eh, Gervase?' the Headteacher had remarked drily as he passed me the letter.

I explained to Julie, therefore, that I was not too disturbed about Mrs Savage, or indeed herself, getting my name wrong and that I didn't want her to go for the poor woman's jugular.

'Huh! If there are any jugulars to go for, Mrs Savage goes

for them,' scoffed Julie. 'It's like arguing with a barracuda.' She raised an eyebrow and curled her top lip. 'Savage by name and savage by nature – that's her. Let anyone else make a mistake and she goes completely off her trolley. She's into Dr Gore's room to complain, like a rabbit with the runs. All her staff are terrified of her. Her management style is an iron hand in an iron glove. Anyway, it's sorted. The free school dinners that is. I have informed Marlene on the switchboard to redirect your calls if there is the slightest mention of dinners or school uniforms. If they do happen to get through, just transfer the call to extension 5989 – or, if you are feeling really mean and vindictive, to Mrs Savage. She'll sort out Kimberley's mum and no mistake.'

'I take it you've had a few skirmishes with Mrs Savage then?'

'More like world war battles. But I am not going into that. It'll spoil my day.'

'Well, thanks for sorting it out, Julie, you're a real gem.'

'Did you ever think of changing it?'

'Changing what?'

'Your name. I know I would get sick and tired of people always getting my name wrong.'

I told her about the one short period in my life when I did change my first name. Just after the sixth form and during the weeks before departing for college, I had secured a part-time job in a large bread factory in the outskirts of Rotherham. On the first morning, the other three students and I had met the foreman, a loud, bald-headed, rotund little man called Chuck.

'What's thy name?' he had fired at the first student.

'Edward,' had come the faint reply.

'Reight, Ted, get thee sen down theer, thar on t'Farmhouse Crusties.' He had turned to the next. 'And what's thy name?' he had snapped again.

'Robert,' the nervous student had replied.

'Reight, Bob, get thee sen down theer,' he had said pointing in the opposite direction, 'tha'r on t'slicers. And watch weer tha' put thee hands. We don't want fingers in t'bread.' He had turned to the third student. 'And what's thy name?'

'Julian,' had come the reply.

Chuck looked as if he had been smacked in the face. '*Julian?*' he had exclaimed. 'Thy name's *Julian?*'

'Yes,' the student had whispered.

Chuck's voice had roared the full length of the factory. 'Hey lads, we have a *Julian* in!' This had been followed by wild guffaws from the twenty or so men, and by Chuck mincing along with his hand on his hip. Then he had turned to me. 'And what's thy name, pal?' he had asked, wiping the tears of laughter from his eyes.

'Dick!' I had replied.

At college I retained the name Dick for a couple of days but then returned to Gervase. I had joined a 'brush-up-your-German' class and had arrived at the lecture room to find Julian, who I had worked with at the factory, sitting in the front row.

'Hello, Dick,' he had greeted me brightly. 'I didn't know you were coming to this college.' We had chatted for a while until the tutor had arrived. At that first lesson the teacher, having introduced herself, had moved from student to student, asking each to say who he or she was.

'*Wie hießen sie?*'

'*Ich bin* Maria Thomas,' the first student had replied.

'*Wie hießen sie?*'

'*Ich bin* Elspeth Ward,' had come the second.

'*Wie hießen sie?*'

'*Ich bin* Julian Witherspoon,' had come the third. Eventually the question had been directed at me.

'*Wie heißen sie?*'

Because of Julian, and not wanting to have to go into a long explanation, I said, '*Ich bin* Dick Phinn.'

This had been followed by a series of giggles and chuckles from those around me.

'We always have one funny man,' the teacher had remarked. 'I shall be watching your progress, my fat friend, with interest.'

I learned later that '*dick*' in German means fat. I quickly abandoned the name Dick.

The day after my conversation with Julie I was sitting with the Head of the English Department in the staffroom of West Challerton High School at the start of an inspection of the English Department, when my unusual name entered the conversation again.

'Is it Welsh?' asked the Head of English, a small woman with hair pulled back in a bun, rimless spectacles and a round shiny face.

'No,' I replied.

'I have a Welsh cousin called Geraint. I thought it might have been of Celtic origin. Is it Irish then?'

'No, my name's not Welsh or Irish,' I replied. 'In fact, the name Gervase —'

'It ees a French name.' The French Assistante, who was sitting behind us, broke into the conversation. 'Gervase ees pronounced "Gervez" with a soft sounding "g", as in zer word "genre". It ees a French-Norman name and ees very common in France. Everywhere you go, you will 'ear zer name Gervase. It ees pronounced "Ggggervez".'

'Would you mind pronouncing it again?' I said. 'I rather like the way you say it.'

'Ggggervez,' she repeated in a most seductive voice. Then she added, 'It ees the name of a yoghurt.'

The first English lesson I observed that morning was taught by an exceptionally garrulous, rather eccentric, but obviously well-intentioned and dedicated teacher. Mr Palmer was nearing the end of a long and undistinguished career in which promotion had evaded him. He was still, nevertheless, resolutely optimistic and cheerful, enjoyed teaching his subject and attempting, in his own way, to share with his pupils his enthusiasm for Shakespeare and Dickens and Chaucer and all the other great classic writers. During the long time I have worked in schools I have met teachers in similar positions – at the same school all their careers, watching others move on to greater and higher things, and becoming wearied and cynical and ready for retirement.

Mr Palmer was not in this category. In his shiny, pinstriped suit, limp bow tie and frayed shirt he looked like a schoolmaster of another century. He was a genial, sandy-haired individual who chattered on inconsequentially, clearly in no way unnerved by the presence of a school inspector. Before the arrival of the pupils, I endeavoured to find out what the theme of his lesson would be. He rattled out words like a Gatling gun, frowning and twitching and gesticulating by turns.

'I've seen so many inspectors in my long career, Mr Phinn,' he confided. 'I've seen them come and I've seen them go, with their theories and suggestions, their pet projects and imaginative initiatives, with their important government directives and weighty educational reports, but I just carry on in my own little way, trying my best to teach.

Now this morning it is a group of eleven-year-olds you will be observing.' He waved in the direction of the classroom door, outside which a group of youngsters was beginning to queue. 'They are bright and keen and willing enough and do apply themselves but like many young people are not greatly enamoured by poetry.'

'So today you –' I tried unsuccessfully to intervene.

'So today,' he continued, 'I intend to read, appreciate and comment upon a poem, a piece of quite exceptional verse, in an attempt to reveal to them how powerful vocabulary, vivid imagery and heightened emotions contained in good quality writing can so enhance their lives.'

'What is the poem which –'

'I feel it is so important to try and instil in young people the love of great literature, to endeavour –' A small boy popped his head around the door and achieved greater success than I had accomplished in stemming the waterfall of words.

'Excuse me, Mr Palmer!' he shouted. 'Can we come in, sir?'

'You *can* come in, Thomas Ashbourne,' replied the teacher. 'You have the legs which will enable you to come in, you have the ability to walk through the door, you have the facility to enter the room but whether or not you *may* come in is another matter entirely.'

'Pardon, sir,' replied the boy entirely confused by the teacher's response.

Mr Palmer sighed. 'Yes, come in, Thomas Ashbourne. You *may* come in.' Turning to me he disclosed, 'Of course, I blame the television and the Americans for the decline in English grammar. I do not possess one myself – a television that is.'

The pupils, who had waited quietly and patiently outside

the door, entered in an orderly manner, sat down, took out their pens and books and prepared for the first lesson of the day. They looked bright eyed and eager and I wondered if any would get a word in during the course of the lesson.

'Today,' began Mr Palmer, 'we have a visitor. Mr Phinn, a school inspector no less, will be remaining with us for the duration of this lesson. I hope he will leave suitably impressed.'

'Good morning, Mr Phinn,' the class chorused.

'What is the name of a person who steals from another?' asked Mr Palmer suddenly. A hush came over the class. Had someone stolen something? What had gone missing? The pupils looked very apprehensive. The teacher repeated the question. 'Now come along, what is the name of a person who steals from another?'

'Thief, sir,' came a tentative reply.

'Yes, there is "thief", but are there any others?'

'Burglar, sir.'

'Mugger, sir.'

'No, no, I wasn't thinking of those.'

'Robber, sir.'

'Shoplifter, sir.'

'Well, yes,' said the teacher, 'but it is not the one I have in mind. They are all words for someone who steals, but none of you has come up with the one I want,' said the teacher. 'Any others?' At this point I really could not see in which direction this lesson on poetry was going. The interrogation continued during which the class exhausted every possible variation of the word 'thief', but still the pupils had not guessed the word which was clearly implanted in the teacher's head, the word he wanted to hear.

'A person who stole from others in bygone days,' the teacher persisted. 'Now, does that give you a clue?'

There was a forest of hands and an eagerness to answer. 'Sir! Sir! Sir!'

'Yes, Thomas?' the teacher asked.

'Pirate, sir.'

'I wasn't thinking of a pirate, but you are getting warmer.'

'Buccaneer, sir,' came a triumphant voice.

'Not a buccaneer. Any more?' The class was silent.

'Well, I was thinking,' said the teacher, 'of a highwayman. And the poem we are going to look at today is called *The Highwayman* by Alfred Noyes.'

'Mr Palmer,' I quizzed, after the lesson, 'what was the point of going laboriously through all the words for "thief" at the beginning of the lesson? What was the rationale for it? Why did you not merely explain the class was to study the poem *The Highwayman*, read it, talk a little about it and get on with the discussion?'

'Ah, my dear Mr Phinn,' replied the teacher stroking the thinning sandy hair and blinking rapidly, 'I believe in getting the pupils' ideas and points of view rather than merely expounding my own. One should always value the opinions and ideas of others. Children are not empty vessels to be filled up with a few arid facts, you know. They are delicate plants that need careful and sensitive nurturing.'

I was stumped for an answer and instead watched as he carefully took a small, polished brass box from his waistcoat pocket, tapped it gently and clicked open the lid before asking, 'Do you take snuff?'

The next English lesson I observed was quite a contrast. The young woman teacher chaired an immensely lively and good-humoured debate on the set examination text of *Macbeth*, with a large group of fifteen-year-olds. She challenged their views, encouraged them to defend their ideas, asked for examples and illustrations and reminded them of the various stage productions they had been to see. She involved the whole of the group in an animated discussion on the play. It was an immensely impressive lesson. These pupils were certainly not empty vessels filled with a few arid facts but had been stimulated to express their own opinions and have some independence of thought.

At the conclusion of the inspection day at West Challerton High School, I read the first draft of my report to the Headmaster, a large, bluff, outspoken Yorkshireman who nodded thoughtfully throughout.

'Aye well, Mr Phinn, you've told me a lot that I already know, particularly about Mr Palmer who I agree is past his sell-by date, but you've added a few ideas of your own that I would take issue with.' He then challenged a number of my conclusions. We argued and debated for a while but I stood my ground steadfastly and said I felt the conclusions were fair and based on firm and extensive evidence. I added that the report in general was a very favourable one and the Headmaster should not dwell on the relatively few criticisms. I added that he appeared to be taking them personally.

'Well, what can I do, Mr Phinn, but take them personally? I am, after all, in charge of the school and when the school is attacked it's the Headteacher who bleeds.'

We parted on amicable terms and he escorted me to the entrance. 'Is it Welsh?' he asked.

'Pardon?'

'Your name? Is it a Welsh name?'

'I've had this conversation before with your Head of English,' I replied. 'No, it's French actually. French-Norman. St Gervase was a Roman martyr put to death under the Emperor Nero. It was a popular name in medieval times. I believe William the Conqueror had several knights of that name with him when he invaded. The name literally means "spear carrier".'

The Headmaster gave a wry smile. ' "Spear carrier" eh? Well, that's very appropriate for a school inspector.'

'Yes, I suppose it is,' I replied. 'I always seem to be on the sharp end of things in this line of work.'

'I wasn't meaning that,' said the Headmaster. 'I have always been of the opinion that school inspectors are like cross-eyed javelin throwers. They hurl a lot of spears in the direction of schools, missing the point most of the time, but occasionally, and by sheer accident, they happen to hit the right target. Good afternoon to you, Mr Phinn.'

7

'I must say when I heard the name Gervase Phinn, I had visions of a huge, red-headed, hot-tempered Irishman,' murmured the tall, bearded, larger-than-life character who sat next to me. 'Gervase Phinn,' he repeated. 'It is such a wonderfully esoteric and imaginative name. It has a sort of ring to it. *The Collected Poems of Gervase Phinn*. Mmmmm. Now take my name – Sidney Clamp. Not much of a ring to that, is there? *A Retrospective Exhibition of the Contemporary Watercolour Paintings of Sidney Clamp*. Doesn't quite sound the same, does it? It's not the sort of name to appear in the annals of Art History: Leonardo da Vinci, Pablo Picasso, Claude Monet, Vincent van Gogh, Salvador Dali and – Sidney Clamp!'

'You could always change your name,' I suggested.

'Too late, too late,' he lamented, and gave me a mournful look. 'Too late for many things now.' It was early evening and I was sitting next to the renowned inspector of creative and visual arts, waiting for the first inspectors' meeting of the new term to start.

'Of course, it could be worse,' he said suddenly. 'I once knew a teacher called Death and he looked like death as well: thin and grey and bent like the Grim Reaper. He used to add an apostrophe and pronounce it De'Ath. It made not the slightest difference, of course. All the children referred to him as Mr Death. Then there was a Mrs Onions. She taught drama at West Challerton High School – did the same and insisted on being referred to as Mrs O'nions. You can imagine the hilarity amongst the students when the new member of staff arrived, a Ms Garlick. My suggestion that they should present a dramatization of *The Lady of Shallot* for the next school production was not well received.' He laughed loudly. 'You know, I've never agreed with old Shakespeare: "What's in a name? That which we call a rose by any other name would smell as sweet." I go along with Oscar Wilde: "Names are everything!" I think you can tell a great deal by a person's name. Have you met Mrs Savage yet by the way?'

I had met Sidney very, very briefly in my first week. He had rushed into the office, puffing and panting, snatched his pile of letters, thrust some documents into Julie's hands for typing, hurriedly shook my hand and disappeared.

'Whoever was that?' I had gasped.

'That,' Julie had replied, sighing dramatically, 'is Mr Clamp. He appears like the genie from the lamp and then disappears into thin air.'

A week later, Sidney had bolted past me on the long corridor at County Hall one lunchtime, stopped suddenly, retraced his steps, stared at me for a moment and announced, 'Hello, Gervase, I thought it was you. Come along with me if you have a moment, I've something to show you.'

I had been whisked along, with Sidney grasping my arm tightly, striding forward and chattering excitedly. We had arrived at a large room full of paintings, pastel sketches, charcoal drawings, watercolours, sculptures and carvings. Sidney had pulled himself up to his full height with conspicuous pride.

'It's the art exhibition of children's and students' work,' he announced with obvious pleasure and satisfaction, waving an arm at all that was before him. 'At the end of each summer term, I collect a selection of artwork from the schools and colleges and then during the holidays mount it, arrange it and display it for the general public to see, to show the high quality of work that well-taught young people achieve in the visual arts. Here is the result. Magnificent, isn't it?

The exhibition had indeed looked magnificent. It had been a mass of brilliant colours and shapes and such a range of work from the bold bright faces painted by the infants to the detailed oil paintings and twisted metal sculptures of the sixth formers. When I had turned to compliment Sidney on the display I found he had gone. I had caught sight of him moving amongst the people meandering between the exhibits, expounding, interpreting, discussing and explaining how the different effects had been created. His eyes had been bright with enthusiasm and ardour, his arms waving in the air like daffodils in the wind. So that had been my first couple of meetings with the renowned Sidney Clamp.

After that first inspectors' meeting, Sidney and I walked to our cars together.

'Harold tells me you are in digs,' Sidney remarked.

'I was for the first couple of weeks but I've found a flat now – above The Rumbling Tum café in the high street. I've paid the rent for a couple of months, then I hope to buy a place. I don't want to rush into anything yet. To be honest, I don't know where to start looking. I'm spoilt for choice.'

'Well, certainly not Fettlesham. You definitely do not want to live in Fettlesham. You'll meet the entire working population of County Hall every Saturday. There's some lovely property – little cottages and converted barns – in some of the surrounding villages. What sort of house have you in mind? Old? New? Large? Small? Cheap? Expensive? In the town? In the country?'

'I just don't know, to be frank. I've been so busy since I started that my feet don't seem to have touched the ground and I just haven't had time to think, never mind look for a house.'

'When you start looking seriously, I shall take it upon myself to give you my undivided help and assistance. I am something of an expert on properties.'

'I shall know where to come,' I replied, smiling. 'Thank you.'

'And Julie tells me that you are unattached.'

'Unattached?'

'No wife, family, fiancée, partner, girlfriend or children.'

'Yes, unattached at the moment. I've been so busy I haven't had time to think about that either.'

'Now that is serious. Never neglect your love life, Gervase. You cannot beat the love of a good woman. Wherever would I be without my Lila – my long-suffering wife of twenty-eight years. When you start looking seriously in the direction of the opposite sex, I shall take it upon myself to give you my undivided help and assistance and introduce you to some eligible young women of my acquaintance. I am something of an expert on women. In fact, come to think of it, I am something of an expert in most things. You aren't looking for a car by any chance, are you?'

One bright Monday morning a couple of weeks later, the door of the office was flung open and there stood Sidney, beard bristling, eyes flashing, chest heaving and his face suffused with colour. 'That woman,' he boomed, 'has got to go!' The name of Mrs Savage immediately came into my mind but before I could inquire into the reason for this outburst, he enlightened me.

'The caretaker from Hell! That's what she is!'

'Who?' I asked.

'Connie, the caretaker, site manager or whatever she calls herself. Have you not met her yet?'

'Ah, Connie!' I replied. 'Yes, I have met her.'

Connie was the caretaker of the Staff Development Centre where all the courses and conferences for teachers were held. She was a woman of a certain reputation. In the fourth week of my new job, I had directed my first course at the Centre. I had walked cheerfully into the main hall early one Thursday morning carrying a large armful of books and folders only to drop the lot a moment later. A voice of stentorian proportions had echoed down the corridor seconds later. That was my first experience of Connie.

'I say,' she had boomed, 'I've just mopped that floor!'

She had watched my every move that day. I would look up from my lecture notes to see her face grimacing at the door; during the coffee at break I found her hovering behind me. I almost expected to see her, arms folded, face scowling, duster in hand, waiting for me in the men's toilets. Her presence was everywhere in the building. Far from thinking that she was controlled, managed or directed by us, it was Connie who felt she had the various inspectors under her command when they were on her territory. She was a great democrat in that she had no conception of status, rank or position in the world and treated everyone exactly the same, usually like naughty children.

About to leave the Centre on that Thursday, I had heard her talking on the telephone to a friend, explaining that she had a young, new inspector to break in, and that she had to get him used to her systems.

73

'Well, you know what they are like, these clever, artistic folk,' she had said. 'They're full of fancy ideas and, whilst they might be good at creating things, they are hopeless at clearing up after themselves.' On hearing this I had scurried back to the room in which I had been working, made certain that everything was tidy, positioned the chair neatly behind the desk, checked that all the cups had been returned to the kitchen and the equipment had been safely put away.

Sidney, extrovert, unpredictable, creative, was the sort of man guaranteed to ruffle Connie's feathers and he had experienced the sharp end of her tongue on many an occasion. On this particular Monday morning he was in a furious bad temper.

'Last Friday,' Sidney snarled, throwing himself into his chair, 'I directed a highly successful course for infant teachers at the Staff Development Centre on the theme of "Creative Modelling in the Infant Classroom". I set the course members a practical task, to build a mythical creature, which I have to say they did with immense enthusiasm and inventiveness – and you will never guess what's happened? What do you think that dictator in the pink overall did? That virago with the feather duster! That tyrant with the teapot! The caretaker from Hell.'

I put down my pen, turned in his direction and prepared myself for a long account of the disaster.

Sidney told me he had provided the infant teachers on the course with a variety of household waste material: kitchen rolls, plastic containers, tin foil trays, milk bottle tops, bits of fabric, brown paper bags, toilet tissues, tin cans and sheets of newsprint, and from this detritus emerged a huge dragon which was later proudly displayed near the entrance to the Centre. This morning, armed with his camera, Sidney had returned to the Centre to take photo-

74

graphs of this truly stunning creation only to find it had mysteriously disappeared. He had searched everywhere without success and had finally run Connie to earth to ask if she had seen the dragon.

'Dragon? No, I can't say that I have,' she had replied. Sidney, in a calm, controlled sort of voice had told Connie that she *must* have seen it, that there had been a four-foot dragon near the entrance – a long, snake-like, fierce-faced creature constructed of waste material.

'Oh that!' Connie had replied casually. 'I put it in the bin.'

Sidney had exploded.

'Can you believe that, Gervase?' he demanded. 'She had put it in the bin, she had disposed of that wonderful, multi-coloured dragon that had taken all day to construct! She had consigned it to the rubbish tip! I said to her, "Connie," I said, "it was a work of art!" and do you know what she replied? Do you know what she replied?'

'No, Sidney, I don't,' I said. 'But I feel certain that you are going to tell me.'

'She looked at me, without the least trace of remorse, regret or contrition, and she said, "Well, you should have written on it then – 'This is a work of art and not a load of old rubbish' – then I would have known not to throw it out." I was completely lost for words. With hindsight I should have replied, "Well, I should think of all people you would recognize a dragon!"'

Sidney and I were at the Staff Development Centre the following week to direct a series of Expressive and Creative Art courses for secondary teachers. We were in the small staffroom having a cup of tea, before the arrival of the course members when Connie entered.

'Don't forget to wash your cups up, please, when you've finished,' she said, her eyes scanning the room for untidiness. 'And could you make certain you break for coffee promptly at half past ten because I've a lot of people in the Centre this morning, including one of Mr Pritchard's PE courses.' She headed for the door but turned back. 'Oh, and another thing, whose are those dreadful stuffed animals cluttering up the entrance?' Sidney, who had retained a simmering silence throughout Connie's harangue, looked up and smiled disdainfully before replying.

'They are mine, Connie,' he said. 'And they are not dreadful stuffed animals, they are the next best thing to first-hand experience.'

'Well, they're a health and safety hazard stuck there. People could fall over them. It could give an old person quite a shock coming face to face with a fox or those big black birds with sharp beaks.'

'The course today is not for short-sighted pensioners, Connie, it's for relatively young, agile teachers,' Sidney replied. 'And I am certain a few stuffed animals and birds will not shock anyone.'

'I shouldn't be surprised if they have fleas,' said Connie, trying another tack.

'Very clean young teachers,' retorted Sidney. 'Quite flealess.'

'I am talking about those animals!'

'Really?' replied Sidney.

'What are they doing here anyway?' she asked bluntly.

'The teachers, the fleas or the animals?'

'The stuffed animals.'

'Those, Connie,' he replied gently, 'those wonderful, carefully preserved creatures will form the focus for today's course on Wildlife Drawing for Non-specialist Secondary School Art Teachers.'

'Well, they don't look very wild to me,' she fired back. 'They're dead.'

'I know they are dead, Connie, they are stuffed, but they are the best alternative to the real thing and I don't want them interfered with.'

'Huh!' Connie threw back her head and screwed up her face. 'There'll be no interference, I can assure you of that. I wouldn't touch them with a barge pole. They give me the creeps.'

'Well that's fine,' replied Sidney. 'If you stay away from them, they will stay away from you.'

'How long are they going to be here?'

'They'll be collected tomorrow morning by the Museum Service. Oh, and Connie,' he continued pointedly, 'I do hope that you will resist the temptation to consign anything we create today to the dustbin.'

'Pardon?'

'Leave everything alone.'

Sidney spent the next half hour arranging the various creatures in the rather overgrown area to the rear of the Centre. The snarling fox glared menacingly through the bushes, the black raven perched on the stone wall, the two hedgehogs could be seen snuffling in the dry leaves underneath the dark trees, the fat badger stared around a tussock of tall grass and the heron peered into the murky waters of the pond as if looking for fish. Connie observed from the window.

Following a practical morning during which Sidney, in particularly enthusiastic mood, taught the teachers some of the skills of pencil and chalk sketching, the teachers moved outside with their sketchpads to draw the animals 'in their natural habitat'. Looking over the shoulders of some of the industrious teachers, Connie had to admit that the results were very impressive and much to be preferred to the 'dustbin dragon' as she called it.

At four o'clock, the sketches were displayed to good effect on the Centre's walls, the stuffed animals and birds were gathered together in the entrance ready for collection the next morning, the teachers departed and Sidney left for a meeting at the Education Office.

'I must say,' admitted Connie as we both admired the sketches and drawings, 'they are more my cup of tea than great big dragons made of litter and junk. Mind you, I don't like having those stuffed animals all over the place. I shall be glad to see the back of them. They make me feel very uncomfortable.'

As we headed down the corridor, Connie suddenly peered out of the window. 'What are *they* up to?' she asked.

Staring over the low, limestone wall which bordered the Centre were a couple of ageing ramblers. One clambered stiffly onto the wall and his companion handed up a camera.

'What *are* they doing?' she asked me.

'I've no idea,' I replied. 'They seem to be interested in something or other at the back of the Centre.' We watched the group for a minute or so.

'He's taking photographs of something. He needs to be careful balancing on that wall at his age. He could do himself a mischief.' Connie opened a window and shouted, 'Hullo! Can I help you?'

The old gentleman with the camera was startled by her voice, tottered on the wall, regained his balance and then hissed back at Connie. 'Sssssshhhhhh!'

'This is private property!' she called.

Again came the response. 'Sssssshhhhhh!' accompanied by gesticulations and waving of hands.

'I'm going out to see what they want,' she said authoritatively and out of the Centre she strode and up to the wall. 'Did you not hear me, this is private property! Get down from there at once.'

'Quiet,' urged the fellow standing on the wall. He was a very tall, elderly, straight-backed man in long shorts, baggy anorak and heavy walking boots. 'You'll frighten him away.'

'Frighten who away?' demanded Connie in a loud voice.

'Do keep quiet,' urged the man, pointing in the direction of the pond. 'See – one of the most elegant, beautiful birds, indigenous to this country, very rarely seen at such close quarters.' Connie turned to see a heron – the stuffed heron – poised over the little pool. It had been forgotten by Sidney and remained rigid but very lifelike.

'Oh that,' said Connie and, leaving the couple with open mouths, approached the heron, picked it up by its long neck and returned to the Centre. She turned in the direction of the two silent, awestruck ramblers when she got to the door. 'It's stuffed!' she shouted. The effect of her words, which may of course have been misheard, was immediate and Connie and I watched with amusement as the old man clambered off the wall and set off up the path and disappeared from sight.

The following day Sidney arrived to make certain the stuffed birds and animals had been collected. Then, under the watchful eye of Connie, he began to take down from the display boards the various sketches and paintings.

'I must say, Mr Clamp,' she remarked as she hovered behind him with a tin for the used staples, 'this sort of art is much more to my liking. I mean, I'd have one of these pictures on my walls. It's proper art, isn't it?'

'I am so very glad you approve, Connie,' replied Sidney. 'Do allow me to present you with a little painting I did.' At this he gave Connie a small, carefully-drawn picture of a tiny furry creature watching with piercing eyes from beneath a fallen branch. 'I think it is just the thing for you.'

'Oh, well, that's very nice,' said Connie, quite taken aback. She peered at the picture of the small creature for a moment. 'Yes, I like this. Thank you very much, Mr Clamp, I shall treasure it.' She continued to stare at the drawing for some time before remarking, 'A little harvest mouse – it's really sweet.'

I did not enlighten Connie – it was the picture of a shrew.

8

Amongst the pile of mail one morning was a lovely letter from a Miss Christine Bentley, the Headteacher of Winnery Nook Nursery and Infant School. She expressed the hope that I might call in and visit her soon and included some delightful little poems written by the children. I looked at the map on the office wall and saw that my route to St Bartholomew's, an infant school I was to visit later that day, passed the village of Winnery Nook so I decided to pop in during the morning and thank Miss Bentley for her letter and the children for their poems.

'Julie,' I said on my way out, 'could you add another school onto my programme for the day? I'm going to call in at Winnery Nook Nursery and Infant School on my way to Crompton. Could you please give the Headteacher, Miss Bentley, a ring and tell her I am on my way?'

'My goodness,' Julie replied, 'what keenness. Not even time for coffee.'

Winnery Nook School was a relatively modern building in honey-coloured brick with an orange pantile roof and large picture windows. The school was surrounded by fields and rocky outcrops and backed by a friendly belt of larch and spruce trees which climbed towards the high moors. Everything about it looked clean and well tended. I arrived just before morning playtime to hear the squealing and laughing of small children as they ran and played in the small schoolyard.

I was just about to enter the main door when a very distressed looking little girl of about five or six, her face wet with weeping and her cheeks smeared where little hands had tried to wipe away the tears, tugged at my jacket.

'They've all got big sticks!' she wailed piteously.

'Who's got big sticks?' I asked, surprised.

'All on 'em. They've all got big sticks!'

'Well, they shouldn't have big sticks,' I replied.

'I want a big stick!' she cried, sniffing and sobbing, her little body shaking in anguish.

'No, you can't have a big stick. It's very dangerous.'

'I want a big stick!' she cried. 'I want a big stick!'

'You could hurt somebody with a big stick,' I said.

'But they've all got big sticks!' she howled again. 'They've all got 'em.'

At this point a very attractive young woman appeared from the direction of the playground.

'Whatever is it, Maxine?' she asked gently pulling the little body towards her like a hen might comfort a chick. She then looked at me. 'It's Mr Phinn, isn't it?'

'Yes,' I replied.

'I'm relieved about that. We have to be so careful these days. The playground supervisor came rushing into the school saying there was a strange man talking to the children.'

I suddenly felt acutely embarrassed.

'Of course, I'm so sorry. I should have come directly to the school office. It's just that this little girl was so distressed and came running up to me.' The child in question was nuzzling up to the teacher, sniffling and snuffling softly. 'I'm looking for Miss Bentley, the Headteacher.'

'That's me,' she replied, giving me such a smile that I was quite lost for words. She had the deepest of blue eyes and the fairest complexion I had ever seen and a soft mass of golden hair. She was one of the most strikingly beautiful women I had ever seen.

'Mr Phinn?' she said. 'Mr Phinn?'

I returned from my reverie. 'Oh, yes, I'm sorry. I was distracted. I do hope you don't mind my taking you up on your offer to call, Miss Bentley. I really did enjoy reading the children's poems and stories and would love to er . . . love to er . . .' I was lost in the deep blue eyes again.

'Look around the school?' she asked.

'Exactly, yes. I would love to look around the school if that's convenient.'

Before she could reply, the small child clutching her began to moan and groan again pitifully. 'I want a big stick, Miss Bentley,' she moaned. 'They've all got big sticks.'

'Of course, you can have one,' the teacher replied, wiping away the little girl's tears. 'You weren't there when I gave everybody one. You don't think I'd leave you out, Maxine, do you? You come with me and I'll get you one, a nice big one. How about that? I won't be a moment, Mr Phinn.'

'A big stick?' I murmured. 'You're giving this little girl a big stick?'

The teacher gave a great grin before replying, 'She means a biscuit.'

The school was a delight: cheerful, optimistic and welcoming and the creative writing of very high quality. Maxine looked a very different little girl when I saw her again, smiling and contented and busily colouring away with a large blue crayon.

'I've got a red crayon,' she said as I looked at her bright picture.

'It's a blue crayon. You've got a blue crayon,' I replied.

'It's red.'

'No, it's blue.' I took the crayon from her little fingers and held it against my suit. 'Like my suit, see – blue.'

'*That's* a blue crayon,' she said with great determination. 'I know that. I'm talking about my red one. It's at home. I've got a red crayon at home.'

I sighed, smiled and nodded. 'I see. And what is your picture about?'

'A king and queen who live in a palace. Do you know how to write "queen"?'

'Yes,' I said and, borrowing her pencil again, carefully wrote the letters. 'It's a very difficult word this one. Can you see it begins with a "q" and a "u" and when you put these two letters together they sound like "kwu".' She nodded, copied down the word carefully and added, 'I know another word that starts with a "kwu".'

'Do you?'

'It's Kwistmas twee,' she replied giggling.

'This little girl,' I thought to myself, 'really does take the biscuit.'

Miss Bentley approached and looked at the little girl's work. 'That really is a lovely picture, Maxine,' she said gently.

As I looked at the teacher leaning over the small child, both of them smiling, I thought the phrase particularly apt: 'That really is a lovely picture.'

'Miss Bentley,' the small child asked suddenly in a very audible whisper, 'Miss Bentley, is that man your boyfriend?'

'No, Maxine,' she replied, colouring a little, 'Mr Phinn's an inspector.'

'He could still be your boyfriend,' she replied with all the openness and honesty of a small child.

At the end of the morning, I sat with the Headteacher in her office, sipping tea from a china cup and listening to her tell me about the school and the children and the good work they produced.

'I do hope you come to love this part of the world, Mr Phinn,' she said, 'and get to know the very special children who live here.'

'I'm sure I will,' I replied. I knew in my heart as I said it that I would. And I thought to myself, I wouldn't mind getting to know you as well.

'Oh, how remiss of me,' said Miss Bentley with a twinkle in those large blue eyes as she passed me a plate of shortcake, 'Do have a big stick!'

St Bartholomew's Roman Catholic Infant School was quite a contrast to Winnery Nook. Sister Brendan, the Headteacher, saw my car pull up outside her office window and was at the door of the school to greet me before I had a chance to straighten my tie and comb my hair. She beamed so widely that, had she worn lipstick, I would have expected to see traces on her ears. The small school was sited in the disadvantaged centre of Crompton, a dark and brooding northern industrial town. Tall black chimneys, great, square, featureless warehouses, and row on row of mean terraces stretched into the valley beyond. The school was adjacent to a grim and forbidding wasteland of derelict buildings and piles of rubble, surrounded by half-demolished houses which seemed to grow upwards like great red jagged teeth from blackened gums. From the grime and dust I walked into an oasis: a calm, bright, welcoming and orderly building.

'Good afternoon to you, Mr Phinn,' said Sister Brendan enthusiastically. 'I got your letter. We are all ready and waiting and raring to go.' She was a slight, thin-cheeked woman with tiny, dark, darting eyes and a sharp little beak of a nose. Sister Brendan looked like a small hungry blackbird out for the early worm.

'Good afternoon, Sister,' I replied, shaking a small cold hand.

'And did you have a pleasant journey, Mr Phinn?' she asked, her little black glittering eyes looking up into mine.

'Yes, indeed, Sister, a very pleasant journey.'

The Headteacher took me on a tour of the school, fluttering along the corridors, pointing and chattering and chuckling away as we went from room to room. Children's painting and poems, posters, pictures and book jackets covered every available space. Shelves held attractive books, tables were covered in shells, models, photographs and little artifacts. Each child we passed said 'Hello,' brightly and in all the classrooms little busy bodies were reading, writing, discussing, solving problems and working at the computers.

'It's a hive of activity,' I remarked.

'Does that make me the Queen Bee?' asked Sister Brendan with a mischievous glint in her shining eyes.

It was clear that for Sister Brendan the children in her care were a source of real delight. She glided through the school, pointing out with pride a painting or a poem displayed on a corridor wall, telling me about the football team and the drama group and the brass ensemble, introducing me on the tour to each teacher with a flourish.

'And here, Mr Phinn, is the wonderful Mrs Webb.'

'Oh, Sister, really,' simpered the small, red-faced teacher, clearly enjoying the praise.

I explained to Sister Brendan the reason for my visit: to hear a selection of children read, test their spellings and look at their writing. The small head nodded like some mechanical toy.

'No child leaves this school unable to read,' she boasted. 'It is the single most important skill and we work extremely hard to achieve success for every child. Most of these children have few books in their homes and many of their parents do not have the inclination nor the time to hear them read so our task is a hard one. To fail to teach a child to read, Mr Phinn, in my book, is tantamount to handicapping that child for the rest of his life. I hope you will conclude, when you have done your testing and heard the children read, that we have risen to the challenge.'

I tested a sample of twenty children in the small and attractive school library. They came one after the other, clasping their readers, bright eyed and keen. All read with clarity and expression and when they spoke it was with enthusiasm and confidence. And I had never met such lively enquiring minds nor so many budding little philosophers in ones so young.

Marie, a seven-year-old with a round saucer face and enormous ginger bunches of hair, read a story about the great fierce lion in the zoo. She paused in her reading for a moment and a meditative expression came to her round face.

'What are you thinking?' I asked quietly.

She thought for a moment, then sighed wistfully. 'Oh, I was just thinking what the old lion was doing before they went and put him behind bars.'

'He does look a fierce old lion, doesn't he?' I remarked.

'I think I'd be very angry locked up in a cage all day and remembering the jungle.' She went on to explain to me how badly she felt humans treated animals. 'My grandpa goes ferreting, you know. He goes with a dog and a ferret and catches rabbits. I told him I think it's cruel but he says it's not and the rabbit doesn't feel anything. I told him he wouldn't like being chased down a burrow by a ferret.'

'No,' I agreed, 'I don't suppose he would.'

John was seven and read from a book about dinosaurs. He could pronounce many of the great monsters' names and concluded his very competent reading with a small lecture on the different kinds of prehistoric creatures.

'Of course,' he remarked, 'they are not really called dinosaurs, you know.'

'Are they not?' I replied.

'Prehistoric lizards is the correct name for them. Did you not know?'

I did not and told him so. Later in the day I asked Rebecca, the youngest in Mrs Webb's class of seven-year-olds, to read to me. She did so in beautifully modulated tones with great confidence and animation.

'That was splendid,' I told her as she gently closed the book. 'And do you like reading, Rebecca?'

'Oh yes! Do you?'

'Yes, I love books.'

'What sort?'

'Oh, books about everything and everybody,' I replied. 'Do you have a lot of books at home?'

'Yes, too many.'

'I don't think you can have too many books,' she replied.

Rebecca next completed the standardized reading test, again without any trace of nervousness or apprehension.

'That was splendid,' I told her a second time. 'You got full marks!'

'Have you another one?' she asked. 'I like doing the tests.'

After I had given some brief and very positive feedback to the Headteacher, Sister Brendan guided me towards the entrance and wished me a safe journey.

'Actually, Sister, I was intending to remain for the rest of the afternoon,' I said genially.

She was rather taken aback. 'It's the school assembly at three o'clock, Mr Phinn. I wasn't expecting you to join us for that. I thought this was just to hear a sample of children read and look at their writing. You never mentioned anything about coming into the assembly.'

'Yes, I know, Sister,' I replied, 'but I would like to watch the assembly if you wouldn't mind.' The nun fixed me with a stern eye.

'Very well, Mr Phinn,' she replied, 'I shall lead on.' She then glided away in the direction of the school hall.

The little ones filed into the hall to a stirring tune hammered out on the piano with great gusto by 'the wonderful Mrs Webb'. I stayed at the back but was ushered by Sister Brendan to a seat next to hers, facing the rows of smiling children.

'Every afternoon, children,' said Sister Brendan in a quiet voice, 'we have a very special visitor who joins us for our assembly, don't we?'

'Yes, Sister!' the infants chorused.

'And who is that very special visitor, Anne-Marie?'

'It's Jesus,' came a confident reply. Then all the faces turned to look at me.

Sister Brendan gave a wry smile. 'Well, this is not Jesus but he is an important visitor – not as important as Jesus, of course – but very important. Mr Phinn is a school inspector and he has looked around our lovely school this afternoon and heard some of you read. He has been telling me how very much he has enjoyed his time with us and how well you read. I know you have made him feel a part of our large, happy family. Now, let's all of us say a really warm "Good afternoon" to Mr Phinn, shall we?'

'Good afternoon, Mr Phinn!' the whole school chorused.

'Good afternoon, children,' I replied.

'You know, Mr Phinn,' continued the nun, 'not only are these children such lovely readers, they are also very good singers as well. Aren't you?'

'Yes, Sister Brendan!' the whole school chorused.

'I'm sure you would like to hear them.' I nodded ostentatiously. 'So we will start off with one of our favourite hymns, "I am Walking in the Footsteps of Jesus".' And the children sang and sang and the hall was filled with the most happy music.

'Did you enjoy that, Mr Phinn?' asked Sister, at the end.

'It was delightful,' I replied.

'Mr Phinn wasn't singing, Sister,' came a small voice from the front of the hall.

'Not singing, Mr Phinn?' remarked Sister in mock surprise.

'I'm afraid I don't know the words,' I responded a little shame-faced. 'It's not a hymn I know.'

'Then we must teach you,' replied Sister Brendan. 'Rebecca, will you come out and teach Mr Phinn the words?'

The little girl stood in front of me, slowly mouthing each word. 'I – am – walking – in – the – footsteps – of – Jesus, I – am – walking – in – the – way – of – the – Lord.' She then added, 'Say them after me.' I struggled through the verse.

'Perhaps you would like a quick run-through by yourself?' asked Sister, a mischievous glint in the small dark eyes. My heart sank when I heard 'the wonderful Mrs Webb' start up on the piano.

'No, no!' I replied quickly. 'I think I've remembered them.'

'But we haven't taught you the actions yet,' said Rebecca.

At the end of assembly, as the children dispersed quietly, Sister Brendan turned to me beaming with pleasure. 'That will teach you to come in unannounced, Mr Phinn.'

Before I left the school, Sister Brendan took me to her office. She talked about the needs of her children, many of whom came from deprived homes, how important it was to build up their confidence and self esteem, to lift their aspirations, to unlock their energies and talents.

'I can see that God has been very good to you, Mr Phinn,' she concluded. 'You had caring parents I guess, grew up in a loving home surrounded by books, and now have a very comfortable life style.' I nodded. 'You've got a well-paid job and you clearly enjoy your work.' I nodded again. 'You have the inestimable opportunity of seeing children every day. My goodness, you are a lucky man. What more could anyone want?' I continued to nod. Suddenly she asked, 'Are you married?'

'No, Sister, I'm not married.'

'Well, that is a pity. You would make a wonderful husband and father.'

'Thank you very much, Sister.' I resisted the temptation to say that she would make a wonderful wife and mother, but instead replied, 'I will certainly know where to come for a recommendation.' I then added, 'This testimony, Sister, sounds like a preface to something.'

This time it was her turn to nod. She slid a cardboard collecting box across the desk. 'I feel sure,' she said, her dark eyes twinkling, 'that you would like to help those less fortunate.' I reached into my pocket. 'In the form of a silent collection.'

'A silent collection?'

'The rustle of five pound notes.'

'Sister, this is blackmail.'

'I know,' she chuckled. 'The charity is called CAFOD – Catholic Aid For Overseas Development – and it does wonderfully good work all around the world. It helps those in the developing countries to earn a living. When I started teaching, it was called "Penny for the Black Babies" and each week the children would bring a copper or two to school for the missions. We stopped calling it that when our first little West Indian boy arrived and I overheard a child in the playground tell him: "We've bought you, you know."'

Before getting into my car I looked across the playground enclosed in a high wire-mesh fence. How different this scene was from Winnery Nook with the large picture windows and the view up to the high moors. I looked across to the tall black chimneys and ugly warehouses, wasteland and cramped terraced houses surrounding St Bartholomew's. Then I caught sight of Sister Brendan waving from her office and I heard little Rebecca pointing me out to her mother.

'He's called Mr Grim,' she said, 'and he's a spectre!'

9

It was a chilly day as I drove along a twisting ribbon of a road on my way to a small rural school set in the depths of the Dales. On such an autumn day, the colouring of the scene was unforgettable: long belts of dark green firs glistening in an ocean of crimson heather, great walls of rusty-coloured rock rising sheer, russet bracken slopes, grey wood smoke rising to the pale purple of the sky. It was a cold, bright and silent world.

Suddenly there was a loud crack and my windscreen shattered. I screeched to a halt. Climbing from the car I realized that the long road was quite empty of traffic, the air still and the scene undisturbed. I discovered the cause of the shattered windscreen – a large pheasant lay prone on the bonnet of the car, its claws sticking skywards. I was about to remove the bird when a rotund, red-cheeked character with a great walrus moustache and hair shooting up from a square head appeared from behind the drystone wall. The figure was dressed in bright tweeds – Norfolk jacket, plus fours and deerstalker hat – and carried a large shotgun under his arm.

'I say!' he boomed. 'Are you all right?'

I assured him that I was only a bit shaken but no damage had been done apart from the windscreen.

'Good show!' he roared.

'It came from out of nowhere,' I said. 'I was –'

'Came from out of the sky actually,' corrected my ruddy-cheeked companion. 'I bagged it. It's the October shoot. Lovely day for it. Plenty of game. Good sport. You're on my land, you see.'

'Oh, I'm sorry,' I apologized, 'I thought this was a public road.'

'It is, it is. It's just that it cuts through my land. Didn't you know it was the shoot?'

'No, I didn't,' I replied.

'Well, everyone hereabouts knows it's the shoot. Out of county, are you?'

'Yes . . .'

'Anyway, not too much damage. Drive your car, can you? Garage in the next village. Send the bill to me. No need to bother with insurance and that ballyhoo. Get in touch with the Estate Manager at Manston Hall. I'll tell him to expect your bill. I'm Lord Marrick, by the way. Take care.'

Before I could respond, he disappeared back behind the drystone wall. I stared after him for a moment and then reached for the pheasant.

'I say!' The tweeded figure re-appeared through a gate in the wall, marched straight past me, snatched the pheasant from the bonnet of the car and made off with the aside: 'My bird, I think!'

I met Valentine Courtnay-Cunninghame, the ninth Earl Marrick, Viscount Manston, Baron Brafferton MC, DL properly some weeks later when I joined the interview panel for the appointment of the Headteacher of High Ruston-cum-Riddleswade Endowed Church of England County Parochial Junior and Infant School. I arrived at the school at a time when a lively debate was taking place between the governors.

'Cost us a pretty packet just to place the advert in the paper!' boomed Lord Marrick as I entered the school's only classroom, which had been set out for the interviews. 'All those words in the name and every one to be paid for. Can't see why we can't just call it the village school or Ruston School, that sort of thing.'

'It's tradition, Lord Marrick,' responded the cleric to whom he was talking – a large, balding individual with a genial face and great bushy side whiskers. 'The school has always been known as High Ruston–cum–Riddleswade Endowed Church of England County Parochial Junior and Infant School as long as I can remember.'

'No, no, vicar, it used to be even longer,' added a diminutive, busy-looking woman in tweed suit and brogues. 'In grandfather's time it was High Ruston–cum–Riddleswade by Lowerwatersthwaite and Chapelwatersthwaite Endowed Church of England County Parochial Junior and Infant School.'

'Good grief!' exclaimed Lord Marrick.

'And a goodly number of the children walked the three miles from Lowerwatersthwaite and Chapelwatersthwaite to attend the school. That was before their own school was built in the Dale. So it wasn't that long ago that those villages were included in the name of the school. Quite a mouthful. I remember grandfather joking once that –'

'I'm all for tradition, vicar,' interrupted Lord Marrick. 'Traditions such as keeping to the King James Bible and the *Ancient and Modern Hymnal* in the Church of England – which I have to say your young curate at St Philip's seems to have abandoned in favour of the Good News Bible and those happy-clappy, sing-along tunes – but I can't see the sense in this. I like things to be short and to the point.' Lord Marrick was still dressed in the tweeds I had first come across him in, but he now sported the largest bow tie I had ever seen. It was huge and a vivid green colour with various assorted pheasants, partridges and grouse flying in every direction.

'As for keeping to the King James Bible and the *Ancient and Modern Hymnal* in the Church of England, Lord Marrick,' responded the vicar looking rather peeved, 'I should say that this is a matter which the Parochial Church Council —'

'Shall we . . . er . . . make a start,' announced the Chairman of Governors, a worried-looking woman, turning in my direction. 'I don't think our school inspector has come all the way from Fettlesham to hear us squabble about the name of the school or to hear about the selection of hymns at St Philip's. Let me do a few introductions. I am Mrs Dingle-Smith, the Chairperson of the Governing Body.'

'Chairperson, I ask you!' grunted Lord Marrick. 'What's wrong with Madam Chairman? There's another instance, you see, of loss of tradition.'

'Oh please, Lord Marrick,' pleaded Mrs Dingle-Smith, 'let's not go over all that again. We did discuss my title at the last governors' meeting.' Before the earl could reply, she sallied on. 'I believe you are acquainted with the Rural Dean, the Very Reverend Bernard Braybrook?'

'We met at my interview,' I said, nodding and praying that we would not get into the discussion about Janus again. The cleric held out a pale hand and smiled benignly.

'And over here is another of our governors.' The diminutive, busy-looking woman in the tweed suit and brogues shook my hand with amazing force and gusto.

'I'm Mrs Pole,' she said. 'Spelled P-o-w-e-l-l.'

'I'm Mr Phinn,' I replied. 'Spelled P-h-i-n-n.'

'And our other foundation governor,' continued Mrs Dingle-Smith, 'is the Earl of Marrick.'

'Met before!' roared the earl. 'Good to see you, Mr Phinn. Car all right, is it? Splendid, splendid. I move we get on with this interview, Madam Chairman, otherwise we'll be here all night at this rate. Things to do and all that.'

Surprisingly Lord Marrick said very little during the interviews. He stared rather menacingly at each of the candidates, grunting occasionally or nodding his head in approval on hearing the answers. When it came to his turn to ask a question he snapped: 'Do you believe in standards?' All three candidates for the position of Headteacher assured him that they did indeed believe in quality education and that they would do everything to encourage excellent academic, sporting and moral standards within the school. Having heard such positive responses, the earl nodded vigorously and growled, 'Glad to hear it!'

The last candidate was a rather intense, nervous young man, immaculately dressed with highly polished shoes, crisp white shirt, sober grey suit and dark blue tie. The stare on the earl's face became even more fixed. He inspected the candidate closely as if looking for dirt and then he suddenly asked, 'What's that on your tie?'

'I beg your pardon?' asked the startled candidate.

'The creatures! You have little animals all over your tie.'

'Oh, I see,' replied the candidate. 'They're natterjack toads.'

'Toads?' repeated Lord Marrick. 'Natterjack toads?'

'The natterjack toad is the emblem of CAPOW.'

'Of what?' snapped Lord Marrick.

'The Countryside Association for the Protection of Wildlife,' explained the candidate. 'One of my hobbies is the preservation of endangered species.' Feeling a little more confident he chanced his arm. 'I see that you too like wildlife. I notice that your tie depicts a variety of birds indigenous to the area.'

'Oh, these?' replied the earl casually, lifting the tie to look at the pattern. 'I shoot 'em.'

It was a week later that a memorandum arrived from the Chief Education Officer requesting me to take a group of governors round some infant and primary schools to give them an insight into the workings of the curriculum. On the list was Lord Marrick of Manston Hall, and I was asked to drive him in my car.

A couple of days later, therefore, I collected his lordship from the Small Committee Room at County Hall and explained the programme of visits I had planned.

'Splendid! Splendid!' he cried eagerly.

The first school we visited was a grey-stoned village primary school. Lord Marrick was something of a talking point when he entered the small classroom and with his red cheeks, great walrus moustache and hair shooting up from his square head it was not surprising. The bright tweeds added superbly to the effect. He was introduced to the very nervous Headteacher who was taking the class, and then sat down solidly, legs apart, on a tiny red melamine chair designed for very small children.

After a while he was approached by a small girl who stared and stared at his round, red face and bristling moustache. Then the following conversation took place.

'What is it?' asked the little girl.

'What's what?' retorted Lord Marrick.

'That on your face.'

'It's a moustache.'

'What does it do?'

'It doesn't do anything.'

'Oh.'

'It just sits there on my lip.'

'Does it go up your nose?'

'No.'

'Could I stroke it?'

'No.'

'Is it alive?'

'No, it's not alive.'

'Can I have one?'

'No.'

'Why?'

'Well, little girls don't have moustaches.'

'Why?'

'Because they don't.'

'Can I have one when I grow up?'

'No.'

'Why not?'

'Because ladies don't have moustaches either.'

The little girl thought for a moment, tilted her head on one side before answering. 'Well, my grannie's got one!'

'Really enjoyed that visit,' Lord Marrick enthused, as we drove away. 'My goodness, these little ones are bright as buttons, aren't they?'

At the next school Lord Marrick joined the lower junior class for mathematics. As he sat at the back of the classroom an interested pupil approached him and asked: 'Can you do add-ups?'

'Yes,' replied the peer. 'I'm very good at add-ups.'

'And take-aways?'

'Good at those as well.'

'And timeses?'

'Excellent at timeses.'

'And guz-inters?'

'Guz-inters?' repeated Lord Marrick looking stumped.

'You know, two guz-inter four, four guz-inter eight.'

'Ah, guz-inters!' laughed the peer. 'I'm outstanding at guz-inters.'

'Well, you shouldn't be sitting here,' said the boy. 'You should be on the top table.'

I got to know Lord Marrick well over the next few weeks. He was an immensely warm, generous, supportive and rather extravagant figure who loved the Dales as dearly as any farmer. There was one famous occasion when I accompanied him to a school on his own extensive estate: Manston Church of England Parochial School. He was a well-known figure there and the children were clearly quite delighted when the larger-than-life figure strode through the door and boomed, 'Morning, children!' We sat beneath a marble plaque placed on the classroom wall by his forebear which stated that the small school had been 'endowed by the Dowager Countess Marrick of Manston Park in the North Riding of Yorkshire'.

A chubby little individual came to talk to us with a bright 'Hello'. I let him chat on for a while and then I asked him the sort of question that adults usually ask small children.

'And what would you like to be when you grow up?'

I was expecting one of the stock answers: fireman, doctor, policeman, train driver – but received a most unusual reply.

'The Earl of Marrick,' he announced without hesitation. I stared for a moment at the sunny countenance of the present incumbent of that title, wondering what on earth his reaction would be, and was surprised when he roared with laughter and patted the boy's head affectionately before the child returned to his work.

'Good lad, good lad,' he chortled.

'You are quite a hit, my lord,' I observed as we walked

to the car. 'It's a pity that the little boy will never achieve his ambition.'

'Nonsense!' Lord Marrick roared back. 'That's the grandson!'

10

'It's Lady Macbeth on the phone!' Julie called as she saw my scurrying figure disappear from the office one morning at the beginning of November.

'Who?' I asked puzzled, coming back into the room.

'Mrs Savage and it's urgent – but then again, everything's urgent to her.'

I snatched up the telephone. 'Hello, Gervase Phinn here.'

'Good morning, Mr Phinn,' said a calm, unhurried voice. 'Brenda Savage here, Dr Gore's personal assistant. The Chief Education Officer would like a word with you.'

The soft clear tones of the Chief Education Officer came down the line a few seconds later. 'I've been trying to have a word with you, Gervase, for the past few days but without success. I wonder if you could call over and see me tomorrow at about five o'clock?'

'Yes, of course, Dr Gore,' I replied. 'There isn't a problem, is there?'

'No, no, not a problem as such, but something I need to discuss with you personally. I look forward to seeing you tomorrow then.' The telephone clicked and he was gone.

'Dr Gore wants to see me,' I said to Julie.

'An audience with his eminence. It must be important.'

'He needs to discuss something with me personally, he said. What do you think that means? It sounds a bit ominous, don't you think?'

As with an agitated teacher or anxious parent, Julie calmed

me down, said it would be nothing serious, and added, 'He probably just wants to hear how you are getting on. Don't worry.'

'Yes, of course,' I said, reassuring myself that that was it, but at the back of my mind there was a small nagging worry.

'Come along in, Gervase,' said Dr Gore when I popped my head around his office door the following afternoon. I entered the large, dark-panelled room of the Chief Education Officer. Great glass-fronted bookcases full of leather-bound tomes lined one wall and framed pictures and prints drawn and painted by the county's children and students were displayed on the other. Opposite the bookcases a huge window gave an uninterrupted view over Fettlesham, busy and bustling. In the far distance were the moors and misty tops.

'Sit down, will you, Gervase,' said Dr Gore. He rustled a few papers on his desk before continuing. 'Thank you for coming to see me. Would you like a cup of tea?'

'No thank you, Dr Gore.'

'And are you still enjoying the job?'

'Very much thank you, Dr Gore.' I sounded like a naughty schoolboy in front of the headmaster.

'You've been with us nearly half a term now, haven't you?'

'Yes, that's right,' I replied, smiling inanely and wishing he would get to the point. 'Well, more than half a term now.'

'Good, good. I've been receiving some admirable reports about you. The headteachers seem very impressed and Harold Yeats tells me you are doing extremely well.'

I couldn't halt a rather audible sigh of relief before I replied, 'That's very good to hear.'

'Have you everything you need?'

'Yes thank you, Dr Gore, I have everything I need.' But what was it on his mind? I had not long to wait.

'Good, good. Well now, Gervase, the principal reason for asking to see you was about this reading survey.'

'Reading survey?' I repeated.

'The County Education Committee naturally takes a very keen and active interest in all matters educational and members have received details of the recent Government White Paper on literacy and reading standards – that children cannot read as well as they could and that teachers are going for all these trendy methods of teaching reading. Off the top of your head, would you say that is the case? Is reading being taught effectively? Can children read as well as they could in the past?'

'As far as the county is concerned, Dr Gore,' I stated, 'I think it's a little early for me to comment on the standard of reading overall, but in the few schools I have visited since I started, the standard appears to be very high. Apart from a few cases, the children I have heard read do so with assurance and fluency and the teachers seem to spend a good deal of time teaching reading.'

'Mmm.' Dr Gore steepled his fingers in front of him in the same manner as he had done at my interview. 'Well, be that as it may, and it's very gratifying to hear you say these things, I have agreed with the elected members that we – and I am afraid that really means you – will present a short report to the Education Committee early in the spring. Now, I know that's a pretty short timescale but does it present a problem for you, would you say?'

'I shouldn't think so. It depends really on the number of schools in the sample, but –'

'I do, of course, appreciate that you have hardly got your feet under the table but the thing is, Gervase, you are the best person, as our inspector for English, to take responsibility for this initiative, and to write and present the report. You will need to devise a questionnaire for the selected schools about the various methods used to teach reading, a set of survey questions about children's reading interests, select an appropriate standardized reading test for schools to administer to the sample of pupils, and you will need to hear a representative group. Committee has decided to limit it to six- and seven-year-olds. The collation of the questionnaire and the survey questions, together with the analysis of the reading test results can be done for you. Now, do you think you can manage it?'

'Yes,' I replied. 'I think so.'

'It should provide some very useful information and hopefully reassure our members, governors, parents and teachers that what we are doing in the county with regard to reading is on the right lines.'

'I will start planning right away, Dr Gore,' I said.

'Well, that's settled then. Can you aim to give me a detailed outline of the programme, say, by a week on Monday, together with some idea of which schools you are using in the sample – Harold Yeats will advise you in this – and some notion of costings and timings and so forth, then we can make a start before Christmas. Mrs Savage will look after the admin. so you will obviously need to liaise closely with her. Have you met Mrs Savage, by the way?'

'No, not yet,' I replied.

Dr Gore became thoughtful, steepled his fingers again and nodded sagely. The room had become unexpectedly quiet.

'Good, good,' Dr Gore said suddenly. 'Well, is that everything you need to know?'

'Yes, it seems very clear, Dr Gore. I'll get right onto it.'

'That's settled, then. Thank you for coming to see me, Gervase. I very much look forward to seeing your proposals and to reading your report.'

Over the next few weeks, in between inspecting, advising, directing courses, and joining interview panels, I set about planning the reading survey. With Harold's help, I selected a small random sample of schools in different parts of the county, chose a simple, easily administered test, devised a list of key words for the children to read and designed a questionnaire and a survey about reading interests and patterns. My suggestions were accepted fully by Dr Gore who instructed me to go ahead. The next part of the process was potentially tricky. I needed to see Mrs Savage to get her to reproduce the material and send it out to the schools.

'Not something I would relish, liaising with Mrs Savage,' said Julie screwing up her face as if waiting for an unpleasant smell to evaporate.

I approached the door on which were large black letters spelling out Mrs BRENDA SAVAGE, Personal Assistant to the Chief Education Officer. I wondered what this menacing woman would look like. Julie had painted a picture of a despot with a heart of iron. I knocked tentatively and entered. A young woman looked up from the desk where she was working and smiled.

'May I help you?'

'Yes, I hope so. I'm looking for Mrs Savage.'

'I'm afraid Mrs Savage is at lunch. Can I be of any help?'

I introduced myself, explained about the survey and handed the draft copy of the questionnaire to her.

'And if there are any problems, please ask Mrs Savage to contact me.'

'If there are any problems,' chuckled the secretary, 'Mrs Savage will contact you. Of that you can be certain.'

The following day a memorandum arrived on my desk. It stated briefly that Mrs Savage had received the questionnaire which she had reproduced, with 'various necessary amendments', and that she had arranged for a copy to be despatched to each school requesting that it be returned completed to her for analysis of the results. I had apparently survived unscathed this time.

The first school I visited as part of the survey was at Mertonbeck. It was a small village primary with high mullioned windows and a shiny, grey slate roof. From the classroom window a great rolling expanse stretched to the far-away moors. The Headteacher, a bright-eyed, bubbly and immensely enthusiastic teacher called Jean, introduced me to the children, ensconcing me on a comfortable chair in the corner of the classroom.

'I'll send the children to you, Mr Phinn, one at a time,' she said. 'They really love to read.'

A small, healthy-looking little girl with long golden plaits, wide, unblinking eyes and a face as speckled as a thrush's egg, was the first to join me.

'Hello,' she said brightly. 'I'm Amy. Miss said you wanted to see me.'

'Would you like to read to me, Amy?' I asked pleasantly.

'Why?' came the blunt reply.

'Well, I would like you to.'

'Yes, but what for?'

'Well, because I would. That's why I am here this morning – to hear the children read.'

'Is it your hobby?' I was asked.

'No,' I replied. 'It's my job.'

'Oh,' sighed the infant. 'It's a funny sort of job!'

'Well, I like it,' I smiled.

'It must be nice,' she mused, 'listening to people read all day.'

'It is,' I agreed.

'And do you get paid for it?'

I finally prevailed upon her to read and she did so in a superbly clear and expressive manner. 'All right?' she asked with the satisfied and confident expression of one who knows she is something of an expert.

'Splendid,' I replied. 'Thank you. You're a lovely reader, Amy.'

'I know,' she said. 'And I'm pretty good at writing as well.'

'Are you?'

'Do you like writing, Mr Phinn?'

'Well, well, Amy, you've remembered this funny name of mine. I am very impressed.'

'No, not really,' she replied. 'You have it written on your folder.' She continued in her confident little voice. 'It's a funny spelling, isn't it?'

'Well, in answer to your question about writing, Amy, yes, I do like writing.'

'Do you write stories?'

'Yes.'

'And poems as well?'

'Yes.'

'Do you get the rhymes?'

'Sometimes.'

'And the rhythms?'

'Oh, I always get the rhythms.'

'Do you draw pictures around your poems?'

'No.'

'I do. I think it makes them look prettier on the page. Do you write poems about animals?'

'Yes I do, Amy, but –'

'And people?'

'Amy,' I firmly said, chuckling. 'It's me who usually asks the questions, you know.'

She gave me the sweetest of smiles before replying. 'I'm interested – that's all.'

The next child, a small boy with a crown of close-cropped black hair and large pale eyes between almost colourless lashes, was an excellent reader too. He read from his book with grim determination in a loud and confident voice.

'You're a very good reader,' I commented when he snapped the book shut.

'Aye,' he replied nodding sagely.

'Do you like reading?'

'I do.'

'And I see from your reading card you've read a lot of books this year.'

'I have.'

'Do you read at home?'

'Sometimes.'

It was like extracting blood from a stone but I persevered. 'And what do you like reading about?' I asked cheerfully.

'Animals mostly.'

'Farm animals? Wild animals?'

'All animals.'

'And do you have any animals at home?'

'A few.'

'What sort?' I asked.

'Mostly black and white on green.'

'Pardon?'

'Cows,' he said quietly. 'I live on a farm.' Then a slight smile came to his lips and his expression took on that of the expert in the presence of an ignoramus – a sort of patient, sympathetic, tolerant look.

'Do you know owt about cows then?' he asked.

'No,' I said feebly. I should have left it there but I persisted. 'Would you like to tell me about the cows on your farm?'

'There's not that much to tell really, cows is cows.'

'You're not a very talkative little boy, are you?' I said peering into the pale eyes.

'If I've got owt to say I says it, and if I've got owt to ask I asks it,' he replied casually.

The following week, on a sunny but cold late autumn morning, I visited St Helen's, a tiny Church of England primary school in the depths of the Dale, as part of the reading survey. The small stone building and adjacent chapel had been built in 1788 from the bequest of a wealthy landowner for the education of his estate workers. It had continued over the years to serve the Anglican community in the two villages of Kirby Crighton and Kirby Ruston and one or two children from the nearby United States Air Force Base at Ribbon Bank. The trees had a golden lustre to them that bright morning, the mists had gone and the air was clear and fresh. The whole land surrounding the small school was a vast and silent panorama of fields and hills. I entered the building armed with my questionnaire, checklist, survey form and standardized reading test. In the small entrance area, sitting on a round, coloured cushion and surrounded by an array of books, was a small girl engrossed in her reading.

'That looks a very interesting book,' I said smiling.

She looked up with a most serious expression on the small face and replied, 'Mrs Smith says we are not allowed to speak to strangers.' She then returned to her reading. having been firmly put in my place, I pressed the buzzer at the reception desk, signed in and was soon in the Headteacher's room looking across the desk at the serene countenance of Mrs Smith.

'You will find that we devote a great deal of time and effort to the teaching of reading, Mr Phinn,' said the Headteacher. 'We pride ourselves on achieving good standards and I think you will find every child well on the road to reading.' I was not to be disappointed.

In the infants, I met Elizabeth. She was in that part of the classroom called the Home Corner, where children can dress up, get into role, practise talking, reading, writing and acting out parts. Mrs Smith confided in me later that she had chuckled when a rather pompous inspector, in her dark and distant past, had referred to this area as The Social Interaction Centre. The Home Corner in this classroom was set out like an optician's shop. There were posters and signs, price lists and eye charts, a small desk with plastic till, appointment book and a large red telephone. Elizabeth was dressed in one of her daddy's white shirts. She had a piece of string around her neck attached to a pair of empty frames and was busy arranging some spectacles on a small stand. She was the first child to be tested for reading so I approached.

'Hello,' I greeted her amiably.

'Oh hello,' she replied cheerily and popped the frames on the end of her nose. 'Is it a pair of glasses you want?'

I hadn't the heart to say, 'No, I'm here to give you the Cathcart-Smitt Reading Test,' so I replied, 'Yes, that's right.'

'What sort have you in mind?'

'I think I'd like a pair which makes me look considerably younger.'

'Well, we'll see what we can do.' Then she added, 'I shall have to test your eyes, you know.'

'I thought you might,' I replied.

'Can you read?'

Here was the school inspector come to test the child's reading and he was being tested himself. I nodded and was presented with a list of letters which I read as she pointed to each in turn.

'You have very good eyes,' she said as she rummaged in a box of frames. 'And you want some to make you look young?' She finally decided on a pair as pink as elastoplast, pointed at the ends, with diamanté studs. I tried them on and looked in the mirror. Elizabeth watched fascinated for a moment and then began giggling. She slapped her hand over her mouth to stop herself but her little body shook with mirth.

'Are you laughing at me?' I asked sadly, peering through the ridiculous pair of glasses. She nodded slowly and stopped giggling.

'And are you the manageress of this optician's shop?' She nodded again, her face taking on a slightly quizzical expression. She really did not know what to make of me.

'I don't think it is very nice, you know, for you to laugh at your customers.' I pulled a strained face. 'I'm very upset.'

She stared for a moment before approaching me and then, patting me gently on the arm, whispered gently, 'It's only pretend, you know.'

Elizabeth then read to me in a clear, confident voice full of expression. She completed the reading test with flying colours and talked to me about her reading interests with enthusiasm.

The following week I visited a real optician's to collect some new reading glasses. The amount of reading small print had put quite a strain on my eyes since I had started the job. I waited a good few minutes to gain the receptionist's attention and when I finally managed to lure her to the desk she was curt and unsmiling and said without bothering to look up from the order book on the desk: 'Ready in a week!'

'That young woman,' I thought, 'would benefit from a lesson in good manners and how to treat customers.' And I knew just the person to teach her.

That Friday afternoon as I climbed the stairs to the Inspectors' Office, I felt weary after a week's work in schools. I had just about completed the last visit of the reading survey and had a weekend ahead of me to draft some early findings.

Julie saw me from the outer office and popped her head around the door. 'You've got a visitor.' She raised an eyebrow and curled her top lip.

'I have? Who is it?'

'Mrs "I could curdle milk with one of my stares" Savage. The Lucretia Borgia of the Education Department.' I entered the office to find a tall, elegant middle-aged woman, of strikingly good looks, casting a critical eye on the spider plant which sat on the window sill. I had certainly imagined, from Julie's description, a very different sort of woman. Mrs Savage was dressed in a stylish black suit, black stockings and shoes and was bedecked in an assortment of expensive gold jewellery. So this was the formidable Mrs Savage.

'Mr Phinn!' There was a clash of bracelets and a wealth of false smiles.

'Mrs Savage?' I replied.

'I thought, rather than communicate by constant memoranda and hurried telephone conversations, we should meet face to face to discuss the collating of the results of the reading survey. I do want things to run smoothly. I just cannot be doing with last-minute arrangements. I like things to be done efficiently and thoroughly.' Her voice had a sharp, strident quality and her eyes shone with intensity. She looked ready for combat.

My mother had always advised that, when confronted by belligerent or hostile people bristling for an argument, the best plan of attack was to disarm them with graciousness and affability. It never failed to work. So – I grinned like a shark and replied in the softest of voices.

'I am sure that, with your assistance, Mrs Savage, the final part of the survey will go exceptionally smoothly.' I motioned her to take a seat. 'Would you care for a cup of tea?'

'I only drink herbal tea,' she replied curtly before continuing. 'It's just that I cannot impress on you too strongly how very important this report is, Mr Phinn.' Her voice was still hurried and strident. 'You are, of course, new to writing reports of this nature and addressing the full Education Committee. Dr Gore has asked me especially to help you organize things. He spoke to me personally on the matter only this morning.'

'Dr Gore, I know, regards your work very favourably.'

'Have you been discussing my work with Dr Gore?' she asked looking quite alarmed.

'No, no, it's just that he mentioned how organized and capable you were.'

'Oh, did he?' She allowed herself a slight smile. 'Well, I do endeavour to respond to requests for help promptly and efficiently. I like initiatives such as this to be well planned from beginning to end and with various contingencies built in. I may be something of a stickler but –'

'I think you are so right,' I cut in.

'Pardon?'

'About the need for careful planning – I think you are so right.'

'You do?'

'But, of course. And I know I will get the highest level of support from you.'

'Oh,' was all she could respond with. She was struck dumb with astonishment. The wind had been sucked from her sails. I guessed she had been ready for a confrontation with this new, jumped-up inspector who had been 'disrupted, disturbed, and disorganized' according to Julie, by her mistake with the telephone extension number. On every occasion when Mrs Savage blustered, I agreed with her. I readily accepted her suggestions and supported her ideas, all of which were, in fact, eminently sensible. After an hour, we had planned the report down to the finest detail and Mrs Savage was a different person.

'Your help has been invaluable, Mrs Savage,' I concluded, giving her the shark-like smile.

'Well, it is nice to be appreciated, I'm sure.' Julie looked up from her desk as we passed and, with eyes like a hawk, watched her enemy head for the stairs. 'And should there be anything else,' said Mrs Savage in a much softer tone of voice, 'please do not hesitate to ask. You have my extension number.'

As she clattered down the stairs in her high-heeled shoes, jangling her bangles, Julie shook her head. '"And if there is anything else,"' she minced, imitating Mrs Savage, '"do not hesitate to ask." How that woman has the brass neck to mention extension numbers after the havoc she caused!

And as for you, Mr Phinn, you really did lay it on thick.'

'Well,' I replied, 'a little blandishment goes a long way. In my experience, people always appreciate recognition for what they do and respond much better to a kind word and a smile. I found Mrs Savage not quite the ogre she is painted when I got to know her. In fact, she was perfectly pleasant and more than helpful. I think her bark must be worse than her bite.'

'You think so, do you?' replied Julie, arching the eyebrow again. 'Well in my experience, her bite is worse than her bark and she can yelp and yap and howl and growl louder than most. You mark my words, you may just have bitten off more than you can chew with Mrs Savage. My advice is to stay well clear of her. Beware of the woman in black.'

I should have heeded Julie's prophecy.

11

David Pritchard, County Inspector for mathematics, PE and games was a small, good-humoured, silver-haired Welshman with the comic-pathetic expression of a music hall comedian. He had that gift for words and power of persuasion often possessed by those of Celtic origins. I had met him during my first week with the County Inspectorate. He had breezed into the office, had greeted me like a long lost brother, had shaken my hand vigorously and had taken me for lunch in the staff canteen, all the while talking incessantly. I had learnt more about the inspection business during that one lunch-hour than I had gleaned from all the documents, memoranda, guidelines, policies and other papers which had been sent to me prior to my taking up the post.

I had been in the job now for eight weeks and felt I was really getting to grips with the varied work. I was gaining in confidence and enjoying both the delights and the demands of the work. It was a mild November Saturday morning and, over breakfast, I was browsing through the local paper's section on 'Houses for Sale'. The flat I rented above The Rumbling Tum café looked over Fettlesham High Street. It was roomy and more than adequate for my needs, but extremely noisy and there was a lingering musty smell in every room which, try as I might, I could not remove. I was thinking I might just look at one of the cottages advertised in the paper when the telephone rang.

It was David Pritchard. His voice, breathless and strained, was like that of a soul in purgatory.

'I'm in a real fix, Gervase,' he explained, 'and I need your help.'

'Well, of course, David, but whatever's happened? Are you –' I was stopped in my tracks.

'It was such a bright, sunny morning when I got up that I thought I'd get a round of golf in while Gwynneth was shopping. I don't know whether you play golf or not, Gervase. I find it such a relaxing game and –'

'David!' I interrupted. 'What's happened?'

'Broke a leg,' he said bluntly.

'*What?*'

'I was heading for the club-house for a drink and tripped on this broken paving slab – mind you, they call them patio squares at the Golf Club as the steward pointed out as they carried me in after the fall. I said, "I really don't care what you call the wretched things, they've managed to cripple me."'

'Broke a leg?' I intervened again.

'Clean break. Went over like a skittle. Snapped like a nut. Laid me out good and proper.'

'And where are you now?'

'Waiting to have a plaster cast put on at the Royal Infirmary.'

'I really am sorry to hear that, David,' I sympathized. 'I suppose you're out of action for a few weeks then?'

'Afraid so. Now the thing is, I had a planned visit on Thursday to Sir Cosmo Cavendish Boys' Grammar School. It's the annual inspection of the P E and games department and they are depending on me spending the day there. It's been planned for weeks. The head of department is retiring at Christmas and is all keyed up for this last visit and, of course, the Headmaster, who's a bit of a dry old stick but quite a decent sort, will be none too pleased if it doesn't take place.'

'Well,' I sighed, 'it can't be helped. These things happen. Will Dr Gore bring in a replacement to inspect games and PE then?' There was a deathly silence. 'David? David? Are you still there?' And that's when the bombshell was dropped.

'Well . . . er . . . that's why I'm calling. I'm afraid it has to be you.'

'Me?'

'I'm very sorry, Gervase, but there is no one else.' I could hear the embarrassment and unease in David's voice.

'But my specialisms are English and drama, David,' I pleaded, 'not sport! I'd feel . . . well, uncomfortable to say the least, inspecting games and PE.'

'But you've taught games and PE, haven't you? You've coached rugger and football. You've got a ref's badge and teacher's swimming certificate. You seem eminently qualified to inspect games and PE. I have every confidence in you.'

'How do you know what I have and haven't done?' I asked, bridling.

'Well, because Harold mentioned it. I've just been speaking to him. He agreed with me that you came out as the most appropriate and best qualified person. I mean, Sidney can't do it. He doesn't know the difference between a lacrosse stick and a cricket bat. He'd fall over his own feet. And as for Harold – well, he's getting on a bit and doesn't fancy the prospect of chasing great big strapping lads around the games field in November at his time of life.'

'Neither do I!' I exclaimed.

'There really is no one else. It would be a waste of my

time trying colleagues in other areas. It's too short notice. Their diaries will be full. Gervase, you *must* do it.'

'But I can't, I just can't. I would make a terrible job of it! You will have to explain to the Headmaster that there is no one suitably qualified to inspect games and PE.'

'I don't think Dr Trollop, the Headmaster, will let me off the hook quite so easily. I know him of old. I know you can do it. *Please* say yes!'

So it was that I arrived at St Cosmo Cavendish Boys' Grammar School on the Thursday morning as nervous as a new boy going to the high school on the first day. The Headmaster, a tall cadaverous man with sunken cheeks, greyish skin, a mournful countenance and draped in a long black academic gown, shook his head and rubbed his chin thoughtfully when I acquainted him with the situation. He would make a good living as an undertaker with that dark, solemn face and those great gloomy eyes, I thought to myself.

'So Mr Pritchard is indisposed you say, Mr Phinn?' he murmured in a soft, low, vaguely ecclesiastical–sounding voice.

'I'm afraid that is the case, Dr Trollop,' I replied rather lamely.

'Very unfortunate, very unfortunate indeed,' he intoned, still shaking and rubbing. 'We have a deserved reputation at SCCBGS for our sporting achievements.' He smiled slightly with thin, pursed lips and took to shaking his head and rubbing his chin again. He then gave me the shrewd, penetrating stare of a psychologist before continuing. 'I was rather hoping for a *specialist* inspector.'

'Well I'm sure you appreciate the real dilemma we are in,' I said.

'And, of course, it's the Head of Department's last term,' he sighed. 'Mr Auchterloonie leaves us at Christmas, after thirty years' service to the school. He was so looking forward to seeing Mr Pritchard and hoping to depart for his much-deserved retirement with his work vindicated in the report.' The Headmaster looked at me sadly with the funereal expression of the undertaker who has just offered his condolences to the bereaved. 'Is there no specialist inspector you could import from another area who could have a look at the games and PE?'

'In all fairness,' I said looking into the doleful eyes, 'I do agree the subjects should be inspected by a specialist but there is no one, I'm afraid.'

'In addition, Mr Phinn, classes are ending early today for the North Yorkshire Schools League rugby matches, the crucial third round, and I did particularly want Mr Pritchard to be here.'

There was something immensely sad in the Headmaster's glance at me. 'It is very unfortunate, Mr Phinn,' he sighed, 'but beggars, as they say, cannot be choosers.'

Mr Auchterloonie was a broad, solid, hard-looking man with a leathery face as crinkled and brown as a walnut. With his tough, straggling white moustache and small sharp eyes, he had the vigorous, tusky look of a walrus.

'We were expecting tae be inspected by Mr Pritchard,' he growled at morning break when he collared me outside the staff toilets. 'I thought you were the English and drama inspector?'

I explained the predicament. 'Mr Pritchard has broken his leg.'

'Well, canna he not inspect on crutches or in a wheel-chair?' came the reply.

'Not really,' I replied. 'However, I am prepared to inspect

games and PE myself. I can make judgements on the quality of the teaching and learning, the available resources and the appropriateness of the accommodation and facilities. Of course, my report will not be as detailed nor perhaps as well-focused as it would have been if Mr Pritchard had been undertaking it but I am accredited to inspect PE and I have taught games in an earlier life as a teacher.'

'Aye, well, Mr Phinn,' growled the teacher, 'I suppose ye'll have tae do.'

Mr Auchterloonie lived up to his reputation. His lessons were well-taught and there was no trace of indiscipline or laziness on the part of his pupils. The boys responded well to the firm but fair approach of a well-respected teacher. They also enjoyed his touches of humour.

As they ran out on that Thursday morning onto the hard pitches, with a cold November wind whistling in their faces, one boy shouted over to Mr Auchterloonie, 'Sir, it's *freezing.*'

The teacher gave a tusky grin before answering. 'There's an old Scottish saying, Farrington, that "Many are cold, but few are frozen!"' The boys who heard that roared with laughter. 'Now let's play rugger!' called the games teacher, rubbing his hands together.

It was the end of the school day and things had gone remarkably smoothly. I was on my way to say my farewells and return to the Education Office when I spotted Dr Trollop near the school entrance. He was in animated conversation with a tall, distinguished-looking man in his mid-fifties, with a thin, neatly-trimmed moustache and dressed immaculately in dark blazer and grey flannel trousers. The Headmaster's mournful countenance had been replaced by a distinctly cheerier look and there was a lightness in his voice when he called out across the quadrangle.

'Ah, Mr Phinn!' he called as he caught sight of me. 'Do please come and meet "Legs" Bentley.'

I approached, nodded and smiled at the visitor. 'I'm sorry,' I said, 'but I didn't quite catch the name.'

'"Legs", "Legs" Bentley,' repeated Dr Trollop before turning to his visitor. 'I've always known you as "Legs". I'm not sure I even know your first name.'

'It's what everyone calls me,' replied the distinguished-looking man genially.

'"Legs" was the fastest wing half in Yorkshire in his day. No one could catch him once he was running down the pitch full pelt. Hence the nickname,' explained Dr Trollop.

'I'm very pleased to meet you,' I said, shaking the visitor's hand.

'Mr Phinn is leading the school inspection of the games and PE department in place of his colleague, Mr Pritchard, who has had an unfortunate accident,' explained the Head-master. '"Legs" is President of Yorkshire Rugby Union this year, Mr Phinn, and has called in to see the rugger matches this afternoon. I guess you were on your way to the pitches when I called.'

I smiled weakly and nodded. The report would have to be written later that evening.

'Well, you won't want to miss the matches, will you, Mr Phinn?' asked his companion. 'They promise to be really cracking games.'

'No, no, I won't want to miss the matches,' I replied, resigned to another hour or so out in the cold.

As I headed back towards the playing fields, I sensed a presence behind me. Then Mr Auchterloonie materialized silently at my side and, greeting me with the tusky smile, said amiably, 'Ah, there ye are, Mr Phinn. I thought you'd want to catch the matches. I'll walk over with ye. One of the boys was telling me that you follow the rugby?'

I nodded. 'Yes, when I get the chance.'

'Do you play?'

'I did, but I stopped playing after a couple of accidents. I was a very indifferent player, I'm afraid. I tended to make up the numbers.'

'Aye, well, it's nae worse fae that. I tell the boys winning is one thing but playing the game is more important. I tell them just to try their best, have a go.'

'Good advice,' I replied.

'The President of Yorkshire RU is here this afternoon,' commented Mr Auchterloonie.

'Yes, that's right. I've just met him.'

'He's something of a legend in Yorkshire is "Legs" Bentley.'

'So I hear,' I replied.

'Incredibly keen on youth rugby.'

'Really?'

'I should think ye know the rules of rugby union pretty well, don't ye?' asked Mr Auchterloonie.

'Well, I suppose I'm reasonably conversant with them.'

'And I hear ye've done a wee bit of refereeing in your time.'

I could feel myself rather like a fish on a line being drawn slowly in – drawn relentlessly, breathlessly, into a net from which it might well be difficult to disentangle myself.

'Yes,' I replied slowly, 'I did coach and referee matches when I was a young teacher but that was some years ago now.'

'Now the situation is this, Mr Phinn . . .'

I could predict what was coming next. 'You're short of a referee,' I sighed.

'There now, I knew you inspectors were pretty sharp but I never realized ye were endowed with psychic powers. You see, the four teams from St Ignatius Boys' Catholic Grammar are, at this moment, changing, but one of their teachers – actually, it's the Head of Department, Mr McGrath – has had to return to school with a boy with stomach pains. We can cover three of the matches but I am desperate for someone tae referee the under-twelves. I'm in a real fix, Mr Phinn, and I need your help.'

'Ah St Ignatius,' I said, desperately trying to change the subject, 'that's the next school on my list for inspecting, I think.'

'Outstanding sporting reputation. Jesuits, you see – they're fanatical about rugger. They win the County Shield every time but this year we are in with a chance. Anyhow, we are desperate. I know you've taught games and PE because you told me so. You've coached rugger and, if I may say so, you're doing a grand job with the inspecting.'

'I was coming to watch, Mr Auchterloonie, not to referee.'

'I appreciate that, but ye just couldn't let those youngsters down, now could ye? I know you'll be just masterful. Please say "Yes"!'

'I don't think I can. I have no kit.'

The tusky smile on the teacher's face seemed to stretch from ear to ear and the small, sharp, clever eyes sparkled. 'Och, no problem at all, I have a spare one.'

'But not in my size,' I replied with some desperation in my voice.

'I think ye'll find that we have.'

So, kitted out in Mr Auchterloonie's spare strip, in boots a size too small and a suspect looking whistle, I jogged out to referee the under-twelves. Earlier that week it had been mild and on occasions quite sunny but by Wednesday the weather had turned bitterly cold. By the Thursday afternoon ragged clouds scudded across an iron-grey sky and thin icy rain like umbrella spokes began to fall.

At the sound of the whistle, there was no stopping the two sides. The youngsters, like nests of frantic rabbits, raced around the field after the ball, moving at a frightening speed. Many of them were felled like trees but would not stay down and jumped up to their feet again, racing and dodging, leaping and weaving. Then the sleet began to fall in earnest. Puddles formed on the pitch, my shorts and socks became sodden and sticky and it was difficult to identify which boy played for which side so caked they were in mud. But the players were undeterred. At the sound of the whistle they formed themselves into a steaming, panting heap for the scrum-down and were soon off again swirling and scuffling, with the ball bobbling muddily in a flurry of grunts and shouts.

It was just after half time that I heard the first roar from the sidelines, after I had made what perhaps was a contentious decision.

'Oi ref! Where's your glasses?' I glanced to the sidelines to see a tall, thin individual, standing in the rain, in a bright orange tracksuit. I returned to the game, which continued to be as fast-moving, furious and frenetic as ever. The field was becoming a swamp, the ball heavy and slippery and I was dripping wet with rain and sweat. After my next decision, for the boys to play-on after a tackle, the voice from the sidelines was heard again booing, protesting, crowing, jeering, exhorting with a real passion. Dazed by the noise and mesmerized by the speed of play I could feel myself losing a grip on the game.

When a series of incidents happened in rapid succession, the voice from the sidelines boomed across the field. 'Come on, ref! You do have a whistle, you know! Is your pea stuck?'

After a number of further comments, I had had quite enough of the orange individual and approached him. He was a thin, chisel-faced man with a long stalk of a neck, bright, glittering blue eyes and scant reddish hair combed in a series of wisps across his balding head.

'Look here,' I said, 'I really could do without your running commentary. Would you please refrain from shouting and barracking.'

'Well, you're making some very dodgy decisions and no mistake. We're playing union, you know, not American football and this is an important match.'

'I'm perfectly aware what we are playing. Now, I would appreciate it if you would keep quiet.'

He gave me a dark and disapproving glance before heading in the direction of the lower pitch where another game was in progress, mumbling under his breath something about 'the decline in standards of refereeing'.

After what seemed an eternity the match came to a close with the home side winning by one try. I congratulated both sides on their enthusiasm and behaviour during the match and joined Mr Auchterloonie who I could see heading towards me.

'Grand decision that, ref, grand decision. What a win!' he boomed. Before I could reply he continued, 'I see you met Gerry.'

'Gerry?'

'In the orange.'

'Oh, the one with the loud voice and all the answers.'

'He's Head of PE and games at St Ignatius. Bit disappointed was Gerry aboot his team losing. First time in years. He was the one you were standing in for.'

I must have looked like a wet rat as I squelched off the pitch towards the changing-rooms, with Mr Auchterloonie whistling merrily by my side.

I caught sight of Dr Trollop and the President of the Yorkshire Rugby Union snug in heavy overcoats and sheltering from the sleet and wind in the entrance to the games and PE block. I was freezing cold, aching all over, exhausted and ready for a hot bath.

'I must congratulate you, Mr Phinn,' said the President as I approached, obviously trying to suppress his laughter, 'on your very individual, indeed your highly-creative style of refereeing. It was quite an experience to watch. What you clearly lacked in knowledge of the game, you amply compensated for by your irrepressible zeal, enthusiasm and commitment. I've never seen a game quite like that one.' He patted me heartily on the back and turned to Mr Auchterloonie. 'Well done, Gus, the boys did you proud.'

Dr Trollop glowed with pleasure. Gone were the great gloomy eyes and the solemn face. 'Yes, indeed,' he added brightly. 'A rather nice retirement present for you to beat St Ignatius.'

As the Headmaster and the President headed in the direction of the school, an orange apparition materialised out of the gloom of the late afternoon, the thin, chiselled face red and glowering, and the wisps of wet hair hanging limp like rats' tails.

'Ah, Gerry,' chortled Mr Auchterloonie.

'I want a word with your ref, if I may, Gus,' the man blustered. 'I was not best pleased, not best pleased at all, with the way he refereed the match.' The shrill voice chittered with a rising inflexion of annoyance, and the glittering blue eyes flashed in anger. He turned to me and pointed a bony finger pistol-like at my chest. 'I just cannot believe some of the decisions that you made, I just cannot believe them. I really think it's about time you hung up your boots. In all my years of –'

'Let me introduce you, Gerry,' interrupted Mr Auchter-loonie in a quiet voice and giving a great tusky grin. 'Gerry McGrath meet Mr Gervase Phinn, oor school inspector, who kindly stepped in tae the breech and helped oot in your unavoidable absence. He's also filling in for Mr Pritchard, his colleague, and is inspecting all the PE and games in the county at the moment. Is that not right, Mr Phinn?' There was a deathly silence. Mr Auchterloonie continued merrily, 'I should think you'll be seeing quite a lot of Mr Phinn, Gerry, in the coming weeks. I believe he's at your school for an inspection in the not too distant future.' Mr Auchter-loonie, trying to suppress his amusement by sucking the corners of his moustache, carried on relentlessly. 'I should imagine that Mr Phinn will be watching you teach PE and, of course, games when he visits St Ignatius.'

Mr McGrath smiled weakly, a smile which was less a mark of pleasure than discomfort, as if he were wincing at the pinching of boots which were too tight for his feet. He held out a limp hand.

I smiled a very friendly smile and shook his hand vigor-ously. 'I very much look forward to seeing you in the near future, Mr McGrath,' I said. 'And I will remember to bring my glasses.'

12

'By the way, Gervase,' said Sidney one Friday morning before the monthly Inspectors' Meeting, 'I saw the delectable Miss Bentley of Winnery Nook yesterday.'

'Oh, did you?' I replied, trying to sound casual.

'You didn't waste much time getting in there, did you?'

'I really don't know what you mean.'

'When I mentioned our new dynamic inspector, she said she had already met you. I believe hers was one of the first schools you visited.'

'Yes, that's right.'

'And what was the excuse for visiting the most desirable, unmarried woman in the whole county?'

'I was invited.'

'This is getting more and more interesting, nay intriguing.'

'If you must know, I received a welcoming letter from Miss Bentley and some poems from the children, and thought I'd call in to thank them.'

'And what did you think of the comely Miss Bentley of Winnery Nook?'

'She seems very nice.'

'Very nice? Very nice?' Sidney spluttered. 'You are supposed to be our county inspector and resident expert on the English language, someone who has a flair in using one of the richest, most descriptive, most beautiful and powerful languages in the entire world and all you can come up with is "very nice". She's absolutely gorgeous, dear boy. Miss Bentley is a veritable vision! A Nordic beauty! If I were not a happily married man, I should be in there like a tom cat with its tail on fire.'

'For someone who has just berated me, Sidney, about my choice of words and about the wonders of one of the richest, most descriptive, most beautiful and powerful languages in the entire world, your choice of simile leaves a lot to be desired.'

'Oh but Gervase, don't you think Miss Bentley of Winnery Nook is something to be desired? Don't you think she's just exquisite – like some pale porcelain figurine?'

'I visited in my professional capacity. That sort of thing just never entered my head,' I lied.

'Ah! Good grief! You do sound an old stuffed shirt. "That sort of thing just never entered my head,"' he mimicked. 'I mean, how old are you, for goodness sake – ninety-five?'

'Thirty-one.'

'Thirty-one, attractive, educated, desirable, generous, good-natured and, more importantly, single and unattached –'

'Please don't go on, Sidney.'

'You're love's young dream, dear boy!'

'Hardly.'

'You want to get in there. Ask the divine Miss Bentley out to the theatre.'

'It wouldn't be right. I mean, it could compromise a professional relationship. It's not ethical.'

'Thirty-one and acting as if he's in his dotage.' He mimicked my earnest voice again: '"It could compromise a professional relationship. It's not ethical."'

'Would you mind not parroting everything I say, please?' I retorted tartly but before he could reply our discussion was curtailed when the giant frame of Harold Yeats appeared through the door.

'Colleagues,' he boomed, 'shall we begin the meeting?'

The conversation about Christine Bentley did start a train of thought which I could not get out of my head. I mean, Winnery Nook was not a school for which I had any specific responsibility and it would be very unlikely that I would ever be in a position to inspect it formally, so why shouldn't I ask her out. Then again, she might have a boyfriend or be engaged and I would make a fool of myself. But I could, of course, make a few discreet enquiries on that count. Then again, if I did ask her out and she declined, it would go around the county like wild fire. 'That's the inspector who asked Miss Bentley out!' I just did not know what to do.

The situation was resolved, or so I thought, the following Sunday. I read in the local newspaper that at an auction at Roper's Saleroom in Collington, the next door town, there would be some early editions of children's books for sale. I had quite a collection of children's stories, picture books, and poetry anthologies and I thought I would see if there was anything of interest. At least it would get me out of the dark, damp flat for a couple of hours.

The auction room was a long, elegant building set back from the road. I browsed around, passed great polished oak dressers and ornate satinwood cabinets, carved mahogany bookcases and walnut balloon-backed chairs, grandfather clocks and inlaid rosewood tables, display cases full of *objets d'art*, porcelain figures, china plates and tea-sets, silver cutlery, lamps and glassware. As I headed for a table piled with books, I caught sight of Christine Bentley gently stroking the top of a highly-polished mahogany table. She did indeed look like a vision. I watched her move around the room with a languid easy grace and felt borne upon a stream of most powerful emotion. She must have sensed that someone was watching for she looked up, saw me staring, waved and then came over.

'Hello,' she said, giving me a stunning smile. 'I thought it was you.'

'Hello,' I managed to reply in a hoarse whisper, looking into the dark blue eyes.

'So you are interested in antiques, are you?'

'Well, no, not really. I came to look at some children's books. I collect early editions.'

'And have you seen anything you fancy?' she asked.

'I beg your pardon?' I spluttered.

'Any books which interest you?'

'Well there's a first edition of *Un Drôle de Chien* but I guess it will be out of my price range.' I realized my voice sounded rather wavery, pure nerves.

She smiled and was just about to reply when a tall, fair, good-looking man approached.

'Not much here, I'm afraid. Did you see anything, Chris?' he asked, ignoring me.

'There's a nice Georgian birdcage table, not too big, which would probably fit into the study. Oh Miles, this is Gervase Phinn. He's an inspector.'

The pale young man glanced in my direction observing the jeans and baggy jumper. 'Plain clothes?' he asked.

'Not a police inspector, silly,' chuckled Christine. 'He's a school inspector.'

'Really? You're that man that puts the fear of God into the poor teachers, are you?' commented her suave companion, brushing back a strand of blond hair like a male model and catching sight of himself in an ornate gilt mirror.

'Not really,' I replied.

'It must be dreadfully dull sitting at the back of classrooms ticking little checklists and writing endless reports all day. And those beastly noisy little children everywhere. Still, each to his own. What are you interested in?' he added in a weary tone of voice.

I looked at Christine and thought I detected a slight smile on her lips as she looked back at me.

'Interested in?' I enquired.

'At the auction. Are you here for a particular piece of furniture?'

'No, no,' I replied. 'I'm looking at some old books?'

'Really? Old books?'

'I collect early editions of children's books but I think the ones on sale today are going to be a little too pricey for me. I was just saying, I . . .' My voice trailed off. I could see he was not the slightest bit interested.

He gave me a patronizing smile. 'Well, we must make tracks.' He took Christine's arm and began to lead her away. 'There's nothing I like, Chris, so we might as well go and get something to eat. There's that nice old pub near Hawksrill I thought we'd try. There wasn't anything you wanted, was there?'

'Yes, there was, as a matter of fact,' she said, releasing herself and flicking through the catalogue. 'There's a Copeland china plate, lot 229, a Hammersley bone china plate with cobalt blue borders and gilding, and an early Davenport blue plate.' She looked up and smiled in my direction. 'I collect blue plates. Miles says I have enough crockery to cover the fields of his farm.'

'Come on, Chris, we don't want to spend all day here just for a couple of plates. It will take ages to reach that part of the sale. If you're really interested in even more plates and Mr Glynn here is staying on to bid for his old books, perhaps he could bid for the plates. We could reimburse him later.'

'I should be delighted,' I replied. 'As Miles says, I will be waiting around for the old books to come up so I might as well.'

'Oh could you?' cried Christine. 'That is kind. But don't go above thirty pounds, will you. There's two plates I'm interested in: the Copeland and the Davenport. The Hammersley will fetch too high a price so leave that one. It's lots 229 and 237 I think, but I'll just check.' She ran a long delicate finger down a page in the catalogue. 'Yes, that's right. There's also "a blue plate of unknown provenance", lot 239. You could go to twenty pounds for that.'

'If you manage to buy the plates, you could pop round with them sometime. There'll be coffee and a biscuit waiting.' Her eyes twinkled as she mentioned the biscuit.

'Oh, do come on, Chris,' urged Miles, tugging at her arm. With that, they left chattering, no doubt including comments about the strange inspector who collected old books. I must have seemed deadly dull.

The book I was interested in, lot 198, fetched a price way above that which I was prepared to pay. There was nothing else I was interested in and could have left the auction room there and then – goodness knows I had enough to do. But I stayed to bid for the plates, and sat thinking about Christine and feeling a strange dull ache deep in the pit of my stomach. I had never felt like this about anybody before. If I bought the plates that would give me the ideal opportunity of calling in to see her again. Perhaps then I could . . .

My thoughts were abruptly interrupted by the auctioneer's announcement: 'Lot 238: a Davenport toy tea-set painted with Pratt coloured decoration, comprising four cups and saucers, a slop bowl and sugar bowl and cover with an impressed mark on the base. Can we start the bidding at two hundred pounds.'

Oh Lord, I had missed the two plates I had been asked to bid for. My mind had been on quite other things. Then I heard the auctioneer announce the next item: 'Lot 239, an attractive pale blue patterned plate of unknown provenance.'

Right, I thought, I'll bid for this and not go away empty-handed. A big, purple-faced individual raised a finger as fat as a sausage when the auctioneer started the bidding at twenty pounds. I raised my hand.

'Twenty-five pounds!' shouted the auctioneer, pointing in my direction.

'Thirty!' barked the purple-faced individual.

'Thirty-five!' I called out.

'Forty!'

'Forty-five!' I was determined to buy the plate. Before I knew it, the bidding was up to fifty pounds. The fat, purple face was now more of a crimson colour.

'Fifty-five pounds!' he roared.

'Sixty!' I shouted with a defiant ring to my voice.

At last, old purple face shook his head and looked down at the catalogue.

'Any other bids, ladies and gentlemen?' called the auctioneer. 'Going once, going twice. Any more for this delightful, blue patterned plate? No? Sold to the gentleman in the jumper and jeans.'

As I signed the cheque for the plate, the purple-faced individual sidled up. 'Nice plate,' he said. 'Very nice plate. Unusual figures. Nice bit of patterning as well.'

'Yes,' I replied, 'I'm sure my friend will like it.'

'Pity about the crack,' he grunted, before pushing his way through the throng.

That evening I sat looking at the plate wondering what to do. In my opinion, it was a very ugly piece of pottery. The three stiff Chinese figures looked quite out of proportion, the perspective of the bridge was all wrong and the depiction of the trees and vegetation was crude to say the least. The picture looked like one executed by a small child. Worst of all, there was a long hairline crack right across the centre. I could imagine the gloating Miles turning it over in his hands with the comment, 'Fancy buying a plate with a crack in it!'

I telephoned Miss Bentley the following Monday.

'Hello, Winnery Nook Nursery and Infant School.'

'Miss Bentley?' There was that tell-tale nervousness in my voice again.

'Speaking.'

'It's Gervase Phinn here. I'm afraid I missed the two plates you were interested in. They fetched quite a high price.'

'Oh, not to worry,' she replied.

'But I did get the other plate. The one of unknown provenance.'

'Oh excellent,' she said. 'How much did you pay for it?'

'As you said, twenty pounds.'

'I'm delighted. Thank you so much for taking the trouble.'

'No trouble,' I replied. 'It was a pleasure.'

'And did you buy anything?'

'I'm afraid not. Everything was out of my price range.'

'I'm sorry. There's no rush to get the plate to me but when you are passing, drop in. The coffee – and biscuit –

are waiting. Now don't forget, when you are passing.'

'I'll look forward to that,' I replied before placing the receiver down carefully. 'I really will look forward to that.'

13

'There has been a veritable harem wishing to speak to you today, dear boy,' said Sidney when I arrived at the office late one afternoon. 'Is that not so, David?' David Pritchard looked up from his papers and nodded. His leg, with the most enormous plaster cast upon it, was thrust out before him.

'I would like to know,' continued Sidney, with mock melancholy, 'your secret with the opposite sex, Gervase. Women seem to be queueing up to speak to you.'

I was ready with a riposte, for both colleagues had been teasing me good-humouredly over the past few weeks about finding 'a good woman' and 'settling down' and giving up my 'lonely bachelor life', but before I could open my mouth Julie bustled in. She held a batch of telephone message sheets which she proceeded to read out, much to the amusement of my two colleagues.

'The phone has not stopped ringing all afternoon for you,' she announced. 'It's been like the switchboard at a dating agency. You've had Mrs "I could turn you to stone with my stare" Savage asking if you were in. She intends to "catch you" later on. You've had Mrs Beighton of Hawksrill School wanting you to get in touch. You've had Mrs Powell (pronounced Pole) about the St Philip's Church fête. You've had Connie from over the way thanking you for the box of chocolates – what are you sucking up there for? You've had Sister Brendan on, asking you to take part in her Victorian Day. You've had Miss – or Miz Isleworth about the drama seminar. And – you've had Miss Bentley of Winnery Nook saying a cheque is in the post. There,' sighed Julie, 'all done. You sound like the Casanova of the Education Department.'

'What it is to be so popular,' sniggered Sidney snatching up his briefcase and breezing out of the office but not before adding, 'and in such urgent demand by the delightful Miss Bentley of Winnery Nook as well.'

'I thought you were finishing that report for me to type before you went?' Julie said to his departing back.

Sidney stopped in the doorway, and said with deadly emphasis, 'Julie, if Mrs Savage is on her way over here I am departing post haste. I'm just not up to seeing her this afternoon.' His words were followed by a clattering of high-heeled shoes on the stairs and jangling of heavy jewellery. Sidney gave a great sigh and pulled a grotesque face. 'Here she comes.' With that he shot out of the door. 'Prepare for the entrance of the Queen of Sheba.'

'If it wasn't for this leg,' sighed David rubbing the plaster cast, 'I'd have been down those stairs with him.'

Mrs Savage swept into the office with all the appearance of assuming she was the most important person there.

'Was that Mr Clamp I saw scurrying down the back staircase? I wanted a word with him.' She did not wait for a reply. 'Ah, Mr Phinn, just the man I want.'

David looked up and arched an eyebrow.

'Oh . . . er . . . Mrs Savage, good afternoon. I can't stay to talk, I'm afraid. I'm attending a governors' meeting at West Challerton High School at five-thirty and am late already. I said I would be there for –' She held up a hand as if stopping traffic. 'It will only take a moment. Firstly, here is the full statistical breakdown of the reading test scores which you asked for, and the results of the survey on reading interests.' She plucked a wad of papers from a large red file. 'They look most impressive, I must say. I hope you will be pleased with the result.' She cast a glance at David who had returned to his report, head down and pen scratching. 'I just wish some of your colleagues were as prompt and adept at getting the material to me,' she said casually. 'It would make my life a whole lot easier.'

David was either too involved in his report, assumed the criticism was not addressed to him or merely chose not to hear the barbed comment, for he carried on scribbling away at his desk.

'You also need these.' Mrs Savage thrust a bright yellow badge and plastic covered card into my hands. 'The identity card had to go back to printing to be re-set, that's why it's a little late.'

'Did you spell his name wrong again, then?' asked David with feigned innocence.

Mrs Savage saw fit to ignore the remark and continued unabashed. 'And here's your badge to be worn at all times when on county business. Your colleagues should all have theirs by now.'

I stared for a moment at my identity card complete with name, title, county crest and photograph, and at the large yellow badge.

'It's a damn silly idea, if you ask me,' grumbled David looking up suddenly. 'Having to wear these wretched psychedelic badges. I don't mind the identity cards but great big, bright, plastic lapel badges, like the ones travel couriers wear, go against the grain – particularly when you have an enormous badge like mine. It's virtually the width of my body. And look at the size of the letters. Whoever designed these monstrosities?'

'I did,' retorted Mrs Savage scowling. 'And if you wish me to convey to the CEO that you think his introduction of identity badges is "a damned silly idea", then I shall be only too pleased to oblige, Mr Pritchard.'

'I have already expressed my views, Mrs Savage, thank you very much. If we have to wear badges, then I think they ought to be smaller, more subdued and certainly less conspicuous than these luminous objects. We will be wielding great red and yellow signs next, like the crossing patrol people, with "Stop, School Inspector".'

'It is not a question of "if", Mr Pritchard,' Mrs Savage replied calmly. 'You are obliged to wear a badge. It is Dr Gore's directive. Anyway, I don't hear Mr Phinn complaining.' She gave me a broad smile.

'Well, if I *have* to wear the thing, why can't I have *Inspector* written on the badge instead of *Mr DAVID R. S. PRITCHARD* and why do we have to have the county crest on?'

'Because –' began Mrs Savage.

'And why is my first name written in full? I'll have all the children calling me Uncle Dave at this rate. And another thing about these badges –'

'Look, I'm sorry but I must go,' I interrupted and rushed from the room, thankfully leaving the altercation behind me.

The next morning Harold was waiting for me in the foyer to the Conference Hall in Fettlesham, a large Georgian-style building with a high-domed ceiling, long elegant windows and great white pillars. We had been asked by Dr Gore to attend a symposium on the theme of 'The Education of Children in a Hospital Environment' and each of us was to chair a discussion group.

'I've saved us a couple of seats down at the front of the lecture theatre,' said Harold, taking my arm and guiding me through the throng. 'If we are chairing the discussions we need to hear every word.'

'I see you are wearing the new official county identity badge,' I remarked, looking at the rectangle of bright yellow plastic pinned to his lapel and bearing the words, in bold capitals: DR HAROLD J. YEATS.

'Excellent idea having a badge. We should have had these years ago.'

'I don't think David would agree,' I replied and regaled him with the lively difference of opinion I had witnessed in the office the day before.

'Well, I'm all for them. A little bright and garish maybe, but necessary. They will save so much confusion. Do you know, if I had a penny for every time someone says when they meet me: "Well you don't look like a school inspector to me!" I'd be a millionaire by now. I shall just point to the badge, flash my identity card and Bob's your uncle.'

We had just settled in our seats awaiting the arrival on the podium of the distinguished speaker when the elderly woman sitting next to Harold, having glanced at the impressive-looking badge on his lapel, held out her hand in front of his face. Three fingers were joined together like the webbed foot of a duck.

'What do you make of that then, doctor?' she asked.

'Pardon?' replied Harold startled.

'My hand. Have you seen anything like that before?'

'No, I can't say that I have. It's . . . er . . . very unusual.'

'It's baffled lots of doctors has that hand. There's not one doctor I have asked could tell me how my hand came to be like this. It's not congenital, you know. I wasn't born with my hand like this.'

'So it was an accident,' remarked Harold.

'Yes, though it happened years ago. Are you a surgeon or a general practitioner?' asked the woman. Before Harold could explain that he was not, in fact, a doctor of medicine, the woman proceeded to explain how, as a child, she had caught her hand in her mother's old washing mangle. There then followed a detailed and gruesome description of the various operations she had undergone, with Harold nodding sympathetically. When she began to talk about a rather more personal ailment, Harold coughed, clearly embarrassed at the way the conversation was proceeding, and gestured to the podium with some relief.

'Ah,' he said, 'I see the speaker is ready to begin.'

During the break for lunch, we were sitting in the foyer when the elderly lady, in quite an agitated state approached, accompanied by a worried-looking attendant and several of the delegates.

'Here he is!' she exclaimed. 'This gentleman's a doctor.'

'Excuse me, doctor,' began the attendant, 'I'm sorry to disturb you but we have a lady who has fainted and the manager wonders if you might take a look at her?'

'No, no, I don't know anything about medicine!' Harold cried to the group of concerned onlookers. 'I'm a doctor of medieval history.'

I saw the woman with the splayed hand scowling as she heard this, and then chattering at her companions. I just caught the words 'that bogus doctor' as she stalked off.

'This badge has got to go,' grunted Harold removing the offending rectangle of plastic from his lapel.

Not long after, I noticed the badge had been amended to read: *H. J. YEATS, Inspector.*

'That should avoid any further confusion,' said Harold confidently. He was mistaken, as he recounted to us later that week.

'You're not wearing your badge, Harold,' chided David one lunch-time. 'Don't let the wicked witch of the west see you without it or she'll put a spell on you.'

'The badge has had to go,' sighed Harold. 'It's been more trouble than it was worth.' Then he gave us a blow-by-blow account of his skirmish the evening before. 'I'd just finished reporting back to the governors about an inspection at St Hilda's. It was late, I was tired and I wanted to get home. I got to the car and it was all iced up. I looked in the boot. No de-icer, no scraper. I have a very efficient de-mister in the Volvo, so I put it on full blast, cleaned a bit of the front window, enough to see ahead of me, and turned out of the school gates. I'd only gone a couple of hundred yards when I heard a siren and saw flashing lights behind me. I pulled over and wound down a window. There was this young policeman. "Are you able to see out of your rear window, sir?" he asked me. I admitted that I couldn't. "Are you able to see clearly what is behind you through your side mirrors, sir?" I admitted that I couldn't. "Do you realize, sir, that it is an offence to be driving a vehicle when your view is restricted in this way?" I admitted that I was aware of the fact. I tried to explain that I usually clean the windows before driving but had no de-icer or scraper. Then he asked me to get out of the car, and was reaching for his notebook. I'm in for it, I thought as I climbed out. He stared up at me and then his eyes moved to the wretched badge which I had forgotten to take off, the one with *H. J. YEATS*, Inspector on it. "That will be all right, sir," the bobby said suddenly. He pushed his notebook into his pocket and saluted me. Then he turned to the other policeman in the car and I heard him mutter "CID." Then they just drove away. Phew, what a let off.'

I had my own problems with my badge. I had made a morning visit to a school in the centre of Collington and over lunch decided to call into Kepple's department store and look for a large bright rug to brighten up my dreary flat. I had completely forgotten about the badge on my lapel and was browsing between the rows of rolled floor coverings and fabrics when an elderly lady approached and tugged at my arm.

'Is this Axminster?' she asked. The large sign above, which she had clearly missed, indicated that it was.

'Yes,' I replied, moving down the row.

'Is it hard wearing?' The elderly lady was at my side.

'Well, Axminster has a reputation, I believe, for being a very hard-wearing carpet.'

'Don't you know?'

'Well, I can't claim to be an expert on carpets,' I replied.

'What's the price of this one?'

'I've no idea,' I replied moving further along the row.

'You're not very helpful, young man,' said the woman.

'I'm sorry but, as I said, I'm not an expert on carpets.'

'Can you tell me about the linoleum and cushion flooring then.'

'No, I'm afraid I can't. I know even less about linoleum and cushion flooring.'

'Curtains?'

'Or curtains.'

'Well, this is a rum do,' she said shaking her head. 'You'll not get any sales the way you're going on, young man. They used to be very helpful in this store.' She walked off but not before commenting to another elderly lady customer, 'I wouldn't ask him, dear. I think I know more about carpets and curtains than he does.'

The other customer nodded in agreement and I heard her replying, 'Shop assistants just aren't as helpful these days, are they?'

It then dawned on me. I did look like an assistant in my grey suit and with the bright badge on my lapel.

A week later a memorandum arrived from Dr Gore explaining that when in schools, inspectors should clip their official identity cards to their lapels rather than use the badges which had not proved to be popular.

'What a pity,' said Sidney, after reading the note. 'I rather liked wearing my badge. It was rather like me – bright, bold and larger than life. It's quite distinctive, don't you think?'

None of his three colleagues replied.

14

Father Leonard was a remarkable priest. I came across him a number of times on my travels around the county's schools. He was a member of the Education Committee, and it amused me the way he would feign ignorance on a matter with a wide, inscrutable smile, ask for clarification and then demonstrate in his quiet, diffident way that he had understood perfectly. He was a man of immense wisdom and erudition, with such a gentle and unassuming manner and such a prodigious knowledge that all who heard him speak could not fail to hang on every word.

He was a tall stick of a man who wore a rather shabby-looking, ill-fitting cassock, threadbare at the cuffs and along the collar, and great scuffed black boots. His eyes, dark and penetrating, nestled in a net of wrinkles and the long, generous mouth seemed to be permanently smiling. He loved the company of children and was constantly re-minding his parishioners, parents and teachers, that we all had a lot to learn from them.

'The young child is the greatest philosopher of all,' he would say. 'He or she is open minded, trusting and honest, and greets people without any pre-conceived opinions. They see the world as it is – something wonderful and new and full of excitement.'

On one occasion recently I had been delighted to learn that Father Leonard would be attending the Presentation Evening at St Walburga's Roman Catholic Grammar School where I was due to address the parents and students, and award certificates and cups. I arrived at the school in good time to find the various guests drinking sherry in the Head-master's room. I spotted the formidable Sister Brendan from St Bartholomew's Roman Catholic Infant School, and joined her.

'How nice to see you again, Mr Phinn,' she said.

'And you, Sister,' I replied. 'Incidentally, the Headmaster knows that I am joining his assembly this evening and, furthermore, I am word-perfect in the hymn "I am walking in the footsteps of Jesus" just in case it appears in the programme.'

'I am very glad to hear it,' she said, smiling sweetly.

The Headmaster crossed the room towards us, bringing a gentle-looking cleric with him. 'This is one of our gov-ernors, Mr Phinn,' he said. 'Could I introduce you to –'

'We have met,' I said and smiled back at the genial figure in black. 'Good evening, Father Leonard, I hope you are well?'

Before the priest could reply, Sister Brendan interrupted: 'No, it's not Father Leonard,' she said. 'It is now Monsignor Leonard. He has been elevated.'

'Ah, well, good evening, Monsignor, and many congratu-lations on your promotion. But should you not be wearing the appropriate clerical garb, so innocents like myself don't get caught out?'

The priest gazed down at his shabby black cassock.

Sister Brendan interrupted again. 'What do you mean?'

'Surely a monsignor is entitled to wear purple, isn't he? Purple beading, purple sash etc?'

'He doesn't *have* to wear those,' said Sister Brendan. 'Any more than His Holiness *has* to wear white.'

'Quite, Sister, but on official occasions I thought it was

de rigueur to wear the appropriate garb?' Then turning to Monsignor Leonard, I said, 'Are you still at Mertonbeck, Monsignor, or have you been moved?'

Once more Sister Brendan spouted forth before the priest could open his mouth. 'Mr Phinn,' she said, 'Monsignor Leonard is now the Vicar General and if there is any moving to be done, *he* does it. He is in charge of moving priests and clergy within the diocese.'

'And if I don't get a word in soon, Sister,' said the monsignor smiling benignly, 'I'll arrange to have you moved to South America.'

On the way to the hall, the priest took my arm and whispered in my ear: 'You have to know how to handle nuns, Mr Phinn. Wonderful woman, Sister Brendan, but very forceful. Had she not taken the veil, I suggest she would have been governing the country by now.'

Now, on the run up to Christmas, I met Monsignor Leonard again. I arrived at the small Roman Catholic primary school at Netherfoot the week before the school broke up for the holidays. I had volunteered to narrate the Christmas story to the infants but never reached the end. Dominic, a massively freckled boy with spiky ginger hair that stood up like a lavatory brush, positioned himself at my feet on the small carpet in the reading corner. To say he was hyper-active would be an understatement. He was lively and interested and his questions and comments came fast and furious.

I began: 'It was cold and dark that December night many, many, many years ago, and on the hillside, where the icy winds whistled through the dark trees –'

'I can whistle,' said Dominic puckering up his lips.

'And the grass was frosted and stiff with cold –'

'Do you want to hear me whistle?'

'Not now, I don't,' I said, 'perhaps later.' I continued with the story. 'Matthew, the little shepherd boy, huddled in a dry hollow with his sheep to keep warm. The cold winter wind blew about his ears, and high above him the dark sky was studded with millions of tiny silver stars –'

'Miss Stirling gives you a star if you do good work,' said Dominic.

'It wasn't that sort of star,' I said. 'These were like tiny diamonds sparkling in the darkness. This was the night that a very special baby was to be born.'

'Jesus.'

'That's right, it was Jesus.'

'I've heard this story already!' exclaimed Dominic. 'I know what happens.'

'We all know what happens, Dominic,' I responded, 'and we are going to hear what happens again.'

'Why?'

'Because we are.'

At this point, I caught sight of the priest quietly entering the classroom and positioning himself unobtrusively at the back.

'Now, very soon a very special baby would be born and his name, as Dominic has already told us, would be Jesus.'

'Was he induced?' asked Dominic.

'Pardon?'

'Was baby Jesus induced?'

'No, he wasn't induced.'

'I was induced.'

'Well, baby Jesus wasn't induced.'

'How do you know?'

'Well, I know because it was a long, long time ago and they didn't induce babies then.'

'Why?'

'Just listen to the story, Dominic, and then we will all find out what happens.'

'But I know what happens,' he replied.

At this point, a little girl, with long blonde plaits and an angelic face, raised her hand.

'What does seduced mean?'

'Oh dear,' I sighed wearily, catching sight of the priest and the teacher attempting to stem their laughter. 'I will tell you another time – when you are older. Now let's get on with the story. And then amidst the tiny diamonds that sprinkled the dark sky there appeared a great shining star, a star that sparkled and gleamed with such a wondrous brilliant light that –'

'How much did he weigh?' asked Dominic.

'Who?'

'The baby Jesus?'

'I've not got to the baby Jesus yet.'

'I was an eight-pounder. My grannie said I was like a plucked turkey when –'

'Dominic!' I said very quietly and slowly. 'Now just listen to the story. You are spoiling it for all the other children.'

'I know how this story ends,' he replied undaunted.

'Then why don't *you* come out here and tell us all, Dominic,' I said, throwing in the towel.

And so he did. Like a seasoned actor taking centre stage he came out to the front of the class and recounted the Christmas story in such a simple, animated and confident way that we all listened in rapt silence.

'Once upon a time there was a man called Joseph and a lady called Mary and they were friends and they played games together and they had fun. Then they had a wedding and after the wedding they went home and then they had some lunch and a drink and then they set off for Bethlem on their honeymoon and they went on a donkey. When they got to Bethlem there was no room at the inn so they had to stay in a barn round the back and then Mary had a little baby and she called it Jesus and she put him in a manger and all the animals were around him and the big star shone up in the sky and then the shepherds all came and then the three kings came and they all gave him presents because it was his birthday and baby Jesus had plenty of milk because there were lots of cows about.'

There was silence at the end of Dominic's story, then he looked at me and said, 'OK?'

'OK,' I replied, 'very OK.'

On my way out that morning the little girl with the blonde plaits and the angelic face approached me shyly. 'I liked that story,' she said quietly.

'Did you?' I replied. 'I'm glad. Thank you for telling me.'

'But Dominic tells it better than you do. Happy Christmas.'

Monsignor Leonard, who had been watching and listening, placed his hand gently on my arm. 'There is an old proverb, Gervase, which goes like this: "Here's to the child and all he has to teach us."'

Later that week, I met Sister Brendan again and she had the last laugh. I arrived at the Church of England primary school adjacent to Sister Brendan's, to find an extremely distraught headteacher.

'Oh dear, Mr Phinn,' she gasped, 'oh dear me.' Teachers are sometimes rather nervous when I arrive in school but I had never had such an effect before. This woman was near to fainting. 'Oh it's not you, Mr Phinn, it's just that Father Christmas has appendicitis and it looks as if we will have to cancel the party. The children will be so disappointed. They were so looking forward to it.'

It turned out that Father Christmas was Mr Beech, the school crossing patrol assistant, who every year took on the arduous role at the infant and nursery Christmas party. This year he had been rushed to hospital and his daughter had telephoned to say that he would not be able to oblige as Santa Claus that afternoon. There were tears in the Headteacher's eyes. 'The children will be so disappointed. They are all so excited about Father Christmas coming.'

What could I do? I was the only available man. Nervously I donned the costume and after a strong cup of coffee entered the hall to find row upon row of open-mouthed, wide-eyed children. They squealed in delight when they saw the familiar red coat and white cotton-wool beard. Everything went well until a bright little spark announced loudly, 'You're not real, you know.'

'Oh yes, I am!' I replied in a deep jolly Father Christmas voice.

'Oh no, you're not,' she persisted, 'your beard's held on by elastic. I can see it. And Father Christmas has big boots. You're wearing shoes.'

'Ah, well, I got stuck in a snowdrift on my way here and my boots were so filled up with snow that I borrowed these shoes from Mr Beech.' School inspectors have to think on their feet when it comes to bright little buttons like this one.

'You can't have because Mr Beech has gone to hospital,' continued the child. 'My mum told me because he lives next door. You're not the real Father Christmas!'

'Oh yes, I am!' I said in my loud, jolly voice and heard a whole school hall shout back: 'Oh no, you're not!'

The Headteacher intervened and bailed me out by starting the singing. After three verses of 'Rudolf the Red-nosed Reindeer' each child came forward to receive a small present.

'What are the names of your reindeers?' asked a little boy.

'Well, there's Rudollf' I started, 'and Donner and Blitzen and er . . . er . . .'

The Headteacher, seeing that I was struggling, helped me out again by explaining that Father Christmas was rather deaf.

'Some of the snow from the snowdrift is still in his ears,' she said.

One child asked me if I knew her name and when I replied that I did not looked crestfallen. 'But I thought Father Christmas knows all the boys' and girls' names?'

The Headteacher explained that Father Christmas's eyes weren't too good either and he had such a lot of letters to read.

One rather grubby little scrap asked if she could sit on my knee.

'No, Chelsea,' said the Headteacher firmly. 'I don't think —' She was too late — the child had clambered up and clung to me like a little monkey.

'Come on down, Chelsea,' said the Headteacher. 'I don't think Father Christmas wants children on his knee. He's got a poorly leg.' Any more ailments, I thought, and I would be joining Mr Beech in the Crompton Hospital.

'Now, you be a very good little girl and sit on the floor, Chelsea,' I said in my jolly voice, 'otherwise all the other children will want to climb up.' Chelsea stayed put and held fast like a limpet. I chuckled uneasily until the child's teacher managed to prise her off. The Headteacher shrugged and looked knowingly at the teachers standing around the hall.

After the children had sung me out to 'Jingle Bells' I was invited into the staffroom. It was extremely hot under the red suit.

'Father Christmas, you were a great hit,' said the Head-teacher. The staff looked on and nodded. 'And we'd like to give you a little Christmas gift.'

'Oh no,' I said, 'it really isn't necessary.'

'Oh, but it is necessary,' insisted the Headteacher and presented me with a small bottle wrapped in bright Christmas paper.

I shook my gift and held it to my ear. 'After-shave?' I enquired. 'Is it after-shave?'

'No, Father Christmas,' the staff replied.

'Is it a little bottle of whisky?'

'No, Father Christmas,' they chorused.

I tore off the wrapping to reveal a small brown bottle of medication. The label read: 'For infestation of the head.'

'Chelsea's just got over head lice,' said the Headteacher. 'It's not advisable to be too close to her for the time being.'

'And she's just recovered from scabies,' piped up a beaming teacher. The rest of the staff then joined in with a hearty 'Ho! Ho! Ho!'

I was already beginning to itch and began to remove the cottonwool beard which shrouded my face.

At this point, there was a knock on the door and the Headteacher of St Bartholomew's entered, clutching Christmas cards for the staff. It was Sister Brendan.

'Ah, Sister, greetings!' exclaimed the Headteacher. 'Now, may I introduce you to Mr Phinn, a school inspector from County Hall?'

A broad smile came to the nun's lips.

'We have met,' I sighed, conscious that I had been caught with the ridiculous beard in my hand and still dressed in the baggy red suit.

'And tell me, Mr Phinn,' the nun inquired, 'is this the appropriate garb for school inspectors these days?'

Hot, flustered and itching all over and no doubt looking like someone who had been dragged through a hedge backwards, I was utterly lost for words. I just clutched the bottle of medication, stared vacantly and wished that Monsignor Leonard had indeed moved Sister Brendan to South America.

15

'I have a cryptic message for you, Gervase,' announced
David Pritchard peering over his gold-rimmed, half-moon
spectacles.

It was late Tuesday afternoon and three days before the
school finished for the Christmas holidays. I was endeav-
ouring to catch up on a backlog of correspondence and
seemed to be making little progress. Harold Yeats, oblivious
to everything and everybody around him, was tapping away
on the computer with two fingers, trying to complete a
school report. Sidney Clamp was scribbling and scratching
at his desk, trying to plan his next art course for early in the
new year and David Pritchard was completing the guidelines
for teachers on 'Sport in School'. Since his accident, David
had spent much more time in the office and, as a conse-
quence, had cleared all his paperwork, written numerous
guidelines and planned all his forthcoming courses. He was,
therefore, at something of a loose end that afternoon.

'I was asked to ask you what has happened to the plate?'
announced David, gazing intently over his spectacles. 'Does
that make any sense?'

'Yes,' I replied, 'it does. Thank you, David.' I returned
to the letter I was writing.

'It sounds very mysterious to me. Like a coded message,'
he observed. 'Like some secret phrase used by spies. You are
not with MI5 are you, Gervase? FBI? CIA? An undercover
agent investigating corruption in the county?'

'David, I'm attempting to write an important letter.'

'It's just that it's a most unusual thing for someone to say, that's all.'

David Pritchard was a man of ebullient personality with a jolly face, a head of silver hair, dark eyes and a big splayed boxer's nose. He had been a great athlete in his youth, featherweight boxing champion for his university college, was a highly-respected rugby referee of long standing and a scratch golfer. But David never used two words if a couple of paragraphs would suffice. His reports were wonderfully entertaining and full of anecdotes and illustrations. They made fascinating reading but it took some time for the lead inspector to pull things together, annotate and summarize his paragraphs for the Report – to see the trees in his very wordy wood of language.

'I wonder if they would have treated the prose of Dylan Thomas like this?' he had said at one lively meeting. He had scrutinized his corrected draft and sighed when he had seen all the amendments, before concluding, 'No, I think not.'

'But you are not writing *Under Milk Wood*, David,' Harold had attempted to explain with some exasperation in his voice. 'You are writing an inspection report – a clear, succinct, unambiguous inspection report.'

David loved words and he also loved mystery, gossip and intrigue.

' "Ask him what has happened to the plate," ' he repeated. 'That's all she said.'

'Yes, David, I heard you the first time.'

'Miss Bentley came over to me as I hobbled around the Staff Development Centre last week, inquired after my leg, placed an elegant hand on my arm, looked deep into my eyes with those limpid pools of hers and said: 'Ask Mr Phinn what has happened to the plate.'

Sidney's ears pricked up at the mention of Christine Bentley's name and his body became animated like a puppet with its strings pulled.

'The ravishing Christine Bentley of Winnery Nook!' he cried. 'And what were you doing visiting Winnery Nook again, Gervase? What was your excuse this time for going to see the most desirable unmarried woman in the whole county?'

'We have had this conversation before, Sidney.'

'You never seem to be out of the place,' he remarked casually. 'You are in and out of that school like a fiddler's elbow!'

'Hardly!'

'I trust that your relationship with Miss Bentley is entirely professional?'

'I have been into the school once, Sidney, only once.'

'What's this about a plate, then?' he asked. 'Or was the word "date"? Did she say, "Ask Mr Phinn what has happened to our date"?'

'No, it was definitely plate,' said David.

'Gentlemen,' said Harold turning away from the computer screen to face us, 'do you think we could return to the serious business of report writing, guideline preparation, course planning and correspondence? It is nearly the end of term, it has been a horrendously hard week and it is only Tuesday. There is much to do, it looks like snow, the roads are busy and I do intend getting home at a reasonable hour this evening. I am late-night shopping tomorrow evening with wife, daughters and son and have to assemble the wretched imitation Christmas tree, get the fairy lights to work and decorate the house with fronds of holly before the weekend, so I would really appreciate a little less badinage in order for me to concentrate on finishing this report. I really do not want to take work home over Christmas!'

'Of course, Harold, old boy,' replied Sidney smiling beatifically. 'It is a dreadfully demanding time of year, I do agree, and we all have such a lot on our plates.' He glanced mischievously in my direction, before saying in an undertone, 'Some more than others.'

We had just settled down to our work again when the telephone rang. Harold snatched up the receiver with a great paw.

'Hello, Harold Yeats here. Yes, yes, he's sitting next to me. I'll pass you over.' He slapped a large hand over the receiver which he passed in my direction. 'Gervase, it's for you. Miss Bentley of Winnery Nook.'

Sidney and David both turned to stare at me with expectant looks on their faces.

'Now,' exclaimed Sidney, 'all will be revealed!'

'Hello,' I answered. 'Yes, yes, he did mention it to me. No, no, that's quite all right. Yes, yes, I have meant to call in with it but have been so very busy. Yes, yes, well, that would be very nice. I should enjoy that. Yes, of course. I will see you tomorrow then. Goodbye.' I put down the receiver carefully. I then returned to my letter.

'Well?' asked Sidney.

'Well what?'

'Do tell, Gervase,' pleaded David. 'Put us out of our misery.'

'You don't need to look at me with those silly expressions,' I said. 'I've only been invited to a nativity plate – I mean play, tomorrow evening.'

'Invited to the nativity play by Miss Bentley of Winnery Nook,' sighed David, 'and the only one in the office to receive an advent calendar from Sister Brendan *and* a

Christmas card from Mrs Savage. My goodness, Gervase, just what *is* your secret with the opposite sex?'

'Gentlemen,' growled Harold, 'please!'

Winnery Nook Nursery and Infant School looked very different from when I had last visited it early in the autumn. The surrounding fields and rocky outcrops were now hidden under a smattering of snow, and the friendly belt of pines had a fine dusting of white. The air was icy fresh. The snow had fallen softly overnight and the whole area around the small school was a vast white silent sea.

I entered the brightness and warmth of the school clutching the blue cracked plate and looking for Christine. A member of staff informed me that she was backstage getting the little ones ready for the play but that a seat had been reserved for me in the front row.

'Shall I take the plate?' asked the teacher, eyeing the piece of pottery.

'No, that's all right, thank you.' I managed a weak smile.

Mums and dads, grannies and grampas, aunties and uncles, neighbours and friends filled the school hall for the nativity play, the highlight of the school year. I found my seat just as the lights dimmed and a spotlight lit up the small stage.

This was the fifth infant nativity play I had seen this year. At the first, I had approached the school to find all the children heading for home. I had stopped a small boy loaded down with Christmas cards, calendars, decorations, presents and all manner of boxes and bags as he tried to negotiate the narrow gate.

'Where's everyone going?' I had asked. 'There's a nativity play here this afternoon, isn't there?'

He had stopped for the amount of time it took to tell me bluntly, 'It's off!'

'It's off?' I had repeated.

'Aye,' he had replied. 'T'Virgin Mary's got nits!'

The second nativity play I had seen had not started off all that well. The seven-year-old introducing the Christmas play had announced, after a number of unsuccessful attempts, 'Welcome to our Harvest Festival.' I learnt later that she could not pronounce the word 'nativity'. Things had improved after this initial hiccup until the little girl with the lead part of Mary had begun to find that the thick robe and headdress made her more and more hot and sticky as the play progressed. As the Magi had presented her with their gifts she had sighed and thrust the large doll representing the baby Jesus with a fair bit of force onto the lap of Joseph, saying in a loud stage whisper as she did, 'You have him a bit, he's getting heavy.'

At the third nativity play I had overheard a conversation at the side of the stage between two cherubic six-year-olds dressed in white silk trimmed with silver and speckled with sequins. It was an exchange not meant for the audience's ears. One child had remarked, 'I feel a right twit in this, don't you, Gavin?' His companion had agreed, nodding vigorously, 'And if she thinks I'm being a flipping snowflake next year she's got another think coming!'

The little actor in the fourth nativity play I watched had looked very disgruntled. I heard later that the lead part of Joseph had been given to another child and he had not been too pleased. He had argued with his teacher to no avail and had been given the role of the innkeeper. On the night of the performance Mary and Joseph had arrived at the inn and had knocked loudly on the door. The innkeeper, who had remained grumpy all through the rehearsals, had opened the door with a great beaming smile.

'Innkeeper, innkeeper,' Joseph had begun, 'we have

travelled many miles in the darkness and the cold. May we come in?'

'She can come in,' he had said, pointing to Mary, 'but you can push off!'

I was now about to watch the fifth version of one of the most famous and powerful stories of all time, and wondered what gem might be produced tonight. The curtain opened to reveal the outlines of various Eastern-looking houses painted on a backdrop and two rather forlorn palm trees made out of papier mâché and green crêpe paper which drooped in the centre of the stage. The little boy, playing the lead as Joseph, entered wearing a brightly-coloured towel over his head and held in place by an elastic belt with metal snake fastener. He took centre stage without a trace of nerves, stared at the audience and then beckoned a particularly worried-looking Mary who entered pulling a large cardboard and polystyrene donkey.

'Come on!' urged Joseph. 'Hurry up!' He banged on the door of one of the houses. 'Open up! Open up!' he shouted loudly.

The innkeeper, with a face like a death mask, threw open the door. 'What?' he barked.

'Have you any room?'

'No!'

'You have!'

'I haven't!'

'You have, I saw t'light on.'

'I haven't.'

'Look, we've travelled all night up and down those sand-dunes, through dusty towns, over hills, in and out of rivers. We're fit to drop.'

'Can't help that, there's no room,' replied the innkeeper.

'And I've got t'wife out here on t'donkey.' Joseph gestured in the direction of a very glum-looking Mary who was staring at the audience, her face completely expressionless.

The innkeeper remained unmoved. 'And you can't leave that donkey there. You'll have to move it!'

'Well give us a room.'

'There is no room in the inn. How many more times do I have to tell you?'

'She's having babby, tha knaws.'

'Well, I can't help that, it's nowt to do with me.'

'I know,' replied Joseph sighing as he turned to the audience, 'and it's nowt to do with me neither.'

To the surprise of the children there were great roars of laughter from the audience. And so the play progressed until the final magic moment. Little rosy-faced angels in white with cardboard wings and tinsel halos, shepherds with towels over their heads and cotton-wool beards, the three wise men in coloured robes and shiny paper hats gathered around Mary and Joseph on the cramped stage to sing 'Away in a Manger' and bring a tear to every eye.

Following the performance, I went in search of the elusive Miss Bentley but, just as I was passing the main door, I was stopped by a mother who wanted to talk to me about her daughter. I put the plate down on a nearby table, and forgot to pick it up again when I moved across the hall to discuss the problem with the child's teacher. When I finally extracted myself, I returned to the entrance to collect the plate.

I looked down in astonishment: the plate was full of coins and even a £5 note. The audience, as they had left the hall, must have thought a collection was being taken. And then I saw Christine heading my way, her face flushed with excitement.

'It went really well,' I said.

'Thanks,' she replied, shaking my cold hand. 'It's nice to

see you again.' Then she caught sight of the plate full of coins. 'I see you've had a collection.'

'Quite by accident, I assure you. Our old plate came in handy. If you want a really worthy charity to donate this to, I know a very persuasive nun who will take it off your hands.'

'Sister Brendan?' she laughed. 'I know her.'

'Well, I must be off. One blue chipped, cracked patterned plate of doubtful provenance,' I announced and presented it into her hands.

'Oh it's lovely,' she replied. 'It's really unusual. Thank you so much for bidding for it. It was sweet of you. I think we got a real bargain here, don't you think?'

'Yes,' I replied thinking the very opposite and remembering the full price I had paid. All that money for a piece of ugly, cracked pottery that I would have consigned to the dustbin.

'And you got my cheque?'

'Yes, yes, thank you and the lovely card.' This was followed by a rather embarrassed silence. I changed the subject. 'And what are you doing over Christmas?' I said, trying to adopt what I thought to be a casual tone of voice. 'Are you going away?'

'Yes,' she replied, 'we are off to Austria, skiing. Miles is a first-class skier. He was an army champion. Do you ski at all?'

'No, but I sledge.'

She laughed. 'And what are you doing for Christmas?'

'Nothing at all special,' I replied. 'I'm spending a quiet Christmas with my brother and his family.' I sounded deadly dull and dreary again. 'Well, I must make tracks. Thank you for asking me to the nativity, Christine. Goodnight and a happy Christmas.'

I walked out into the cold night. Army champion! Well, of course, he would be, I thought. The white moon lit up the landscape, luminous and still. Cars growled along the road through the soft snow, throwing cascades of slush in their wake. Lights twinkled and flickered in windows and there was the smell of pine in the air. It was the magic atmosphere of Christmas.

'And I hope he breaks his bloody leg!' I said aloud.

16

Julie bustled into the office balancing a potted plant in one hand and a wire tray full of letters in the other.

'So what sort of Christmas did you have?' she asked, placing the tray of mail on my desk and the potted plant on the filing cabinet. Before I could reply, she continued, 'I've brought the spider plant to brighten up your office. This place looks like a crypt with books.'

'I spent Christmas with my brother's family, nice and quiet. I slept for most of the time in front of the great log fire. It was quite a shock coming back to my cold and damp flat in Fettlesham. It was like a morgue. I really must make an effort to find somewhere when the weather gets a bit better. I will start to look seriously in the spring. A little country cottage would suit me, if you happen to hear of anything. What was your Christmas like?'

'About as quiet as the D–Day landings. Arguments about the presents which didn't suit, screaming, overfed children who never stopped whingeing, family feuds over the Christmas dinner, quarrels about which television programmes to watch. It was four days of disagreement, dissension, squabble and strife. Whoever said that Christmas was a time of peace and goodwill to all men should have spent it with us. I'm glad to be back, to be honest. There's a message from Dr Gore somewhere in that pile of papers, by the way, asking you to call him urgently.' As she headed for the door Julie turned and smiled impishly. 'Probably heard about your secret liaisons with all those women.'

Julie was typical of many 'a Yorkshire lass' – cheerful, good-humoured and, on occasion, blunt to the point of rudeness. Several people had complained about her out-spoken manner, constant chatter and clever comments but she was such a big-hearted, self-effacing young woman and an excellent secretary – efficient, organized and ready to stay late at a moment's notice – that I found it very difficult to criticize her. I did once take her aside and ask for a little more restraint and deference when she dealt with callers. It was prompted by a particularly patronizing and rather pompous headteacher who wrote a letter of complaint about Julie's 'very familiar manner' and 'bluntness' down the telephone.

'Oh her,' said Julie dismissively, when I mentioned the name. 'Like my old mum says: "All fur coat and no knickers!"' I saw this particular headteacher some weeks later when I visited her school. She approached me across a crowded playground in heavy sheepskin coat with a wide wool collar. I had to suppress a smile as the grim face came into view.

Dr Gore stared at me across the desk with a smile like Dracula before he sinks his teeth into a victim.

'I've a little job for you, Gervase,' he said.

I glanced at him despairingly. I had been an inspector in the county a little over four months but knew Dr Gore's 'little jobs': a county-wide reading survey, an audit of the secondary school libraries, chairing a working group on gifted children, accompanying members of the Education Committee around schools, compiling a discussion paper on the state of drama teaching, organizing a poetry festival. They were never 'little jobs'.

'Now don't look so worried,' he murmured languidly. 'It *is* a little job — well, relatively little.' When I did not reply but continued to stare at him morosely, he carried on. 'Under normal circumstances I would have asked a more experienced inspector to take on this sort of thing but David Pritchard is still not a hundred per cent with that leg of his and, as you know, Sidney Clamp is directing the Arts in School Conferences for the next couple of weeks, so it falls to you.' This was beginning to sound less and less like a little job. 'I've received a letter from the Department of Education and Science asking if it would be convenient for the Minister of State for Education and Science to visit the county. Being newish to the job, he's trying to get a feel for things before he puts together a White Paper. He wants to learn something about the education system at ground level up here in the north.'

I sighed and gave the CEO a mirthless smile. I predicted what was coming next.

'He'll be with us in five weeks' time and I would like you to manage the visit and arrange an itinerary. Harold Yeats felt, and I must say I agreed immediately, that you would be able to cope admirably with the responsibility for making the visit run smoothly.' He performed his Dracula smile again.

'Thank you, that's very gratifying,' I replied. 'Of course, I'll do my best.'

'Good, good,' said Dr Gore enthusiastically. 'Now the Minister will only be here for the morning and I want him to leave with a favourable impression. Your task will be to present him with a picture of the life and work in our schools. You know the sort of thing — organize a display of children's and students' work at the Staff Development Centre, get a few headteachers and teachers together to meet him, produce an explanatory booklet for him to take away. Mrs Savage will help you co-ordinate things. There will be one of the Minister's assistants, probably one of Her Majesty's Inspectors, contacting you shortly to discuss arrangements.' He beamed across his desk. 'Now do keep me fully informed of the progress of the visit, won't you, Gervase.'

'Of course.'

'See – quite painless. I think you will find this little job most enjoyable.'

The task, I had to admit, promised to be a most interesting and challenging one and I set about it with gusto. First of all, I dropped a memo to Mrs Savage asking for her help in producing a programme of events and received a prompt reply in which she said it would be a pleasure. I booked the Staff Development Centre, asked colleagues to call in the best displays of work they had seen recently during inspections, and arranged for a representative group of people to meet the Minister.

'There's been another woman wanting to speak to you!' shouted Julie from the outer office two days later. 'With a funny name! Sounded like Miss Deadly Stare.'

'Did you get a number?' I asked.

'I got the number but not the name. She sort of growled down the telephone like a grizzly, something like Deadly Stare. Said she wanted to speak to you about some visit you're organizing and left her number. Then she hung up. She'd get on really well with Mrs Savage – peas out of the same pod, by the sound of her.'

I rang the number which was a London one, and asked

for a Miss D. L. Stare. I thought it was a reasonable guess.

'De la Mare,' corrected the receptionist in high-pitched, artificial tones. 'Miss de la Mare, Her Majesty's Principal Divisional Inspector of Schools. I'll put you through.'

'De la Mare,' came a loud and strident voice down the line. I explained who I was. 'Right, now I am arranging things this end for the visit of the Minister of State and, of course, we all want things to go as smooth as clockwork, don't we?'

'Oh yes, indeed,' I spluttered, 'as smooth as clockwork.'

Miss de la Mare then barked various instructions and requirements down the telephone. The Minister, Sir Bryan Holyoake, I was told, was a man of few words and strong views, and was a perfectionist. He did not like a deal of fuss, drank only mineral water, liked to see the detailed itinerary before his visit and was punctilious about keeping to schedule. The information filled me with a silent dread.

I spent a full day at the Staff Development Centre the week before the visit making certain everything was in readiness for the Minister's visit. There were colourful and varied exhibitions in each room, and the walls were covered in displays of children's work.

Connie watched my every move like some manic guard dog. 'I can't see what all this fuss is about anyway,' she remarked pursuing me from room to room and along the corridors as I checked the details. 'Anyone would think the Queen herself was visiting the Centre.'

If the Queen were to walk through the door at that very moment, I thought to myself, Connie would be calling her 'luv' in next to no time. The caretaker had not the slightest conception of rank, status or position and treated everyone in the same blunt manner.

'And I hope you're going to take all those staples out

when you've finished,' she said, staring intently as I made some small adjustments to the children's poems and paintings. 'They are the devil's own job to pull out and they clog up the vacuum cleaner.'

'Of course, Connie,' I replied.

'It's just that I like things to be left as people find them.'

'Of course, Connie,' I repeated.

'I've seen how you inspectors leave this place after your courses. That Mr Clamp, with the coloured suits and fancy ties, left a trail of destruction and debris behind him last week after one of his art courses. I had to have a word. And Mr Pritchard has made marks on the polished floor with those crutches of his.'

'There will be no destruction and debris, Connie,' I replied. 'You can be certain of that.'

'Mmmm,' she murmured sceptically. 'And I've heard that one before as well.'

I had completed the last of the displays and was admiring the final effect with great satisfaction when Mrs Savage arrived. She was dressed in a cardinal red suit with matching accessories. Over the week prior to the visit she had telephoned and met me a number of times to tie up the loose ends and we had got to know each other well, so much so that we were now on first-name terms.

'This looks very impressive, Gervase,' she said scanning the walls. 'I have a feeling that this visit is going to be a great success. Here are the programmes and the itinerary for you to look over.'

'That's very kind, Brenda. It's saved me a trip into the office. Thank you very much. I think everything's in order and –'

'Is that your car?' Connie appeared from nowhere. 'That blue car – is it yours?'

'Yes, it is,' replied Mrs Savage brusquely and swivelling on her high heels to face the questioner. 'Why?'

'You're blocking the main entrance. You'll have to move it. It's a health and safety hazard. If there was a fire it would prevent people from getting out.'

'I hardly think so,' replied Mrs Savage in a patronizing voice. 'There appears to be only three or four people in the entire Centre at the moment. I hardly imagine one small car, parked against the wall, would constitute a health and safety hazard.'

'Yes it would!' snapped Connie.

'Perhaps you could then explain,' responded Mrs Savage with a slight curl of the lip, 'how a small car, parked well away from the door, could possibly impede the exit of a handful of people.'

'Rules are rules!' replied Connie curtly. 'So would you move it – please?'

'I have only popped in to deliver some papers,' explained Mrs Savage giving Connie a very condescending look. 'I shall be going in one moment. Now if you wouldn't mind –'

The formidable Mrs Savage, however, had met her match in Connie, who clearly did mind and she persisted with all the tenacity of a Yorkshire terrier.

'There's a sign which says: "Do not block this entrance." It is there so people do not park their cars in front of the main door and cause a health and safety hazard.'

'Oh for goodness sake!' cried Mrs Savage thrusting the programme and itinerary into my hands and scrabbling for the car keys in her handbag. 'I shall move the wretched car.' She gave Connie a look of undiluted venom.

'Well, just so long as you do,' replied Connie, quite undaunted, before strutting off down the corridor, holding her feather duster like a field-marshal's baton.

'I hope you will have a few well-chosen words with that Connie!' exclaimed Mrs Savage, her face the colour of her suit. 'Give me a ring if there are any problems with the programme.'

Several minutes after Mrs Savage's hasty departure, Dr Gore arrived. 'Splendid! Splendid!' he said striding cheerfully through the entrance and rubbing his hands together. 'It really does look good. I've just called in to see if everything is in order for Monday.' As I assured him that all was in readiness for the Minister's visit, Connie approached and hovered within hearing distance.

'Ah, Connie,' I said waving her forward, 'I am sure you know the Chief Education Officer. He's just popped in to see how things are progressing.'

Dr Gore held out a hand. 'Very pleased to see you again, Connie,' he said. 'It's quite some time since I visited the Staff Development Centre. It looks as spick and span as usual.'

'And I'm very pleased to meet you again too, Brian,' replied Connie. No one in the office referred to the Chief Education Officer by his first name. It just was not done. It was always Dr Gore or 'sir'. As he chatted amiably with Connie there was no trace of irritation on his face; in fact, quite the opposite.

'Now, Connie,' he was saying, 'this visit on Monday is an important one and we want the Centre to look really good – bright, sparkling, the best it's ever looked.'

'Don't fret on that account, Brian,' she said with nonchalant good humour. 'It'll look cleaner than a baby's bottom.'

'Well,' replied Dr Gore, one corner of his mouth twitching upwards uncontrollably, 'I'll leave you with Mr Phinn to get on with things and I will see you both on Monday.'

'There is one thing, Brian,' said Connie catching his arm.

'Yes, Connie, what's that?' he replied amiably.

'When you come again on Monday, don't park your car in front of the main door. Blocking the entrance constitutes a health and safety hazard.'

'I'll remember that,' he replied smiling and not a trace irritated.

'He's a very nice man,' concluded Connie as she watched the departing figure. 'I used to clean his office years ago.'

On the Monday morning I waited nervously at the entrance of the Centre for the arrival of the important visitor. A large black car pulled in front of the main entrance at exactly 9.00 a.m.

'The car's here!' I shouted down the building to those assembled, in a voice taut with apprehension.

Through the main entrance came the Chief Education Officer accompanied by the Right Honourable Sir Bryan Holyoake, MP. The Minister of State was a tall, imposing man with a Roman-nosed face and short, carefully-combed silver hair. He was surrounded by a knot of dark-suited, serious-looking men who intermittently whispered things in his ear in response to which he gave a slight nod. Sir Bryan was barely through the door when Connie sidled into sight. A dreadful thought crossed my mind. Connie was going to tackle him about blocking the entrance and causing a health and safety hazard. I intercepted her just before she reached the assembly of dignitaries.

'Don't mention the car, Connie, for goodness sake,' I hissed. 'I will tell the driver myself to park away from the door. Please do not mention the car!'

She nodded but as the C EO passed her, smiling benignly, Connie leaned forward. 'Brian!' she said in a stage whisper.

Dr Gore turned at the sound of his name. 'Shall I take the coats?'

The CEO smiled gently and mouthed, 'No, thank you, Connie. We're not staying long.'

The important party moved down the main corridor of the Centre, resplendent with the displays of children's writing and painting, models and artefacts. The Minister paused to read a poem, stare at a picture, scrutinize a piece of design engineering, but maintained an unsmiling taciturnity.

'Brian!' Connie came into view a second time. The CEO turned again at the sound of his name. 'Would you like a cup of tea?' He shook his head. 'Would your friend like one?' she persisted.

He shook his head again before whispering, 'No, thank you, Connie.'

The Minister and his entourage entered the main hall where an extensive exhibition of models and constructions was arranged. As he wandered around, pursued by the blue-suited minions, he appeared to show little interest in his surroundings and occasionally glanced at the distant hills framed by the window. His companions continued to whisper in his ear and he nodded slightly in response.

'Brian!' Connie appeared again. 'Watch the step if you go outside.'

Dr Gore nodded, smiled weakly and took a long breath before motioning for me to join him. 'Get-rid-of-Connie!' he whispered slowly and distinctly. 'Take her somewhere and keep her occupied. She keeps on turning up like a bad penny.'

I guided Connie to the entrance where I tried to keep her occupied, but the nervous movement of her head, the twitching of her lips and the fidgeting fingers betrayed her agitation.

'I do hope that old gentleman doesn't trip on the step,' she said in a very anxious voice. 'He didn't look all that good on his feet. In fact, he didn't look too well at all, if you ask me. I bet he could murder a cup of tea. I think I'll just pop down and –'

'He doesn't drink tea, Connie, really.'

'Is he *the* important visitor then? Is he royalty?'

'His name is Sir Bryan Holyoake, Connie,' I replied, 'and he's the Minister of State for Education and Science and he is *very* important.'

'He won't be any relation to Ivy Holyoake who owns the tripe shop down Fitzwilliam Road, I don't suppose?'

'I shouldn't imagine so,' I said smiling.

Connie and I were still near the entrance when the entourage passed by. The Minister paused for a moment to speak to one of his minions so Dr Gore took the opportunity of whispering in Connie's ear.

'Connie,' he said, 'I would just like to say how spotless the Centre looks. It's a real credit to you and I am most grateful.'

Colour suffused Connie's face. 'Well, thanks very much, Brian,' she replied, clearly very touched by the generous comments. 'It's very nice to be appreciated, I'm sure.'

Sir Bryan and his party were moving for the exit so the CEO joined the Minister. When they reached the door a stentorian voice carried over everyone's heads. It was Connie.

'Ta-ra, Brian!' she boomed after the CEO. The silence could have been cut with a knife. Then the Right Honourable Sir Bryan Holyoake, MP, the Minister of State for

Education and Science, turned and gave Connie the most charming of smiles.

'Oh, goodbye, Connie,' he replied.

17

I was once told by a grizzled old farmer that the county of Yorkshire is bigger than Israel and covers more acres than words in the Bible. It may be something of an exaggeration, although Yorkshire folk are not prone to embellishing, but the county is certainly large. It is in winter, when the strings of caravans and crowds of 'off-comed-uns' have disappeared and only a few hardy, red-faced ramblers can be seen striding the fells, that the vastness and beauty of the great Dales fill me with that real sense of wonder. You can travel mile after mile, along a narrow grey ribbon of road, without seeing a soul – just the tumbling acres of green or the rolling empty tracts of rusty brown to either side of the car, or the grim, silent moors stretching ahead of you to the purple hills in the far distance.

It was on one such cold, raw January day, when the sky was an empty, steely grey and the air so icy it almost burnt your cheeks and ears, that I visited Bartondale. The drive from the nearby market town was uphill all the way along a narrow, twisting, slippery road. Barton Moor Parochial School, an austere building of dark grey stone and mean little windows, was surrounded by the bleakest of country. It was set high up above a panorama of dark green hills flecked with snow, deep valleys with long grey farmhouses and a meandering river. Nearby there was a little cluster of houses and an ancient squat church, all surrounded by a fleecy mist. This was the hamlet of Barton Moor.

The inside of the school was as warm and welcoming as the Headteacher, a large woman with the wonderfully-Dickensian name of Miss Sally Precious. She bubbled with enthusiasm when she saw me walk through the entrance.

'It's so good to meet you, Mr Phinn,' she said, shaking my hand vigorously. 'I'm so pleased to see that you have arrived safely. The roads are quite treacherous at this time of year. We get so few visitors up here. You see it's *so* isolated and *so* very bleak in winter that it's such an effort. We get the occasional historian in the summertime looking at Barton Moor, of course, but that's about it really.'

I opened my mouth to say, 'Good morning,' but Miss Precious gushed on excitedly. 'When I received your letter saying that you would like to spend a morning with us, it was like winning the Lottery. Everyone's *so* excited.'

This was not the reception school inspectors are generally used to. We generally fill teachers with a certain amount of fear and dread.

'Well, I'm delighted to be here, Miss Precious,' I replied, when at last I got the chance to respond. 'I thought I would arrive a little early before the children, to have a look around the school and discuss a few things with you.'

She nodded enthusiastically.

I was taken on a tour of the small school which took less than fifteen minutes. Miss Precious chatted on amiably, describing how she organized the curriculum, the methods she used to teach reading, how she developed handwriting skills and the strategies she employed to help the gifted children.

'I've put all the various policies, guidelines and test results in my room for you to look through later,' she concluded triumphantly. 'I also want you to see the old school log books which make very interesting reading and to talk about a particular pupil of rare ability and get some advice on the best sort of education for him.'

There were only two classrooms: one for the infants and one for the juniors. Both were long square rooms with high beamed ceilings, both very bright and showing clear evidence of a range of high-quality work. In the infant classroom I met a small nervous-looking woman busy arranging a spray of flowers and ferns. She smiled weakly and introduced herself as Mrs Durdon, 'the teacher of the little ones'. Her hand trembled slightly and she blinked rapidly as she introduced herself.

In the junior classroom the small high-set windows had been removed and replaced by a large picture window which gave an uninterrupted and quite magnificent view across the moor and down into the valley.

'I had this window put in a few years ago,' said Miss Precious proudly. 'When the school was built, a hundred and fifty or so years ago, I expect the teachers thought the view would be a distraction for the children, but it seemed to me we were missing so much beauty. Here we were in this plain little box surrounded by high walls and tiny windows and outside was one of the finest views in the county. When the frames began to rot and the stonework needed repair, I nagged the governors to put in the larger window. We had the devil's own job to get permission. You see, the school is a listed building. When the school finances allow, and I can convince my governors and the various heritage groups, I want another window on the world for the infants.' She smiled mischievously. 'I do believe in preserving what is good from the past but not to be a slave to history. We must also look to the future. You might wish to comment in your report on the educational value for the children of having the benefit of such a view, Mr Phinn.'

From the classroom window, the cold bleak moor stretched before us, strange and desolate. A light grey mist hung low to the hard ground and the few dark skeletal trees, blackthorns and dwarf scrub, twisted skywards as if writhing in agony. No wind stirred, no birds sang. All was still and silent. It was a grim and gloomy picture but, at the same time, quite awesome.

'It's very beautiful in its own way, isn't it?' commented the Headteacher.

'It is,' I agreed. 'It must be fascinating to see how the seasons change from this classroom window.'

'Yes,' she sighed, 'we are very fortunate.' The noise of excited chatter outside interrupted our reverie. 'If you'll excuse me for a moment, Mr Phinn,' said Miss Precious, 'I can hear the first children arriving. Mrs Durdon and I like to welcome them each morning and say a few words to the parents.'

I was left alone and was still staring from the window when a small serious-faced boy with thick-lensed glasses like the bottoms of milk bottles entered and came across to me.

'Good morning,' he said. 'You must be the school inspector.'

'That's right,' I replied.

'Miss Precious said you would be coming today. Did you have a pleasant journey?'

'Yes, thank you.'

'We don't generally get visitors up here.'

'You are a bit out of the way, certainly.'

'I'm Joseph Richard Barclay.' He held out a small hand which I shook.

'And I'm Mr Phinn.'

'I'm pleased to meet you, Mr Phinn,' he said. 'Were you looking at the moor?'

'Yes. It really is a desolate scene. I don't think I've seen such a bleak and barren view quite like this one.'

'There was a famous battle there, you know, over four hundred years ago, between the Roundheads and the Cavaliers. A lot of men perished on that moor. They say the ground was red with blood.'

'Really?'

'It was called the Battle of Barton Moor but it was really only a skirmish. It wasn't your proper full-scale battle like Marston Moor or Naseby. The Cavaliers were pursued by the Roundheads up the valley but made a stand at Barton Moor. We sometimes get people visiting from the university.'

'You're quite the expert, aren't you, Joseph?'

The boy nodded seriously. 'I do like history. If you walk across the moor in the late afternoon, it's full of shadows and shapes and some say the ghosts of the dead soldiers wander about.'

I stared for a moment at my companion. He was a strangely old-fashioned looking boy of about eleven, with a curiously old-fashioned way of speaking. Eleven-year-olds generally do not use words like 'perished' and 'skirmish' and 'pursued'. His hair was of the short-back-and-sides variety, a style that I had sported when I had been his age and he wore long grey trousers, a hand-knitted grey pullover, long grey stockings and sensible shoes. He could have been a schoolboy of the 1950s. Miss Precious's precocious pupil, no doubt.

'Well,' he said suddenly, 'I must get on. I have to collect the register. If you'll excuse me.'

The school, which had been silent a few moments ago, was now full of business-like noise and bustle. One real pleasure in my job is to hear the animated conversations, lively exchanges and uninhibited laughter of young children as they arrive at school in the morning. Through the classroom door I heard a hubbub of excited children obviously clustering around their teachers as they hung up their coats and changed into their indoor shoes.

'Miss, t'watter in t'hen coops froz up last neight. It were as 'ard as Brimham Rocks.'

'T'calf were born last neight, miss – it's a really big 'un. Like a babby helephant, it were. I was up 'til ten with t'vet!'

'Miss, my mum says it's cold enough to freeze t'flippers off a penguin this mornin'.'

'Miss, did you see the heronsew on t'bank? Reight big 'un miss, looking for t'fish in t'stell.'

'Miss, t'pipes in our outside lavvy are frozzen solid. Mi dad couldn't oppen yat this morning, it were that stiff wi t'cold.'

I learnt later in the day that a 'heronsew' was a heron, a 'stell' a large open ditch and a 'yat' a gate. When the children caught sight of me, I was surrounded and treated to the same lively chatter, full of the richness of a Dales' dialect.

'Come on, come on, chatterboxes!' said Miss Precious, moving into the midst of the children like a great mother hen gathering up her chicks. 'You will have plenty of time to talk to Mr Phinn later this morning.' She turned in my direction. 'Could you start in Mrs Durdon's class with the infants, please, Mr Phinn, and join us after morning break?'

Mrs Durdon, despite her trembling and frequent blinking at the start of the lesson, proved to be a very good teacher and she soon relaxed after I had given her a few reassuring smiles and friendly nods. The classroom was neat and tidy and the children's work was well-displayed. A large bright alphabet and key words for children to learn decorated a wall and an attractive reading-corner contained a range of colourful picture and reading books and simple dictionaries. The standard of reading was high as was the quality of the written work.

A small rosy-faced child of about seven years old was busy tapping away at the computer in the corner, copying a piece of writing from her book. It was a delightful account and quite poetic in its use of language:

> On Saturday we went for a pizza in Pickerton.
> My brother Timmy had a pizza the size of his head.
> He did not eat much because he sniffed some pepper up his
>   nose.
> He kept on sneezing and crying.
> Mum was mad but my Dad laughed and laughed.
> He said he will not do that in a hurry again.

At play-time Mrs Durdon donned a thick black coat, heavy scarf, white woolly hat and white boots and, explaining that she was on yard duty that morning, waddled off in the direction of the small playground. As I watched her, I recalled the comment I had heard earlier that morning: 'Miss, my mum says it's cold enough to freeze t'flippers off a penguin.'

A cup of coffee in a fine china cup was awaiting me in the Headteacher's room.

'Now,' she said taking two heavy, black leather-bound tomes from the shelf, 'I want you to have a look at the school log books. They are really fascinating and go back well over a century. We get all these visitors from the university to study the battlefield but these log books,

Mr Phinn, contain much more interesting history in my opinion.'

She opened the first tome and passed it across her desk. The first page had the following entry:

September 5th, 1898
Took up my position as Headmaster of Barton Moor Parochial
School in the County of York. 24 children on role, all from farming
familys. Most of them iliterate.

'Isn't it just priceless,' chortled Miss Precious. 'Can you see how he's spelled "illiterate" and "families" and "roll" and it gets better.'

The next entry read:

September 6th, 1898
Morning spent on arithmetic, handwriting and scripture. Afternoon
spent on rhetoric. I learned them a poem..

'And they say standards have declined,' said Miss Precious. 'Now if you look at the page I've marked with a piece of paper, you will find the classic entry. It's the report of the school inspector.'

December 10th, 1913
The Inspector's Report to the School Board as follows: 'The affairs
of this school are ill-managed by a committee of languid, inept
amateurs and the school is staffed by two incompetent teachers. To
form the minds of children and direct their efforts into beneficial
channels, the teachers must at least know more than their charges.
The Headmaster is so absorbed in administrative and financial
concerns that he neglects the intellectual and spiritual development
of the children.'

I looked up smiling. 'The inspectors could be pretty savage in those days, couldn't they?'

'Of course, the Headmaster was sacked,' continued Miss Precious. 'He seems to have just upped and gone following the inspector's visit. Just after the First World War the new Headmaster arrived, a Mr MacMillan. He is still remembered by some of the very old inhabitants in the village. He was known as Captain Mac, and was prone to ranting and raving and was a demon with the cane. Evidently he had seen action in the trenches and suffered terrible wounds, mental and physical, and wanted a quiet, untroubled life in Bartondale.' She flicked the pages. 'Captain Mac was a man of few words and stern disposition.'

The entries read:

Monday, December 9th
Heavy snow. Eight children absent. Direful day.

Tuesday, December 10th
More snow. Twelve children absent. Frozen pipes in boys' lavatory. Awful day.

Wednesday, December 11th
Still more snow. Only three children present. Frozen pipes in girls' lavatory. Appalling day.

Thursday, December 12th
Thaw sets in. Two absentees. School full of mud and water. Horrible day.

Friday, December 13th
Full complement of children. Burst pipes, flooded toilets. School inspector, Mr Thoroughgood, visited. Calamitous day!

'This is really interesting,' I said. 'Have you thought of writing a short history of the school and including all this material? It would make an excellent piece of action-research for the children.'

'We've done it,' she replied proudly. 'The children researched the history of Barton Moor Parochial School, collected photographs and old maps, made copies of parish records and interviewed parents and grandparents. We discovered a host of fascinating characters from the past: eccentric parsons, dyed-in-the wool farmers, hedgers and ditchers, colourful landlords of the local inn, a footpad who was hanged at York and the Lord of the Manor who ran off with a serving maid. We amassed a great deal of information and Joseph put it all together. I think you met Joseph Barclay earlier this morning. He's the young man I wanted to pick your brains about. It was Joseph who produced a short but very readable account of the school's history.' She reached up and plucked a booklet from the shelf. The chronicle was word-processed in bold clear lettering and written in a style unusually mature for an eleven-year-old. It was illustrated by small line drawings, carefully executed maps and well mounted photographs.

'It's good, isn't it?' Miss Precious said. 'You'll see Joseph's other work next lesson. I would be very interested to know what you think of it and then I would really welcome some advice on his education. He's a very unusual little boy is Joseph Barclay, very unusual indeed.'

The very person we were talking about was in the classroom when I arrived at the end of morning break. He was busily tidying the books in the small corner library.

'Hello, Mr Phinn,' he said.

'Haven't you been out to play, Joseph?' I asked.

'No, sir.. I had a few jobs to do in the classroom. I keep things ship-shape.'

'It's good to blow a few cobwebs away, you know, get a breath of fresh air, have a run around in the morning.'

'Oh, I get enough fresh air. I walk a mile to school each morning and a mile home in the afternoon. That keeps me hale and hearty.' I smiled at the old-fashioned turn of phrase.

When the children had settled at their desks after the morning break, Miss Precious began her lesson.

'Now children,' she said, 'Emily's mother has been gardening again.' There was loud, good-humoured laughter and a few children groaned, 'Oh no!'

'And she found something.' Miss Precious turned to the corner of the classroom where I sat watching with interest. 'I should explain, Mr Phinn, that Emily, like most of the children in the class, lives close to Barton Moor and her garden goes right up to the site of the battlefield. Emily's mother has found some really interesting things in her garden, hasn't she, Emily?' A bright-faced little girl nodded. 'Tell us what your mother found yesterday.'

'Well,' began Emily, 'it's a sort of buckle. It's maybe from a belt or a bag. It's all rusted up but there is a little silver rose in the middle. My mum was pulling up some dead flowers and there it was.'

'We'll add that to our collection, shall we, Emily, and when someone comes up from the university in the better weather we can find out exactly what it is.'

'So other things have been found, have they?' I asked.

'Yes, sir,' announced a boy waving his hand and arm in the air as if hailing a taxi. 'My grandad found some lead musket balls and three brass buttons when he was mending a gate.'

'My dad found a sort of spear thing,' chimed in another. 'It was under the foundations when we built the extension. It's at the museum now. What was it called?' he said, turning to Joseph. 'You know that spear thing that my dad found. Can you remember what it was called?'

'It was a halberd,' replied Joseph, 'a sort of hatchet with a spike on the top which would have been mounted on a long wooden pole and used by the pikemen during the battle.'

'That's it!' shouted the boy. 'A halberd.'

'Has anyone else found anything in their gardens?' I asked.

'I found a dead cat, sir!' announced a large boy with a big placid face. This was received with some kindly laughter but I noticed that it failed to bring a smile to Joseph's lips. He sat sober-faced at the front desk like the receptionist at a funeral parlour.

'I don't think somehow that a dead cat, Ben,' chuckled the teacher, 'dates back to the Battle of Barton Moor. Soldiers were not in the habit of taking their pets into battle with them. I should think –'

'Excuse me, miss,' interrupted Joseph, 'some of the commanders did take their pets into battle with them. Prince Rupert had a dog – it was a toy poodle – called Boy which he sat on his saddle and he took everywhere with him, even into the thick of the fighting.'

'Do you know, Mr Phinn,' said Miss Precious amiably, 'Joseph has more history in his little finger than I've got in my entire head.'

I spent the remainder of the morning listening to the children read confidently and clearly and examining their written work.

When it came to Joseph's turn he collected his reading book and several folders and arranged them on the desk before me. His record of the books he had read over the year was wide and challenging, and mostly historical in theme. He had listed the title of each book neatly with the author's name, date and brief comments about how interesting or otherwise he had found the book. When I asked him to read a paragraph or two to me, his reading was slow but deliberate and without any stumblings or hesitations at the difficult words. His writing was beautifully presented and accurate but entirely serious in theme. There were no amusing poems, entertaining stories or lively, funny accounts. It was all solemn and pensive. One poem, in particular, I read several times. I had never come across such a melancholy and poignant piece of writing from a child before.

When I was little I thought that God was like Santa Claus,
A smiling, wrinkled face, a great white beard, a gentle
  voice.
Now I am older I think that God is like an old man
With a tired, lined face and furrowed brow
Who weeps to see the world he has made.

'So what did you make of our Joseph?' asked Miss Precious at lunchtime. 'He's a most remarkable boy, isn't he?'

'He's one of the brightest children I have ever met,' I replied. 'A highly intelligent, articulate and, for his age, immensely knowledgeable boy, very polite but . . .' I paused for a moment to try to think of the most appropriate word, 'I find him a melancholy, a quite disconcerting child. That's my opinion, for what it's worth.'

'You are very perceptive, Mr Phinn. He's such a pleasant boy is Joseph, always helpful and courteous. He produces wonderful work and has never been an iota of trouble but he has such a mournful, pessimistic nature and is so very old for his years, too old. The other boys come in from the playground with scraped knees and grubby hands, their hair like haystacks and shirts hanging out, but Joseph appears pristine – not a hair out of place. I just wish sometimes he'd run in panting and laughing like the others as if he'd been pulled through a hedge backwards – but he never does.'

'Is he bullied?' I asked.

'Oh good gracious, no, the other children tolerate him remarkably well. You saw that in the lesson. They just accept him for what he is. The boys tried at first to involve him in their games but he prefers to be alone. I wish he would kick a football around with the others or play conkers or climb trees as boys do, but he prefers his own company. In summer he can be seen sitting quietly reading on the bench in the playground like an old man enjoying his retirement. In winter he potters about the classroom tidying up, cleaning the blackboard, sharpening the pencils.'

'What do his mother and father say?' I asked. 'Are they worried about him?'

'Well, that's part of the problem, I feel,' sighed the Headteacher. 'He lives with his grandparents. I won't go into the reasons why he doesn't live with his mother and father, it's very sad and also confidential. His grandparents are well meaning and caring and they try their best with him. They send him to school spotless and attend parents' meetings without fail but they are like many older people, they've slowed down and want a quiet, unhurried life.'

'Well I have to say, Miss Precious, that I don't think he could be in a better school than this. There is a spirit of happiness and endeavour here. The children talk freely and knowledgeably about their work and most write with excellent fluency. The work Joseph undertakes is certainly challenging enough and he seems, in his own way, a contented child. I will, however, have a word with the educational psychologist and see if she can be of any help. Mrs Richards is much better equipped than I to advise in this sort of thing. Joseph's a very unusual young man and I guess we'll all be hearing a great deal about him in the future.'

Before I set off for my appointment at the next school, I said goodbye to the teachers and children.

'I do hope you will mention the window in your report, Mr Phinn. It would certainly give me ammunition with my governors,' smiled Miss Precious. Then she added: 'Joseph, perhaps you would care to show Mr Phinn out and put the catch on the door after him. Do have a safe journey, Mr Phinn, and thank you so much for coming.'

As we walked towards the entrance, Joseph asked, 'Are you writing a report on this school?'

'Yes, I am,' I replied.

'Well, if you want my opinion, I think this is a very good school with many positive features. Miss Precious really tries her best and works very hard.' It sounded like the comments from one of my own reports. 'I hope you'll put that in to your account of the school.'

'I shall certainly consider doing so, Joseph,' I said. At the door he held out a small hand and stared up at me through the thick lenses of his glasses.

'Well, I must get back to my work,' he said as I shook his hand. '"Time waits for no man" as my grandfather says. Have a safe journey. Goodbye, Mr Phinn.'

'Goodbye, Joseph,' I said.

I arrived home late that evening when all was still and silent and the air misty and cold. The lights of the shops and houses lit up the high street, casting bright bars of yellow across the road. My flat above The Rumbling Tum café was in darkness. I let myself in but paused for a moment before I turned on the light. I could not stop thinking of a lonely little boy with thick-lensed glasses walking home along the narrow path that bordered the vast and friendless Barton Moor.

18

Connie was washing the cups and saucers in the small kitchen at the Staff Development Centre. I heard the clinking and clanking of crockery from way down the corridor so guessed she was not in the best of moods.

'Good morning, Connie,' I greeted her breezily, popping my head through the serving hatch.

'Oh!' she jumped. 'You gave me quite a start. I was miles away.'

'Yes, I could see that. Is everything all right?'

'No, everything's *not* all right, if you *must* know! I've just had one of Mr Pritchard's PE courses — great big gallumping games teachers in track suits, jumping up and down and running all about like whirling dervishes, and trailing mud right into the Centre all over the carpets. I had a mercifully quiet time when Mr Pritchard broke his leg — apart from the marks he made all over the floor with his crutches. Now he's back with a vengeance. You will never believe the amount of tea they consumed — it would sink the *Titanic*! *And*,' she stressed the word, 'I've got another of those art courses in the offing. All those stuffed animals and paint everywhere. It takes me a full week to recover from one of Mr Clamp's in-service sessions.' She glowered and shook her head.

I changed the subject. 'Harold was telling me you have a grandson, Connie.'

The transformation in Connie was nothing short of

miraculous. The tight lips relaxed, she smiled coyly and her eyes took on a sparkling gleam of pleasure. She ceased clinking and clunking the crockery, dried her hands and emerged from the kitchen.

'Oh, he's a bobby dazzler, Gerv,' she began. 'The things that little lad says never cease to amaze me. He's the spit-and-image of his grandad is little Damien. His expressions are exactly like my Ted's.'

'Has he started school yet?'

'Yes, he started at Willingforth Primary last September, same time as you started here. He's in his second term now. My daughter, Tricia, she lives in Willingforth and sends him to the village school. His sister Lucy is in the juniors. That Miss Pilkington's the Headteacher.' When Connie prefaced a name with the word 'that' as in 'that inspector with the fancy car' or 'that teacher who never returns her cup to the kitchen' or 'that Savage woman' I was pretty certain it would be followed by a diatribe. But I was wrong in this case.

'I take it Miss Pilkington is not the flavour of the month, Connie?' I said casually.

'Oh no, she's very compis mental.' I assumed this to be a compliment. 'My daughter's no grumbles in that direction. My grandson loves his school, bless him. He's come on leaps and bounds since he started. He knows his alphabet and his words and can do some of his tables. He brings a reading book home every night and is that keen. And he's so well behaved. He was quite a little character before he started, asking for sweets all the time and when he didn't get them shouting and screaming blue murder. But that Miss Pilkington got the measure of him in no time at all. She was having none of it. A couple of weeks in her class and he was as good as gold. She's excellent is Miss Pilkington. A woman after my own heart. She doesn't stand any nonsense, I can tell you, not like some of these airy-fairy, wishy-washy teachers you hear about. Miss Pilkington's one of the old school.'

I often heard about these airy-fairy, wishy-washy teachers who supposedly believed that children learned to read by osmosis and that spellings are caught rather than taught, but I had yet to meet one.

'Have you been out to Willingforth school yet then?' Connie asked.

'No, I have that pleasure to come.' I reckoned Miss Pilkington sounded like a real virago.

'Well, when you do, you're in for a rare treat. You could eat your food off the floor in that school, it's so clean – and the toilets, you have never seen toilets like . . .' It was as if I had wound up some talking mechanical toy. Connie continued in her eulogy for a good ten minutes more. Why had I ever raised the subject of her grandson?

It was a month later, on a frosty February afternoon, that I had occasion to visit Willingforth Primary School. Everything looked bleak and grey as I drove slowly along the empty road beneath a dark overcast sky. The fresh bursting life of spring, the bright summer sunlight dancing on the fells, the mellow golds of autumn seemed many months away.

The village of Willingforth itself looked deserted. I searched in vain for a school sign, drove up and down the main street, peering this way and that, did a circuit of the gaunt Norman church and the picturesque duck pond, until I accepted defeat and decided to ask at the local inn. There were a couple of old farmers leaning indolently against the public bar and putting the world to rights. They stopped talking and turned in my direction when I entered.

'Shut that door, lad, thy're lettin' a rare old draught in,' growled one of the ancients.

'Could you tell me where the village school is, please?' I asked amiably.

'Tha' wants school, does tha'?' asked the first local, eyeing me over his spectacles as if I were some rare specimen.

'Yes, if you could point me in the direction, I should be most grateful.'

'Tha's got business up theer then, has tha'?' he asked.

'Yes,' I replied simply, 'I have.'

The landlord, who had been busy washing glasses at the other end of the bar joined his two customers.

'Young mester's wantin' school.'

'Oh aye?' said the landlord, staring fixedly at me.

'Willingforth Primary School,' I said.

'Tha's got business up theer then, has tha'?' he asked.

'Yes,' I replied again, 'I have.'

'If tha's selling owt,' said the first ancient observing my grey suit and black briefcase, 'my advice is to get back in thee car. Tha'll be out o' that door before thy 'and's off t'door 'andle.'

His companion chuckled. 'Tha' will that.'

'Oh aye,' agreed the landlord.

'No, I'm not selling anything.'

'And if tha's a parent wantin' to send thee kiddie theer, be ready for a rare old grillin'.' His companion and the landlord nodded.

'No, I'm not a parent.'

'Aye, well whatever, thas'll have to watch thee p's and q's when tha' get up theer and no mistake.'

'Tha' will that!' agreed number two. 'She dunt mince 'er words that Miss Pilkington. By heck, she's a fierce woman and no mistake. She could put the wind up a banshee could that teacher.'

'Actually, I'm a school inspector,' I said.

There was an audible in-drawing of breath and the three men's faces took on the most excruciating expressions – as if they had swallowed their teeth.

'Well, I'm glad I'm not in thy shoes, young man,' said the first old man.

'Nor me,' added the other with a grave expression. 'I don't reckon she'll take kindly to being inspected, Miss Pilkington.'

'It'll not be *'im* who'll be doin' t'inspectin'!' roared the landlord to the great amusement of his customers.

Miss Pilkington sounded as welcoming as a scrapyard rottweiler. I finally extracted directions to the school and five minutes later was parked outside a four-square and imposing stone building, facing open countryside, on the edge of the village. There was no indication that it was a school. Usually these small village schools have playgrounds adjacent to the buildings, tall black iron railing fencing them in and large school signs but not this one. It looked like a private, carefully-maintained private residence. There were shining white shutters at every window, a large oak panelled door with brass knocker and a neat, lawned garden to the front. I braced myself, clambered from the car and approached the school with great apprehension. Taking a deep breath I turned the heavy brass handle and entered.

The door opened straight into a large airy classroom, the like of which I had never seen before. Instead of the small melamine-topped tables and modern chairs usually found in the primary schools I visit, the room was furnished with hard straight-backed wooden chairs and highly-polished desks complete with lids and holes for inkwells. The walls were a pale blue and the beams and curved wooden supports stretching across the high ceiling were painted navy blue and cream. I caught sight of a large coloured sampler with the words: 'STRAIGHT WORDS, STRAIGHT DEEDS, STRAIGHT BACKS'. Framing the high windows hung long blue floral drapes, while the reading corner had a soft pale carpet and large matching cushions. There was a Victorian fireplace, its mantle of dark slate and inlaid marble and its heavy black iron grate filled with carefully arranged dried flowers in various shades of blue and white. I had never seen a colour co-ordinated classroom before. If there were a prize awarded for schoolrooms from one of these glossy magazines – *Creative Decorating* or *Imaginative Interior Design* – Willingforth Primary School would have won hands down.

At the far end of the long room stood, who I presumed to be, the formidable Miss Pilkington. I had rather expected a Dickensian character, a dark, brooding, aggressive individual with cold, glassy eyes, steel-rimmed spectacles and a thin bony frame. Her hair would be white and scraped back savagely from her lined face and she would have a hard beak of a nose. But I was wrong. Miss Pilkington was a tall, elegant woman approaching middle age, and dressed in a pale green silk suit.

'Do come in, Mr Phinn,' she said, 'I was expecting you.' As I headed in her direction she addressed the forty or so children, ranging in age from five to eleven: 'This is Mr Phinn, children. He is the school inspector and he will be joining us for the remainder of the day.'

The class chorused enthusiastically: 'Good afternoon, Mr Phinn.'

'Good afternoon, children,' I replied.

'If you could bear with me for a moment, Mr Phinn,' continued the teacher, 'I just need to explain to the children what they will be doing this afternoon. My assistant, Miss Bates, who teaches the infants, telephoned in sick this morning so I need to tell the little ones what they will be doing. I will then be continuing some work started with the juniors on spelling.'

She ushered me to a chair next to the blackboard where I watched with great admiration as she outlined clearly to a very attentive and interested class the work to be undertaken. I was filled with even greater admiration as the older pupils re-arranged the desks quietly without direction from the teacher, made sure the younger ones had the necessary equipment and paper and started them off on their work, before returning to their own desks ready for their lesson of spelling.

'Please don't let me interrupt the lesson, Miss Pilkington,' I said. 'I should be very pleased to discuss the reason for my visit after school.'

'Very well,' said Miss Pilkington. When the junior children were seated and all eyes were on her, the Headteacher began the lesson. 'How many did you find, Tom?'

A large boy with a shock of ginger hair and a face full of freckles answered. 'Six, miss.'

'Well, that is a very good effort, Tom. Did anyone find any more than six?'

'I found eight, miss, but had a bit of help from my mum,' answered a tall pale-faced girl at the back.

'That is excellent, Janine.' Miss Pilkington turned to me. 'We have been undertaking a little research to find out how many different ways we can find of spelling the sound "shun". We have done some work on the prefix and the suffix and now are looking at the various spelling patterns and word endings.' She turned back to the class. 'Remember I said that good spellers do not make wild guesses but make sensible predictions, didn't I?'

'Yes, miss,' chorused the class.

'Now, in nine out of ten cases the sound "shun" is spelled "t-i-o-n" as in the words "disruption", "investigation", "examination", "interruption" and, of course, "inspection".' She glanced in my direction. There was obvious significance in the particular words chosen. 'There are over a thousand words which have the sound "shun" at the end and are spelled "t-i-o-n" for every four exceptions so you can be pretty sure that if a word has the sound "shun" in it, it will be spelled "t-i-o-n". Let's see how many other possible spellings there are of the sound "shun".'

There followed a lively discussion and the various ways of spelling the sound were listed, with the pupils quick to provide different examples: 'comprehension', 'ocean', 'fashion', 'Russian', 'politician', 'suspicion', 'truncheon', 'complexion'.

'That's excellent, but there are just two more rather difficult and unusual exceptions to the rule which only a real expert on the English language would know.' She glanced again in my direction. I just knew what was coming. I was sitting at the front of the classroom, next to the blackboard in full view of the children, a supposed expert on the language, an inspector of English no less. Miss 'I don't reckon she'll take kindly to being inspected' Pilkington was going to turn in my direction, fix me with a confident stare and ask me to provide the two other ways of spelling the sound 'shun'. And I, for the life of me, could not think of any more alternatives. My mind quickly raced through various words but with no success. It kept focusing on the picture of the landlord at the local inn roaring with laughter as he predicted: 'It'll not be *'im* who'll be doin' t'inspectin'.' But the teacher let me off the hook.

'The two other spellings are "chian" as in Appalachian, that's a range of mountains in North America, and "chion" as in the word "stanchion" which is an upright bar used as a support. I cannot find any others. I don't know if you know of any, Mr Phinn?'

'No, no,' I replied quickly.

She looked back at the children. 'Now the first task this afternoon is to add the spellings and the rule neatly to your word books, spending a little time learning them, and then I would like you to complete the stories you started yesterday. Do use some imaginative words but remember to use a dictionary if you are unsure of a spelling. I shall be spending a little time now with the infants so I would like you to get on quietly. Mr Phinn, perhaps you would like to have a look at what they are doing.' With that, Miss Pilkington moved to the other part of the classroom to teach the infants.

After school I accompanied Miss Pilkington into her small office. 'Now, Mr Phinn, you wished to ask me some questions about this survey you are conducting?'

'That's right,' I replied.

'And what is the focus of the survey?' she asked.

I sighed before answering, 'The teaching of spelling.'

It was a lovely sunny afternoon when I visited Willingforth Primary School a couple of weeks later. I had to return some of the children's work I had taken to assess. I was also going to take assembly. I stole a few moments when I pulled into a gateway and got out of the car. Leaning on the gate and looking at the peaceful Dales pastures shimmering in the late winter sun below me, it seemed that spring was just around the corner. But I could not linger long.

As I approached the heavy door of the school a growl of a voice stopped me in my tracks. 'Tha'are a glutton fo' punishment, thee.'

I turned to see the old farmer I had met in the village inn on my last visit. He leant on his stick at the side of the road and grimaced.

'Oh,' I smiled, 'good afternoon.'

'Tha' not come inspectin' ageean, has tha?'

'No, no, not today.'

'Aye, well I reckon she wunt put up wi' a repeat performance.' He laughed before going his way in the direction of the village.

'I had a very pleasant visit last time,' I called after him. 'Very pleasant indeed.'

He turned and winked dramatically. 'Aye, well, tha' wants to watch thi'sen, young man. Appearances can be perceptive. Her bite is worse than her bark.'

One of the poems I had assessed, 'by Christa aged 10', was exceptionally good. Miss Pilkington had told me that the little girl had already had a poem accepted for publication in a very prestigious national collection of children's writing. The teacher had been delighted for, as she had explained, Christa was a particularly shy and under-confident child who found the work rather demanding and often frustrating. She had a whole host of medical problems and had experienced very little success in her short life. She found reading difficult, number work arduous, while games were her least favourite class. The poem, therefore, was a real triumph and her teacher had told me how delighted little Christa had been to see her poem in print and her name beneath it.

Inside the school, the children's bright, expectant faces were as sunny as the afternoon outside. I was hardly through the door when I heard some very excited welcomes: 'It's Mr Phinn, miss!' 'Miss, Mr Phinn's arrived!' 'He's here, miss!' 'Hello, Mr Phinn!'

'Good afternoon everyone,' I said loudly. 'My goodness, what a welcome!'

'Good afternoon, Mr Phinn,' said Miss Pilkington. 'Come along in. We are all expecting you. The children are just finishing their spelling corrections and are reading quietly for a moment. Perhaps you would care to have a walk around and see how they are getting on.'

I moved from one highly-polished desk to another until I arrived at Christa's. She was a small, pale-complexioned child with great round eyes. She lowered her head and I could sense her nervousness.

'This is lovely work,' I commented gently, leafing through her book. 'You've written such a lot of stories and poems and your writing is coming on a treat.' Her head remained lowered as if in prayer. 'And what is your name?'

'Christa Fennick, sir,' she murmured.

'Not *the* Christa Fennick?' I asked with great surprise in my voice.

'Pardon, sir?' She looked up.

'Christa Fennick, the poet?'

'No, sir,' she whispered.

'Oh, I thought you might be *the* Christa Fennick who wrote the wonderful poem on autumn which appeared in this book.' I took the anthology of children's poems from my briefcase.

She looked up and smiled ever so slightly. 'Well, I did write *that* poem.'

'It was excellent and I really enjoyed reading it. I wonder if you would do me a great favour, Christa?'

'Yes, sir?'

'Would you sign your poem for me, please?' I said. 'I don't often meet many published poets.'

Miss Pilkington, who had been watching this exchange, said nothing but nodded and smiled as Christa wrote her name in the book in a spidery hand.

It was soon time for assembly and I had agreed to talk about stories and storytelling. All the children gathered around. 'One of the greatest storytellers that ever lived,' I began, 'changed people's lives with his wonderful stories. He never wrote them down, they were never put in a book during his lifetime and we have to depend upon his friends who heard him to know what he said. They weren't adventure stories or mysteries, horror stories or funny ones, but everyone who heard them just had to listen. We know that this storyteller was a wonderful speaker, that hundreds of people would come to listen to him and to his fascinating tales, and we know that his stories told us how to treat others and how to live good lives. Does anyone know who I am talking about?'

'Jesus!' chorused the children.

'That's right. Now Jesus told stories like The Good Samaritan and –'

'Parables,' interrupted a large boy with very blond hair. 'Those sort of stories are called parables.'

'That's right they are and Jesus told many parables to teach us how to live better lives. In the Old Testament of the Bible there are many exciting stories and I am going to read one to you today.'

I then read the story of David and Goliath, how the young shepherd boy with only a sling and a pebble defeated the champion of the Philistines. All the children, with the exception of just one, listened in rapt attention, their eyes widening at the part where Goliath, in his bronze armour and with his great spear roared at David: 'I will give your body to the birds and animals to eat!' Their facial expressions changed with the story and there was an audible sigh at the end when the Israelites cheered their champion who had killed the giant and saved his people.

The exception was a small, pink-faced girl whose big eyes bulged unblinkingly. She sat right under my nose, expressionless – not reacting in any way at all. As I closed the Bible I asked her, 'Did you like the story?' She nodded. 'Did Goliath frighten you a little bit at the beginning?' She nodded. 'And did you feel happy at the end?' She nodded. I found this pretty hard going.

Then I caught sight of Miss Pilkington at the back of the room, smiling widely. Her expression said: 'Let the inspector get out of this one.'

It was obvious that this little girl did not find it easy to communicate. She probably lived on an isolated farm and had little opportunity to interact with others. Perhaps she had special educational needs.

I tried again. 'Did you think Goliath would win?' She nodded. 'Have you read any other Bible stories?' She nodded. 'Can you think of a word to describe Goliath?' She nodded. I mouthed the words slowly and deliberately. 'WHAT – WORD – COMES – INTO – YOUR – HEAD – WHEN – YOU – THINK – OF – GOLIATH?' She stared up at me without blinking. I tried again. 'AT – THE – BEGINNING – WHAT – WORD,' I tapped my forehead, 'WHAT – WORD – COMES – INTO – YOUR – HEAD?' She continued to stare. My voice rose an octave. 'WHAT – WORD –

COMES – INTO – YOUR – HEAD – WHEN –
YOU – THINK – OF – THE – GIANT – AT –
THE – BEGINNING – OF – THE – STORY?'

After a thoughtful pause she said in a clear and confident voice: 'Well, I should say aggressive.' Then she added, 'You know my nannan.'

It was Connie's grand-daughter.

'You were speaking to the brightest and most prolific reader in the room,' Miss Pilkington told me later. 'She's an absolute delight to teach – but very quiet and thoughtful.'

'I felt such a fool,' I confided.

'Don't worry, Mr Phinn,' she replied, 'you did a lot better than the vicar. When the Reverend Braybrook took the Harvest Festival assembly last autumn, he fared rather worse.'

She told me how the vicar had started his assembly as I had done by asking the children to try and guess what was in his head. He had told them that, as he had walked through the churchyard on his way to the school that morning, he had seen something behind a tree. It had been grey and hairy with a great bushy tail and little darting, black, shiny eyes like beads.

'And what do you think I'm talking about?' he had asked the children.

Tom, the large boy with the very fair hair had replied, 'I know it's Jesus, vicar, but it sounds like a squirrel to me!'

Towards the end of the school's afternoon I said goodbye and headed for the Staff Development Centre where I was to direct a course later in the day. It was a glorious drive. The sun was still shining and cloud shadows chased across the fellside. A magpie strutted along a white stone wall and a pigeon flapped across the road just in front of the car. A fox appeared, stepping delicately across the road ahead of me, his brush down and snout up, unafraid, unconcerned. In the fields the sheep grazed lazily; lambs would start to arrive in a month or so. This surely was the best of seasons. Suddenly a large hen pheasant shot straight out in front of the car and I heard a thud as it hit the bumper. I quickly pulled over and jumped from the vehicle to see its prone body in the middle of the road, eyes closed and legs sticking skywards. All around me was silent and still. Not a person to be seen – not even Lord Marrick. I picked up the bird, popped it in the boot of my car and thought of the wonderful roast game I would be having for my Sunday lunch.

At 4.30 that afternoon when I arrived at the Staff Development Centre to prepare for the course, Connie, as usual, was standing like some great Eastern statue in the entrance, watching the comings and goings with a face like a death mask and the eyes of an eagle. She watched as I parked the car – well away from the entrance – and clambered out with an armful of folders before she opened the door to the Centre for me. When I had deposited the folders I headed back to the car to collect some books and equipment from the boot. Connie was still guarding the entrance, and I stopped to talk to her.

'I saw your grand-daughter today, Connie,' I said.

'Did you?' She perked up immediately and her face brightened. 'Our Lucy?'

'She's a very sharp little girl, isn't she?' Connie's face suffused with colour and she nodded approvingly. 'Miss Pilkington has very high hopes for her.'

'She's a wonderful teacher, that Miss Pilkington,' said Connie with great emphasis. 'And she keeps that school a picture. It always looks nice but you wait until summer. She has all these window boxes and stone troughs and wooden tubs full of the most wonderful colourful enemas, and inside it's all matching like in one of these smart fashion mags. You could eat your food off the floor in that school, it's so clean and the toilets, you have never seen toilets like –'

'You'll be seeing Miss Pilkington later on, Connie, so you can tell her yourself. She's coming to the writing course at the end of the afternoon.'

'That's nice,' said Connie, heading for the kitchen. 'I shall go and put some of my special Garibaldi biscuits out to have with the tea.'

Mine wasn't quite such 'a nice surprise' a few moments later. I returned to my car and opened the boot to take the books and equipment into the Centre – only to find everything a complete jumble. In the very middle of the mess crouched the pheasant I had run over and had assumed was dead. It was, to my amazement, very much alive and kicking. Connie returned to the entrance just in time to see something squawking and pecking and fluttering its wings madly. I had stunned the creature, not killed it; now fully recovered, it was not at all pleased to have been incarcerated in the cramped dark boot of a car for a couple of hours, bumping along mile after mile.

'Shoo!' I cried, trying to encourage the bird to leave the boot, but every time my hand came within pecking range it lunged at me. 'Shoo! Shoo!' I exclaimed again. Then, turning, I realized I had attracted a crowd of interested teachers who stood in a half circle with Connie, watching proceedings.

'Not wild animals now,' wailed Connie. 'You know I can't stand the stuffed variety that Mr Clamp brings into the Centre, never mind savage beasts!'

'Is it a visual aid?' asked one teacher mischievously.

'No, it is not!' I snapped.

'Are we going to write bird poems,' asked another teacher chuckling, 'from first-hand experience?'

'No, we are not!' came my angry reply.

'Well, I don't want it in the Centre,' said Connie. 'I'm not cleaning up after that. I have enough trouble with the stuffed heron.'

'It's not going in the Centre, Connie,' I said getting as flustered as the bird. The bird made another loud, plaintive squawk and beat its wings and thrashed its tail.

'What sort of bird is it?' asked Connie peering through the dusky evening light.

Before I could answer, Miss Pilkington, who was now amongst the amused onlookers, responded. 'Oh, I should say aggressive,' she said with a twinkle in her eyes. 'Wouldn't you, Mr Phinn?'

19

'Hello, Winnery Nook Nursery and Infant School.'

'Miss Bentley . . . er . . . Christine?' There was that tell-tale nervousness in my voice again.

'Speaking.'

'It's Gervase Phinn here. You left a message for me to ring you.'

'Oh yes, thanks. I must see you. Can you call in sometime?'

'Yes, of course. You mentioned it was urgent.'

'It is urgent in a way,' she replied. 'I can't really explain over the telephone, but I would very much like to see you, there's something I need to discuss with you. It's not to do with school, it's a personal matter.'

My heart began to beat nineteen to the dozen. 'I can call in later today after school, if that's convenient, but it would be about six o'clock.'

'That will be fine. I usually stay late on a Monday. I look forward to seeing you then.'

Whatever could she want? I thought. Why was it urgent? What was the personal matter about? What was there to discuss? Did she really say that she would very much like to see me? I racked my brains to think of what it could be about. Well, by the end of the day, I would know – and predictably spent the day clock-watching.

Just before six I arrived at Winnery Nook. The school looked deserted. On my first visit, when I had arrived at morning playtime, it had been teeming with tiny children, squealing and shrieking delightedly, laughing and playing, and everything had seemed so bright and sunny. On my second visit, to attend the Nativity play, the place had been throbbing with parents, teachers and governors and there had been a Christmassy atmosphere in the frosty air. Through the car window the honey-coloured brick building with its orange pantile roof and large picture windows now appeared strangely silent and prison-like in the early evening.

Over the last few months I had seen Christine very briefly at a couple of courses, and had bumped into her in Fettlesham one Saturday morning when we exchanged a few pleasantries. I had received the lovely card with an enclosed cheque for the plate but I had had no chance to see her for any length of time since before Christmas. She had certainly been in my thoughts. I sat in the car now day-dreaming, wondering what could be so urgent – and personal.

There was a sudden tap on the window which made me jump like someone who has just sat on a firecracker. 'Are you going to sit out here all evening?' It was Christine smiling through the side window of the car. Flustered and embarrassed, I clambered from the vehicle. 'I've been watching you from my room,' she said, 'sitting there motionless like a corpse. You can come inside, you know, I don't bite.'

I followed her into the school and down the corridor to her room. She sauntered ahead in that languid easy grace, leaving an alluring whiff of perfume in her wake.

'I've had a tiring day,' I said, in a feeble attempt to explain the odd behaviour. 'I was just sort of unwinding and then I got to thinking.'

'What about?' she asked.

'Oh just this and that. Nothing of any importance.'

'I thought at one point, you'd died at the wheel,' she chuckled. 'You looked so still and serious. Anyway, you're here now and I will explain the mystery and why I just had to see you.'

This sounded ominous. I wondered if Sidney had said something flippantly to her about my liking her, or whether David had indiscreetly linked my name with hers in the company of some gossipy teacher. They had both been teasing me for several weeks about asking her out and clearly guessed that I was attracted to her, despite my protest to the contrary and the constant retort that she had a boyfriend already. Maybe she wanted to see me to ask me to put a stop to the rumours. We arrived at her room and she motioned for me to take a seat.

'Are you still enjoying the job?' she asked.

'Oh yes, very much,' I replied but I could not cope with pleasantries, I just had to know why she wanted to see me. 'What is it ... er ... you wanted to speak to me about?'

'It's that plate!' she exclaimed.

'Pardon?'

'The plate, the "blue patterned plate of unknown provenance" as the catalogue said. The one you bought for me at Roper's Saleroom in Collington.'

'This is all about the plate?'

'Yes.'

'You wanted to see me so urgently about the plate?' I was thoroughly puzzled.

'The plate, yes. Look, let me explain. We had a school fund-raising event a week ago when parents, friends, governors and members of staff all brought in old items of interest to a social evening. We ran it on the lines of the television programme when people bring paintings, glass and china and other family heirlooms which are talked about by the experts and valued. They have to be small and antique and interesting – the items, that is, not the experts.' She laughed softly. 'We arranged for a valuer from Burton's Fine Arts in Fettlesham to come and talk about the different objects and estimate how much they were worth. Well, I brought the "blue patterned plate of unknown provenance". Mr Burton commented on a few objects on the table until he saw the plate. Then he went really quiet, picked it up and asked to whom it belonged. He asked me how much I had it insured for. He said later that when he first saw it, he nearly swooned. That plate, Gervase, is a Delft blue patterned plate, probably made in Lowestoft at the end of the seventeenth century and will fetch, according to the valuer, over six hundred pounds at auction.'

'What?' I exclaimed.

'Over six hundred pounds. I nearly fainted.'

'That old chipped plate? But it had a crack right the way down it!'

'That's a kiln crack according to Mr Burton and will not affect the value all that much.'

'Well, that's incredible.'

'So you see my dilemma,' sighed Christine.

'You mean, whether to sell it or not?'

'No, I shan't sell it but I feel I ought to give you some money. After all, you bought it. Without you I wouldn't have it at all.'

'Well, neither would I for that matter. I only bid for it – you wanted it.'

'Yes but –'

'And I wouldn't have looked twice at it had I been on my own.'

'Yes but –'

'There are no "buts". The plate is yours. I merely bought it on your behalf and you have paid me for it.'

'You really are kind, Gervase,' she said. 'I must do something to thank you.'

'You can treat me to a meal sometime,' I answered, chancing my arm.

She gave such a disarming smile and then replied, 'Yes, I'll do that. I would like that very much. What fun!'

'I was speaking to a young teacher yesterday,' remarked Sidney casually the next day. 'Said she had been on one of your courses.'

'Really?' I replied, only half listening.

'Said how much she enjoyed it and what a wonderful lecture you gave.'

'Really?'

'Quite taken with you, she was. Said you were quite inspirational. Are you listening to me, Gervase? You won't receive exactly an avalanche of admiration and accolade as a school inspector so when a small amount comes your way, relish it, dear boy, delight in it, bask in the sunshine of the praise and recognition but don't just mumble and murmur "Really".'

'Sidney,' I replied, 'can you not see the mountain of paper on my desk? I am trying to work. I am very pleased this person found the course useful and I am delighted that my lecture in particular was well received – but I really must get on.'

'It is lunchtime, you know, Gervase. You are not obliged to work every hour of the day. You are allowed to stop for a few minutes for some sustenance. Even the workaholic Dr Gore has a cup of coffee occasionally.' I sighed, put down my pen and gave him my undivided attention. 'That's better. Now this young teacher said you were encouraging them to chance their arms, to experiment, to have a go and that you said that few advances are made in life unless one takes a few measured risks.'

'Yes, that's right,' I replied. 'Is there some sort of a problem with that?'

'Not at all, not at all. I thoroughly approve and endorse such a view. After all, where would the art world be if painters like Van Gogh and Manet, Dali and Picasso had failed to experiment and try something different.'

'Sidney,' I said, getting rather irritated by what appeared to be a quite meaningless exchange, 'is this conversation leading somewhere? Is there something you want to say to me?'

'Well, now you come to mention it, there is. Doctor heal thyself.'

'What?'

'Take your own advice, dear boy. Chance your own arm, go for it, take a measured risk, grab the bull by the horns.'

'I still haven't a clue what you're talking about.'

'I'm talking about the heavenly headteacher of Winnery Nook, the delectable Miss Bentley.'

'Oh, don't start again, Sidney. You really are getting tiresome. I am not going to ask her out.'

'Now, come along, Gervase,' he said. 'You know you like her, I know you like her and I should imagine she herself knows you like her. She's always ringing you up. She's attractive, educated and unmarried. Why, for goodness sake, don't you ask her out?'

'You're joking.'

'Why should I be joking?'

'As I've already told you, she's got a boyfriend already.

217

He drives a fast sports car, lives in a huge house, owns half of the county and seems to have money to burn. He's young, handsome, well-connected and successful, speaks with the right accent and jets around the world. I could go on and on with numerous other reasons but I would only be repeating myself.'

'I have to admit,' said Sidney thoughtfully, 'you do sound somewhat insignificant compared with Prince Charming. Money, looks and property are weighty factors.'

'So do you think we could let the matter drop?'

'But if you don't chance your arm,' persisted Sidney, 'you will never know.'

'I'll think about it – and now may I be allowed to return to my work?' I buried my head in the mound of paper on my desk and attempted to continue with the report I was half way through writing but had just settled down to completing the first paragraph when Sidney started again.

'Just thinking about it is no use. "Faint heart never won fair maiden", as Shakespeare or somebody or other once said. You need to take action, dear boy. Anyway, you shouldn't denigrate yourself. You're young, well relatively so, still in your prime, personable, intelligent, reasonably good-looking, have your own hair, full set of teeth and a good, secure job with plenty of prospects. You keep saying you are looking for a nice country cottage. In fact, in an ideal position from which to launch yourself into married life.'

'*Married!* I haven't even asked her out yet!' I exclaimed. 'And if I do get married I shall not launch myself into it like some ballistic missile. I shall consider it carefully.'

'So you *are* thinking about it?'

'Look, Sidney, I've not been in the job for a year. I'm

just settling into things and I'm not ready for another relationship at the moment.'

'*Another* relationship!' he exclaimed. 'Do tell.'

Julie's entrance to the office with a pile of papers, however, curtailed any further discussion.

'Not much work seems to be going on in here this afternoon,' she remarked.

'I give up,' I sighed picking up my pen again.

For the remainder of the day I just could not concentrate on my work or get Sidney's words out of my head. Maybe he was right. Maybe I should chance my arm. After all, she'd promised to treat me to dinner. She could only say no. So I picked up the telephone and rang Winnery Nook.

'Hello.'

'Christine?' There was that tell-tale nervousness in my voice yet again.

'Speaking.'

'It's Gervase Phinn here.'

'Oh hello.'

'How are you?'

'Oh I'm very well. How are you?'

'I'm fine.'

'Good.'

There was what seemed like an interminable silence before I heard her voice again. 'Did you want something, Gervase?'

'Yes, I did really. I would like to see you.'

'Well, we saw each other last week. Have you changed your mind about the plate?'

'No, nothing like that. Could I . . . would it be . . . I phoned on the off-chance that . . . well, I'd like to see you.'

'Yes, of course. To do with what?'

'To . . . to . . . take you up on that offer of a meal.' My

heart began to beat like a stampeding herd of cattle. 'I would just like to see you.' My voice sort of trailed off at this point. I must have sounded very foolish. 'I would understand, of course, if you . . .'

'I would love to.'

'Pardon?'

'Would you like to come round for supper? I haven't asked you before because, well, I wondered if it was the right sort of thing to do – inviting round a school inspector. I mean, a headteacher . . . it's just . . . I really am expressing myself badly, aren't I? What about this Sunday?'

'Pardon?'

'Have you anything on in the evening?'

'N-no,' I stammered, 'I don't have anything on.'

'Right then, Sunday it is. Come about seven. I'll send you a map showing directions. I live with my parents in Collington.'

'Are you sure Miles won't mind?' I asked gingerly. 'You inviting me round for supper. I mean, would he mind?'

'I couldn't care less whether Miles minds or not, to be honest,' she replied. 'After the dreadful holiday in Austria, where all I heard was how expensive everything was and how good he was at this and good he was at that, I became heartily sick of Miles. So we don't see each other any more.'

I gulped – and there was another of those embarrassed silences.

'Gervase, are you still there?'

'Yes, yes, I'm still here. So Sunday, I'll see you on Sunday.'

It was fortunate that no one else was in the office or they would have jumped out of their skins at hearing the deafening, ear-piercing whoop for joy that I emitted.

★

The house was large. It was a high-gabled, stolid, stone, three-storeyed Victorian town house, the sort mill owners lived in and were now often converted into residential homes for the elderly or flats. It looked very imposing and grand. A long gravel driveway swept in a graceful curve between carefully tended lawns and borders to the large porch.

As I pressed the bell my stomach began to churn and my throat became hopelessly dry. Christine opened the door and my heart thumped at the sight of her smiling face. She shook my hand, led the way down a long entrance hall and into an elegant room where I was introduced to her mother. Mrs Bentley was an older version of Christine. She had the same warm blue eyes, slim figure and the same gentle manner.

'Mr Phinn, Gervase,' she said softly. 'I'm so very pleased to meet you. I've heard such a lot about you from Christine and from my husband. I must say, I'm a little nervous meeting a school inspector.' Not half as nervous as I am, I thought. 'I imagined them to be rather frightening figures, watching points and criticizing anything that moved, but my daughter and husband have put me right.'

'Oh, really?' Well, I'm glad about that,' I replied.

'My husband tells me you're a very different sort of person.'

'Have I met your husband, Mrs Bentley?' I asked.

Before she could reply, the man in question entered.

'Now then, young man, let's get you a drink, shall we, and talk over some of the finer points of refereeing a rugby match.' It was 'Legs' Bentley.

20

Early in March I was asked by Harold Yeats to give the opening talk on the Newly-Qualified Teachers course, to a group of new entrants to the teaching profession.

'This is always a successful and good-humoured course, Gervase,' Harold explained enthusiastically, 'and you can be sure of having a captive audience. Everyone is so eager and interested. No pessimists, no cynics, no weary, care-worn teachers. All bright and interested. I want you to introduce the day, if you will, by speaking about some of the qualities you consider the good teacher should possess.'

'Why me?'

'Well, you're relatively new to the team and bristling with fresh ideas. I should imagine you'll relate to the young teachers rather better than Sidney or David, or myself for that matter.'

I considered hard and long about what I should say and spent the preceding weekend planning the lecture carefully. A good teacher, I thought, should be committed, hardworking, enthusiastic, dedicated and well-organized. He or she should have good discipline, be able to command respect and, of course, relate well to children. And then I got to thinking about those of my own teachers whom I considered 'good', those I remembered with admiration and affection. They all possessed the qualities I had considered and felt important, they were all industrious, intellectually astute, enthusiastic and committed but they all had one extra characteristic in common: they encouraged their pupils to chance their arms, to experiment, to try out ideas without the fear of being criticized or disparaged. My lecture finished, therefore, with a heartfelt plea to those young, keen teachers.

'To move forward, both teachers and pupils need to take a few measured risks,' I said in conclusion. 'So – don't be afraid to chance your arm.'

One young teacher who had heard me speak that Monday morning certainly took the advice to heart. I was visiting St Anthony's Boys' Secondary Modern School to observe the morning lessons of a newly-qualified young teacher called Miss Isleworth. She had an engaging brightness and enthusiasm and clearly was enjoying her first year of teaching.

'I heard you speak on the course last Monday, Mr Phinn,' she said rather nervously, 'and I did so enjoy your talk.'

'Thank you very much,' I replied. 'It's always nice to hear the occasional appreciative comment. It tends to be something of a rarity for an inspector to be complimented on his advice.'

'And you know you mentioned about good teachers "chancing their arms"?' she continued.

'Yes.'

'Did you really mean it?'

'I most certainly did. I don't think we move forward unless we take a few measured risks now and again.' I was beginning to sound very pontifical.

'Well,' said Miss Isleworth with a great in-drawing of breath, 'I'm certainly going to chance my arm this morning.'

'Really?'

'I have quite an adventurous drama lesson planned with thirty-five thirteen-year-old-boys who are not too motivated, I'm afraid. I just hope it will be all right and the risk I'm taking is worth it.'

I reassured her as we walked across the playground to the drama studio – a grandiose name for a temporary classroom, perched on four large concrete blocks and sited on a muddy patch of ground. It resembled those POW huts one sees in the old war films: plain wooden walls, dark brown paint the colour of gravy, and grey, sloping asphalt roof. The glass in the windows was painted black.

'This is the drama studio?' I asked in disbelief, as we tiptoed around the puddles in the playground in the direction of the hut.

'Yes,' she replied smiling, 'I'm afraid so. The Headmaster wanted it as far away from the main building as possible so that the other classes aren't disturbed by the noise. It's a bit grim, isn't it?' As we climbed the steps to the temporary classroom, the heavens opened.

'What is the theme of the drama lesson?' I inquired as we lumbered in out of the rain.

'We're re-enacting the sinking of the *Titanic*,' she replied cheerfully.

It was my turn for a great in-drawing of breath. 'Good heavens!' I said. 'That *is* a pretty adventurous undertaking.' The sinking of the *Titanic* in a wooden hut with thirty-five lively teenage boys. She really *is* chancing her arm, I thought with some concern.

In the musty darkness of the hut, the drumming of rain on the wooden roof was all that could be heard. It was pitch black inside.

'Oh dear,' sighed the teacher, as she searched for the light switch, 'I don't think they've turned up. I said we would be having a school inspector in. I think they may have decided to give the lesson a miss.'

'I can hear breathing,' I whispered. The teacher clicked on the lights to reveal all the pupils in complete silence and frozen as in a tableau. They were arranged in various positions and attitudes on five large, grey staging blocks, which presumably represented the *Titanic*. In a corner three shadowy figures stood behind two large drums and a table of assorted percussion instruments. Another boy stood behind a large spotlight on a stand.

'Just relax for a moment will you, boys,' said Miss Isleworth. The figures on the blocks came slowly to life. 'I am really really pleased to see the very responsible way in which you have prepared for the play.' She turned in my direction. 'This is Mr Phinn who will be joining us this morning. There's a chair in the corner, Mr Phinn.'

'Miss, can we start?' asked an excited, diminutive little figure on the highest block, who sported a battered bus conductor's cap.

'In a moment, Dean. First, let me recap what we are doing this morning. This is the climax of the drama where the great ship hits the iceberg. The night is still, the sea is calm. It is dark and the air is icy. Most of the passengers are in bed. On the bridge Captain Smith and his first officer peer into the night unaware of the mountain of ice floating slowly towards the ship. Are you ready on the lights?'

'Yes, miss!' came a chorus.

'Are you ready on the drums?'

'Ready!'

'Actors, are you ready?'

'Ready, miss.'

'Right then, action!'

The room fell into complete darkness. A spotlight picked up two small figures on the highest staging block.

'It's a cold night, Captain Smith, and no mistake,' said one.

'It is indeed, especially for this time of year,' replied the other.

'In the Atlantic.'

'On our maiden voyage.'

'To America.'

'In 1912.'

'On the unsinkable *Titanic*.'

Light illuminated the other pupils on the different blocks miming various actions. Some were sleeping, others walking the deck.

Both boys peered into the darkness. 'What's that then?' asked the first.

'What?'

'That in the water in front of us.'

'It's . . . it's an iceberg!'

'Stop engines!' they both shrieked. This was followed by booming drums, clashing cymbals, screams and shouts, panic and mayhem. All the pupils who had arranged themselves on the various staging blocks lurched forward together, then fell back struggling as they sank beneath the icy waters. All was still. Then the spotlight picked out one lone figure with his hands in his pockets, standing in the water ahead of the *Titanic* and looking round self-consciously.

'Robert,' called Miss Isleworth, 'what are you doing?'

'I was away last week, miss,' came the reply. This was followed by good-humoured groans and laughs.

'Right everybody!' shouted the teacher. 'Just get up a moment. We'll run through this again. Robert, you get on the *Titanic*.' Robert joined the captain and the first officer on the highest block.

'You're not here!' they both snapped. 'This is the bridge. There's only us two up here.'

Robert descended a block. 'And you're not here either!' said another boy. 'This is first class and we're full up.'

Down another block went Robert. 'This is the engine room and there's no room for you down here either.'

Robert appealed to Miss Isleworth. 'Miss, there's *nowhere* for me to go!'

'He can be a seal in the water, miss,' suggested a helpful individual in first class.

'I'm not being a seal. I want to be on the *Titanic*,' moaned Robert and wandered over to where I was sitting. 'There's no room for me on the *Titanic*,' he said to me in the saddest of voices.

'Aren't you the lucky one,' I replied.

Miss Isleworth, thinking on her feet, called Robert over to her. 'You can go in the galley, Robert,' she said.

'Miss, I don't want to be a slave.'

'It's not that sort of galley, Robert. It's the ship's kitchen.'

'What was it called again, miss?'

'The galley, Robert. You can be cooking when the *Titanic* hits the iceberg.'

So Robert assumed the lowest position, looking distinctly unhappy with his assigned role.

'Right, let's go through it again,' said Miss Isleworth. The room fell into complete darkness. The spotlight picked up the two figures on the highest staging block.

'It's a cold night, Captain Smith, and no mistake,' said the first officer.

'It is indeed, especially for this time of year,' replied the other blowing on his hands.

'In the Atlantic.'

'On our maiden voyage.'

'To America.'

'In 1912.'

'On the unsinkable *Titanic*.'

Light illuminated the other pupils on the different blocks miming various actions. Some were sleeping, others walking the deck. Robert was moving his hands backwards and forwards as if poking an imaginary fire.

Both boys peered into the darkness. 'What's that then?' asked the first.

'What?'

'That big thing in the water in front of us.'

'Blinking heck!' shouted the captain. 'It's a great mountain of ice coming our way. It's an iceberg. It's . . . it's an iceberg!'

'Stop engines!' they both shrieked. Booming drums, clashing cymbals, screams and shouts, panic and mayhem followed. All the pupils lurched forward, then fell back struggling as they sank beneath the icy waters. All except Robert who was still merrily cooking in the galley.

'Robert!' shouted a rather exasperated Miss Isleworth. 'What *are* you doing?'

'I'm cooking the chips on the *Titanic*, miss.'

There was a groan from the captain, officers, passengers and crew.

'Robert,' said the teacher, 'the *Titanic* has hit the iceberg. The front of the ship has been ripped open like tinfoil, the watertight compartments are flooding, the icy waters are rushing in, people are panicking to get to the lifeboats, crockery is falling on your head, knives are flying past your ears, burning fat is splashing in your face – and you are cooking chips in the galley.'

'Yes, miss.'

'Well, just think what you *would* be doing. Imagine what

it would be like in the hot steamy kitchen at the bottom of the boat when the disaster happens.'

'Yes, miss.'

'Right, let's go through it one more time,' said Miss Isleworth.

'Again, miss? We're going through it again?' asked an angry Captain Smith, pulling his bus conductor's hat off his head.

'Last time,' the teacher assured him.

The room fell once again into complete darkness. The spotlight picked up two small figures on the highest staging block.

'It's a cold night, Captain Smith, and no mistake,' said the first officer in a very matter-of-fact voice.

'It is indeed, especially for this time of year,' replied the other, blowing half-heartedly on his hands.

'In the Atlantic,' said the captain casually.

'On our maiden voyage,' sighed the other.

'To America.'

'In 1912.'

'On the unsinkable *Titanic*.'

Light illuminated the other pupils positioned on the different blocks, miming various actions but with little enthusiasm – except for Robert who was enthusiastically cooking his chips in the galley.

Both boys on the highest staging block peered into the darkness. 'What's that then?' asked the first.

'What?'

'That big thing in the water in front of us.'

'Could be an iceberg, I suppose,' mumbled the captain.

'Shall we stop engines?' asked the other.

'We might as well,' sighed his companion, 'otherwise we might hit it.'

There followed a few lukewarm drum beats, an occasional cymbal, the odd scream and a shout, then some unenthusiastic movements on the blocks. All the pupils leant forward then fell back before slowly disappearing beneath the icy waters. All was still. The spotlight picked out a lone figure gradually sinking beneath the waves with one arm held aloft. It was Robert. Then 'glug, glug, glug' and he was gone.

'Robert,' asked Miss Isleworth, 'what was all that about with the arm?'

'I was holding the chip pan up, miss,' he explained. 'Didn't your mum tell you that if hot fat hits water, it can be very dangerous? At your age, I would have thought you'd have known that.'

Miss Isleworth's voice came to me through the darkness. 'I think, Mr Phinn, that is what is called "chancing one's arm", is it not?'

21

I arrived at Mrs Savage's office in the County Hall Annexe late one March afternoon. The first draft of the guideline booklet on 'The Teaching of Spelling' was ready and I had been asked to call to collect it for its final check before printing. Mrs Savage's office was palatial compared to mine. It was dominated by a huge mahogany desk behind which was a vast swivel chair – it would have accommodated a baby elephant. There were filing cupboards and cabinets of all sorts, an occasional table, two easy chairs and a state-of-the-art computer area in one corner. From the window there was an uninterrupted view over the market town, busy and bustling at rush hour, and in the far distance were the grey moors and misty peaks.

I was shown into Mrs Savage's office and told by the harassed-looking clerk who was just getting ready to go home to make myself comfortable and that Mrs Savage would be along at any moment. It had been a tiring day. I had chaired a lively working group on 'Raising Pupil Achievement' that morning, shortlisted for a teaching post over the lunch period, dealt with several contentious telephone calls, visited two schools in the afternoon and delivered a lecture at a twilight session for nursery teachers at four o'clock. I had driven up and down the Dales, missed lunch and was ready for a hot bath and something to eat. The clock on the County Hall bell tower struck six and there was still no sign of Mrs Savage. I had just about decided to call in another day to collect the draft booklet when the door opened and she breezed in. She was in a scarlet and black suit with enormous shoulder pads and great silver buttons. This was 'power dressing' taken to extremes.

'Sorry to have kept you waiting. But my little den is quite comfortable, isn't it?' she said closing the door behind her.

'Yes, very,' I replied.

'I cannot work in an environment which isn't homely. I like a warm, comfortable environment. I just don't know how you survive in that cramped, musty, dark little office with those noisy, difficult individuals around you. Dr Yeats is pleasant enough – but the other two! I really don't know how you can stand it.'

'Oh, I enjoy their company,' I replied, springing to my colleagues' defence. 'They're super people to work with when you get to know them. And we don't spend all that much time in the office actually. We are mostly in schools during the day. No, I like it. It has character.'

'You are just too good-natured. Mr Clamp is one of life's mavericks. He just goes his own merry way regardless of others. And as for Mr Pritchard, well – he's a very prickly individual indeed. We've had quite a few cross words about a number of things. It's his Celtic temperament – terrible temper.' Before I could reply she moved to her desk. 'But we don't want to talk about your colleagues, do we?' She smiled like a shark. 'Now, let's get a cup of coffee organized. I only drink decaffeinated myself. Or you might prefer a herbal tea. Then we can make ourselves comfortable. I'll ring down and see if someone can arrange it.'

'No, I won't have anything to drink. Actually, I'm in rather a hurry. I have quite a lot of work to do this evening and I haven't eaten today.'

'It's not good to miss a meal, you know.' She sounded like a school ma'am. 'And you know what they say about all work and no play.' The tone of voice changed to a softer lilt. 'We could always adjourn to The Rumbling Tum if you wish. They do a very nice spinach soufflé.'

'No, no,' I replied hurriedly, 'I really do have so much work this evening. I only popped in about the guideline document. You said it was ready for its final proof-reading.'

'You know, Gervase,' said Mrs Savage skirting the desk and moving in my direction, 'I really feel you and I liaise rather well.'

'Pardon?' I moved back a step.

'I was only saying to dear Dr Gore this morning that there are some people with whom one can work, can relate to, can co-operate with, establish a close working relationship, and others one cannot. I feel you are one of the former. We do work well together, don't we? We do have a certain rapport. Do you feel the same about me?' She fluttered her eyelids.

Good gracious, I thought panic-stricken, this cannot be happening. 'Well . . . er . . . I do think we managed to work well together on the Minister's visit,' I managed to mouth, 'but on a strictly professional and –'

'Exactly! Exactly!' She moved closer, breathing heavily. 'That's just what I mean. We sort of clicked, didn't we?'

'Clicked?' I repeated.

'It's so nice when two people get on so well together, isn't it?'

'Er . . . now about the guidelines . . .'

'You know, Gervase, when we first met, I thought this man will be like all the others up in that ivory inspectors' tower but I was wrong. That offhand secretary of yours quite got up my nose. Do you remember we had a little contretemps about extension numbers. Merely a small mix up but she made *such* a drama of it.' She smiled almost coyly. 'Having worked with you on a number of initiatives, Gervase, I know that you are different.'

'I am?'

'We relate. We talk the same language. We sing from the same hymn sheet, we dance to the same music.' I moved back another step. 'Do you like dancing, Gervase?' she asked.

I was lost for words. 'Well, I . . . I . . .'

'You certainly look like a good mover to me.'

'Well, I . . . I . . .'

'There's the County Ball at the end of the month.'

'Really, the County Ball?'

'I've been asked, in my capacity as the PA to the CEO to distribute the tickets.'

'Have you indeed?' I simpered.

'And Dr Gore always makes two available for me for all my hard work and as a little appreciation. Now I was wondering –'

I predicted how this sentence was going to end so made a pre-emptive strike. 'You know, I have always wanted to be able to dance but this leg of mine gives me so much trouble. It takes me all my time to get up the stairs at County Hall. An old rugby accident, a nasty break, never been quite right, you know. I have to have an operation when they can fit me in.'

'My mother always told me to beware of people with operations,' she replied moving closer. 'They always want to show you their scars.'

'Well, I certainly don't!' I snapped, taking another reverse step. Not much room, I hazarded, before my back would be up against the door.

'The County Ball is not an occasion for wild jigs and rowdy reels. The dancing is very often slow and stately – like the "Anniversary Waltz" – where couples move slowly together around the floor in each other's arms. I should imagine that you need to exercise your leg.'

'About the guidelines, Mrs Savage . . .'

'It's quite a wonderful occasion, the County Ball. The highlight of the year. Exquisite food, beautiful music, everybody who is anybody will be there.'

Well, I certainly won't, I thought to myself.

'I used to go every year to the County Ball when Conrad was alive.'

'Conrad?'

'My dear departed. You knew I was a widow, didn't you, Gervase? That I live all on my own. You live alone, don't you?'

'I do yes but I like living alone. I really like living alone. I do enjoy the peace and quiet after a hard day's work.'

'We had such a short time together.'

'Who did?'

'Conrad and I – before his untimely death.'

'I'm very sorry,' I said.

'He didn't suffer.'

'I'm glad but about the guidelines –'

'Now, Gervase, I was wondering if you might like –'

I made a second pre-emptive strike. 'My goodness!' I suddenly exclaimed, pulling at the door, 'I quite forgot. I said I was meeting Sidney Clamp a little after six and just look at the time. I must make tracks.' Before she could answer I gabbled on. 'I'll collect the guidelines another time. Must rush. Bye!' and made as fast an exit as I could.

*

'Could you ask Mrs Savage to send over the draft copy of the spelling guidelines?' I asked Julie the next morning before sallying forth into schools.

'She left a note asking you to call over for them.'

'Yes, I saw it, but I haven't the time today, I'm afraid.'

'Well you could pop over now. The Annexe is on your way out. It isn't at the other side of the world, you know.'

'Julie, I have not the time to go over now. I have just said. Please give Mrs Savage a ring and ask her to send them over.'

'Shall I ask her to drop them in to you here?'

'No!' I snapped.

'I don't blame you not wanting to enter the spider's parlour, Gervase,' commented David looking up from his work. 'I gather she has taken quite a shine to you. Connie was commenting how well you two get on and I heard Mrs Savage singing your praises to Dr Gore, about how well you relate to each other. I believe the term she used was "clicked". Thank goodness this little fly is too old and crusty to be of any interest to her. You do know she has a man-mad disposition, Mrs Savage, don't you? Had two husbands already so I am reliably informed.'

'Two!' I exclaimed. 'But she can't be more than forty.'

'A strikingly attractive woman, Mrs Savage,' added Stanley. 'Goes through husbands like a dose of salts. Always on the look out for an unattached man of adequate means and submissive personality so popular rumour would have it. I would watch out if I were you.'

'Well thank you very much for warning me, Stanley,' I said. 'As for my pen-portrait – "of adequate means and submissive personality" – that's highly flattering!'

'Shall I give Mrs Savage a ring,' asked Julie mischievously, 'and say you are popping over then?'

'No!' I exclaimed. 'And should Mrs Savage call, I am NOT in.' With that I left the office.

Over the next few weeks I avoided Mrs Savage sedulously. If I saw a glimpse of a red dress on the top corridor of County Hall I scurried into the gents'. If I heard a sharp voice emanating from a room I was passing, I hurried on like an Olympic walker. If I heard the click, clicking of high heels on the marble floor of the main corridor I shot behind a pillar. If the telephone rang I picked it up gingerly, hoping it wasn't the famous black widow herself. It was inevitable that we should meet again – and it was at Castlesnelling High School that our paths crossed.

I had been asked to write a report on the state of the library and had arrived at the school to be shown into a bare, cold, featureless room with a few ancient tomes and dog-eared textbooks scattered along the high wooden bookcases. The atmosphere carried a warm pervasive smell of dust, and the grey walls did not help. This was Castlesnelling High School library, the supposed central learning resource, the foundation of the curriculum, the place of academic study, reading and research. The books on the shelf bore witness to the fact that there had not been a full audit or clear-out of the old and inappropriate material for some time. There were books entitled *Wireless Studies for Beginners*, *Life in the Belgian Congo*, *Harmless Scientific Experiments for Girls*, and *Our King: George VI*. The newly-appointed Head of Library and Resources, Mr Townson, gestured with upturned hands as we surveyed the room.

'Well,' he said, 'you can see what needs doing.' He was a young, eager-faced, dapper man in his early thirties who was obviously keen to change things as soon as possible. 'The Head wants me to develop the library and has persuaded the

Governors to release some capital to improve things but I would be so grateful for any advice and support you could give.'

I wrote a full report with recommendations, secured some funding for improvements and, a few weeks later, returned to the school to deliver the good news that the county would refurbish the room and replace the furniture, help stock it with a good balance of appropriate and interesting texts suitable for teenagers and install some modern computers. I entered the library to find Mrs Savage in a powder-blue suit with shoulder pads which would not have disgraced an American footballer. She was firmly ensconced in the one easy chair, basking in a pale ray of sunlight which cut across the room and which made her earrings sparkle. Her eyes bulged with disapproval. My heart sank.

'Do you know Mrs Savage?' Mr Townson asked innocently.

'Yes, yes, indeed,' I replied. 'Good morning.'

She gave me a cold look, the look of a woman spurned, and nodded. 'Good morning, Mr Phinn,' she replied. Her voice sounded hollow and distant.

'Brenda has been so very helpful,' explained the Head of Library and Resources enthusiastically. 'We've been re-vamping the school library prospectus and various other documents. She's been a real gem.' He turned and smiled warmly at the seated figure.

'It's nice to be appreciated,' she commented caustically. 'Quite often people take you for granted.' She caught my eye with an icy glance. I felt it politic not to say anything.

'Mrs Savage is helping me to sort out the library,' continued Mr Townson.

Mrs Savage made a sort of humming noise before looking at her watch, as if entirely bored by this conversation.

'If it's not convenient,' I began, 'I can call –'

'No, no!' snapped Mrs Savage rising to her feet. 'I was about to go.' She swept for the door but turned on her high heels. 'I will be in touch, Simon,' she said sweetly. Then she nodded in my direction before saying in an icy voice, 'Goodbye, *Mister* Phinn.' Then she was gone and I inwardly gave a great sigh of relief.

'An absolutely delightful woman,' enthused the young Mr Townson rubbing his hands. 'She's been so supportive and sympathetic. Cannot do enough for me.'

I ran my finger along a shelf on which were a number of books on the art of ballroom dancing.

'Do you dance by any chance, Mr Townson?' I asked casually, plucking a tome from the shelf.

'Yes, I do, as a matter of fact. Why?'

'Oh nothing,' I replied. 'Nothing at all.'

22

It was Thursday and I was thankful the end of a dreadful
week was in sight. Problem after problem, pressure after
pressure, had risen their ugly heads one after the other. On
Monday Dr Gore had asked the whereabouts of a committee
report I had promised to write, and which I had completely
forgotten about, and Harold Yeats had left a note on my
desk saying he was still awaiting answers to a number of
important queries. My attempts to respond were dashed
when an overworked and overstressed headteacher had
poured out his woes over the telephone and I had agreed
to call in and be of what help I could. In his room, later in
the day, I spilt a cup of coffee over the chair, the carpet,
the coffee table and the school secretary.

On Tuesday, the course which I had carefully planned
and directed for thirty teachers had not been the roaring
success I had hoped it would be, judging by the appraisal
sheets. The various comments – 'quite interesting', 'of some
use', 'helpful handouts' and 'satisfactory' – damned me with
faint praise. On Wednesday I had a dreadful toothache, a
difficult school visit and Mrs Savage had telephoned three
times asking me to return some papers she had sent to me
to look over. It was now Thursday and I still had letters to
write, the summer term's courses to plan, reports to complete and three schools to visit. In addition, that evening I
had agreed to talk to a group of parents about reading
development.

I was feeling weary, full of the troubles of the world and very sorry for myself, therefore, when I arrived at the first school that morning. A small boy, of about seven or eight, stood in the entrance hall feeding a tank full of tropical fish.

'Hello,' he said brightly.

'Hello,' I replied.

'I'm the fish monitor.'

'Yes, I can see,' I said peering into the tank at the colourful creatures scooping up the floating food with open mouths. 'What sort are they?'

'Hermaphrodites.'

'Pardon?'

'Hermaphrodites. They're neither one thing nor t'other.' There followed a small lecture on the life of the fish. 'I do the frogs and toads as well,' he added. 'We've got a tank down here where they live. You can have a look if you like. We collected the frogspawn from the pond last weekend. We'll hatch it out and look after the tadpoles until they've grown into frogs big enough to fend for themselves. You see, when they've just turned from being tadpoles into little frogs and toads they're . . . now, what's the word miss said . . . er?'

'Tiny?' I suggested.

'No, no.'

'Weak?'

'No, no.'

'Delicate?'

'Vulnerable, that's what they are, vulnerable.'

'Yes of course,' I replied, 'vulnerable.' I was feeling pretty vulnerable by this time.

'You see, hundreds of tadpoles hatch out and most get eaten by fish or birds and the weaker ones die.'

'Well, that can't be helped, I suppose.'

'Unless it's a maternity toad. Now you take the maternity toad. That's a funny creature and no mistake. She keeps her tadpoles in her mouth where they are safe and sound. Normally frogs and toads don't do that but inside the maternity toad's mouth the tadpoles are protected. She's got a really big mouth that she can blow out, sort of inflate like this.' He puffed out his cheeks to demonstrate. 'I've got a picture of the maternity toad if you want to see it.'

'So she keeps all her tadpoles in her mouth, does she? It must be uncomfortable for her but I suppose they are safe from any harm.'

'Aye,' said the little boy and then added with a short laugh, 'unless, of course, she sneezes!' He continued to chatter on as he checked the temperature of the water.

'I think your mother's got a little chatterbox at home,' I said.

'Oh no,' he cried, 'my little brother's got asthma, so we aren't allowed to have pets.'

'Would you take me to the Headteacher's room, please,' I said, smiling for the first time that day. 'Mrs Sevens is expecting me.' When we arrived at the room the Head-teacher emerged to greet me.

'Miss, I think your dad's here.' The little boy waved a grubby hand at me and departed to feed the frogs and toads.

That evening I was billed to speak to parents at a primary school where eighty per cent of the pupils were from ethnic minority homes. It was an inner-city school of red brick, sprawling, flat roofed and surrounded by busy roads, tower-blocks and row after row of long terraced housing. Inside, however, it was gleaming and welcoming, and the children's backgrounds, religions and cultures were celebrated in the drawings and pictures, the colourful range of writing and the careful displays of artefacts.

All through my talk a most attentive young woman of Asian origin smiled from the front row and as I was packing up my books and papers she approached me.

'Do you remember me, Mr Phinn?' she asked.

'I'm afraid, I don't,' I replied. 'I meet so many people and have such a poor memory for faces, I'm afraid.'

'My name is Rahila Hussain. You used to teach me.'

There have been a number of occasions when young men or women have approached me in the street or in a school, a shop or a library with the words: 'You used to teach me, Mr Phinn,' and then they would reminisce about their times at school, recalling lessons and incidents I had long since forgotten.

'I used to teach you, did I? You will have to jog this memory of mine. I am trying to place you.'

'I came from Pakistan without a word of English when I was fifteen. You taught me English.'

'Well, I think I did a pretty good job, Rahila, listening to you now.'

'You did an *excellent* job and I shall always remember your lessons. I passed just one exam at the end of my schooldays and it was English. All those extra lessons of yours paid off.'

'Well, that's wonderful,' I replied. 'It's lovely to see you, and thank you for coming to listen to me speak.'

'You used to teach several pupils who couldn't speak much English and those who needed extra help, every Wednesday and Thursday lunchtimes, in the school library.'

'I remember now,' I said. 'You were in the same group as Jamuna and Jason.'

'That's right.'

I had met Jamuna several years after she had left school when I had been a patient at the Rotherwood General

Hospital. I had been asked to take all my clothes off, was given a square of tissue paper for modesty's sake and told to wait for the doctor in a small examination room. A smart, efficient-looking sister had entered to take my details and as our eyes met there was instant recognition.

'Hello, Mr Phinn. Do you remember me? You were my teacher.' It was Jamuna. She extended her hand for me to shake – but I declined, smiling weakly.

I had met Jason again just before moving to North Yorkshire. I was coming out of the post office in Doncaster town centre one cold, overcast Saturday morning when a tall, fair-haired young man as broad as a barn door, blocked my path. 'Now then, Mester Phinn!' he had shouted in a loud, friendly voice. 'How tha' doin'?'

'I'm doing very well, thank you,' I had replied.

'Tha' dun't remember me, does tha'?'

'I'm afraid not. I meet so many . . .'

'Tha' used to teach me.' When he saw no recognition on my face he had continued, 'I reckon thas'll remember me when I tell thee my name. Once taught, never forgotten. Jason Batty, that's me.'

'Ah,' I had said. 'Yes, I do remember you, Jason.'

He had chuckled. 'I thought tha' would. I were a bit of a rogue, weren't I?'

'Well, yes, you were, but a likeable rogue. More of a rascal really, Jason.'

'Aye, well, I reckon you and t'rest of t'staff 'ad yer 'ands full wi' me and no mistake. I were a bit of a tearaway. You were all reight though, Mester Phinn. You were strict but fair and you were all reight. I never did get mi 'ead round old Shakespeare but I did enjoy them English lessons. It were that French teacher, Mrs Faraday, I had trouble wi'. "Batty by name and batty by nature," she used to say. I din't like that. She din't have much time for us "thickies". She used to say what were t'point of teaching French to groups like us. She used to say we wunt mek much of us lives. I don't think she liked kids very much. She were allus shoutin'. She had this gret big bowl o' plastic fruit on her desk. She'd hold up an apple and ask, "*Que'est-ce que c'est?*" and we were supposed to shout back, "*C'est une pomme.*" Then she'd pick up a pear and ask, "*Qu'est-ce que c'est?*" and we'd shout back, "*C'est une poire.*" Once, she had this reight big plastic banana in her hand. "*Qu'est-ce que c'est?*" she asked but caught sight o' me talking at t'back o' classroom. She let fly wi' that plastic banana. It flew straight through t'air like a missile and 'it me straight between eyes, ricocheted off mi forehead and flew back to her like a boomerang. She put up her 'and and caught it. All t'class jumped to their feet and give her a standing ovation. She went ballistic! I din't learn much wi' that Mrs Faraday.'

'Well, you seem to have remembered quite a bit of French, by the sound of it, Jason.'

'Nay, Mester Phinn, I learnt a bit o' French after I'd left school. I do a bit of importin' and exportin' – fruit and veg, you know. I go over to France quite a bit. I've picked up a bit o' the lingo. I mean, you have to, don't ya?'

'So you're a greengrocer then, Jason?'

'Aye, in a manner o' speakin'. I've six market stalls. "Batty's High Class Fruit and Vegetables". Started wi' one stall in t'outdoor market and built up ovver t'last few years. I 'ave twenty folk workin' for me now.'

'You've done really well. I'm really pleased for you.'

At this point, drops of rain had begun to fall.

'It's goin' to chuck it down in a minute, by the looks of it,' Jason said staring at the grey sky. 'Are you in yer car, Mester Phinn, or can I give you a lift?'

'I did actually come into town on the bus and it's very kind of you to offer me a lift but I live just outside the town on the Doncaster Road. I guess it's too far out of your way.'

'Nay, not a bit of it, Mester Phinn, I can go that way. You must come round one evening. I live in King's Wooton. You can't miss our house. It's that big stone un. Used to be t'vicarage. Got a nice bit o' land at back.'

I made my way to a small van parked nearby, but Jason called me back. 'Nay, nay, Mester Phinn, I'm not in t'van.' He had opened the door of a new, brilliant white, shining sports car with gleaming chrome, great fins on the back and tinted windows. My astonishment must have shown. 'I can see that tha' thinking, "What's a gret big bloke like him doin' driving a piddling little car like that?" Well, I'll tell thee. Wife's got t'big car today, so I've got 'ers. Come on, Mester Phinn, before tha' gets soakin' wet.'

I remembered Jason with affection – and admiration because he was obviously well-established on the fast track.

'There were about ten or eleven of us,' continued Rahila now. 'Sadhu, Javaid, Popinder, Thomas, Jason, Balvinder, Jamuna, Larchvinder, Kim, Florence and myself.'

'Yes, that's right, I remember now.'

'Once you were angry with us for not doing our homework. You asked how did we expect to learn English unless we were prepared to put some time and effort in and to practise using the language. It was at the end of the lesson I remember when Jamuna asked you to try writing a few words in Nepalese, and Sadhu showed you how a Sikh would write. Javaid wrote you a sentence in Urdu, and Kim in Cantonese. We then looked at some Arabic script – all very, very different from English.'

The memory of those lessons came back as she talked. I had been a young English teacher, in my very first year in the profession, with little understanding or appreciation of the linguistic skills of those multi-lingual pupils of mine, of how exceptionally difficult it must have been for them to grasp a writing system so very different from their own and how incredibly well they had managed, in such a short time, to cope with this tricky and troublesome English language I was trying to teach them. It had been a humbling and salutary experience to see the range of different languages before me that day.

'It was the only time you shouted at us, Mr Phinn, so don't look so glum. You didn't make a habit of it. We all of us knew that you gave up a lot of your time to help us and we were very grateful. You were a really good teacher and we loved your lessons.'

'Thank you very much, Rahila. What a nice thing to say. Comments like that make the job of teaching very worthwhile.' I could feel a lump in my throat so changed the subject. 'So you have children of your own now, and they attend this school?'

'Oh no, I'm not married,' she replied. 'Believe it or not, I'm a teacher in charge of English.'

As I drove home later that evening, the week had ceased to be so dreadful after all and the problems and pressure which had risen their ugly heads one after the other, were forgotten as I remembered those pupils I had taught so many years ago. The memories had reminded me why I had come into education and why those who teach the young take on the most satisfying, challenging, and perhaps the most important role in society.

23

'Lord Marrick is keen to have a county inspector along with him on this visit, Gervase,' explained Dr Gore over the telephone. 'He takes his responsibility as Vice-Chairman of the Education Committee very seriously.'

'It will be a pleasure to accompany him, Dr Gore,' I replied.

'Good, good. You should be very flattered. He asked particularly for you. You must have made quite an impression.'

I collected Lord Marrick from the Small Committee Room at County Hall as arranged. We left the bustle of the market town, the crowded streets, the grumbling noise of the traffic, and headed for the open country. We were soon in the awesome world of the Dales, and the dusty acrid smells of the town were replaced by the sharp freshness of spring. I drove along the twisting empty road, past grey farmhouses and cottages, trees displaying their bright new leaves, long hedgerows of twisted hawthorn, the May blossom not yet out, and fields dotted with sheep and their new-born lambs.

Lord Marrick took a long contemplative breath. 'The best place in the world, Mr Phinn. The best place in the world. "Oh to be in England now that spring is here,"' he slightly misquoted, and then looked at me sideways. 'I can be quite poetic when I want to be, you know. I'm not the blunt old buffer many people take me to be.'

'I am sure you're not, Lord Marrick,' I replied.

We had an appointment at Pope Pius X Roman Catholic Primary School in the small market town of Ribsdyke, deep in the heart of the Dales. Lord Marrick, apart from being Vice-Chairman of the Education Committee, had recently been appointed an LEA representative governor. He explained that he had asked particularly for a paired visit with an inspector 'to compare notes' while he learned something about the life and work of the small school. He had visited the school once before but, despite his short acquaintance with the place, he was fiercely defensive of it and made his views known before we clambered from the car.

'I think this is a cracking good school, Mr Phinn. But I look forward to having your opinions. Your school inspector's eyes may see it in an entirely different light.'

Pope Pius X Roman Catholic Primary School was a long, sombre, featureless edifice, built just after the last war and resembling an army barracks. The walls were dark pebbledash, the windows small, the roof was flat. It looked such an uninspiring, utilitarian sort of building, so unlike the small, solid, stone-built Victorian village schools of the Dales with their high windows and patterned slated roofs or the high and imposing polished red-brick schools in the larger towns.

Had the architect who had designed this construction ever considered the needs of children? I thought to myself. Did he not realize how an attractive, spacious and bright building can make such a difference in their education? Obviously not. Perhaps the stumbling block had been money. Many a post-war Catholic school had been built on a shoestring, as a result of the efforts of the parish priest and the small Catholic community who saved long and hard for a school of their own.

The Headteacher and her staff had tried valiantly to create a warm and welcoming atmosphere in the entrance hall. There were colourful books displayed and photographs of the smiling children, there were paintings and poems, arrangements of bright flowers and a parents' notice board but the plain dark doors, cold stone steps with tubular metal banisters, pale yellow walls and the faint but distinctive smell of disinfectant and floor polish reminded me of a hospital rather than a school.

Mrs Callaghan, the Headteacher, was a handsome woman with bright eyes and light sandy hair tied back to reveal a finely-structured face. As she watched us approach the school entrance, her expression took on the look of an explorer who has just caught sight of the ocean after weeks in the desert. Her smile was wide and welcoming.

'It's so nice to see you both,' she said in a friendly voice. 'We are all expecting you.'

We were taken on a tour of the school. Mrs Callaghan stopped at each classroom to tell us about the 'dedicated teachers' and the 'lovely children' within, before ushering us inside and introducing us. The children were busy, interested and clearly enjoyed the various activities. I heard them read, looked in their books, tested them on their number work and asked many questions while Lord Marrick discussed the school budget with the Headteacher. I liked the atmosphere of the school.

When we arrived at the small library I spotted a girl, about nine or ten years of age, tapping away industriously at the computer. Lord Marrick and the Headteacher were busy in discussion about problems with the fabric of the building and examining some hairline cracks on the yellow walls, so I approached the child.

'Hello,' I said brightly.

The little girl looked up and beamed. Her hair was raven-black and she had the bluest eyes I had ever seen — large, open, honest eyes, with long, dark lashes.

'How you doin'?' she asked in the lightest of Irish lilts.

'I'm doing all right,' I replied. 'And how about you?'

'I'm doin' fine. I'm composing a poem about horses. Do you want to see it?'

Lord Marrick's ears pricked up like those of one of his hunters when he heard the word 'horses', and he joined us.

'Horses, eh?' He peered at the computer screen. 'That's very good, very good indeed. When you've finished composing your poem, young lady, perhaps you'd write it out neatly and let me have a copy. I'll pop it on the wall in my study.'

'If you wait one moment, I'll give you a print out,' she replied with a tilt of the head and a disarming smile.

We were moving away when the small girl took Mrs Callaghan's hand and whispered, 'It's still there, Miss — in the girls' toilets.'

'Is it, Bernadette?' replied the Headteacher calmly.

'It is so and it's got bigger.'

'Well, I shouldn't worry about it too much. It won't hurt you.'

'But it's got great curved claws and gigantic jagged jaws and it's turned a mouldy green.'

Mrs Callaghan smiled. 'It can't harm you, Bernadette.'

'But, Miss, it puts the very fear of God into me every time I looks at it.'

'Well don't look at it then.'

'Sure aren't your eyes just drawn to it?'

I could not restrain myself. 'What is it?' I asked, fascinated by this exchange.

'Sure isn't it a monster, a great, dark, green, frightening

251

monster with popping eyes and sharp teeth,' said the girl without seeming to draw breath.

'A monster!' I exclaimed.

'In the girls' toilets,' she added.

'A monster in the toilets?' I repeated.

She patted my arm. 'Sure it's not a real monster,' she chuckled. 'It's a great dark stain from water leaking through the roof but it gives me the shivers right enough just to look at it.'

The Headteacher explained that the flat roof always leaked after heavy rain and that the water had left a ugly stain on the walls of the girls' toilets. It had grown in size.

'Is it a very bad leak?' asked Lord Marrick.

Before Mrs Callaghan could respond, the small girl piped up: 'A bad leak? Sure it'd baptize you!'

Bernadette was from a travellers' family. She had moved around in the white caravan for most of her young life, attended a range of different schools and this had developed in her a great confidence and an outgoing and lively personality. She was a clever child with an astute grasp of life, a vivid imagination and a great gift for conversation.

'She must have kissed the Blarney Stone a good few times,' confided Mrs Callaghan. 'Bernadette could talk the hind legs off a donkey.'

The tour ended with a scrutiny of the dark stain in the girls' toilet.

'I must admit,' I said, staring at the dark outline, 'it does look rather like a monster.'

'It may look like a monster, Mr Phinn,' spluttered Lord Marrick, 'but it can't be doing the kiddies any good, can it? These flat roofs are the very devil.'

'They are indeed,' agreed Mrs Callaghan. 'One section is repaired after one dousing of heavy rain and then the leaks appear in another part of the roof the next downpour. It's one repair after another.'

'I must check to see what the Education Department is doing about it,' said Lord Marrick briskly. 'The governors, from what I have read of the minutes of their meetings, have brought the poor state of the fabric to the attention of the Premises and Maintenance Department on a number of occasions, and still the school has leaks and cracks and I don't know what! Children cannot be expected to work in a damp, unattractive environment. Don't you agree, Mr Phinn?' Before I could reply, he continued. 'Well, I am determined to get things *done*.' He fixed me with a stern eye. 'I mean, Mr Phinn, aren't you inspectors supposed to comment on the poor state of buildings and the effects upon the children's education?'

Mrs Callaghan came to my rescue. 'To be honest, Lord Marrick, I think everything is being done that can. Mr Davies from Premises and Maintenance has been really very helpful. He always seems to be here. We joke about giving him an office here, he's that frequent a visitor.'

'It's no joking matter, Mrs Callaghan,' said Lord Marrick staring at the ceiling and shaking his head.

'No, it's not, I agree,' replied the Headteacher. 'It's just that one problem follows another and if I didn't smile, Lord Marrick, I think I would weep. Last winter it was the faulty boiler, then the dreadful condensation. Then the cracks appeared down the walls in the hall and in the corridors. Then we discovered the exterior wood facings were rotting and found rising damp in Reception. I really can't fault the support and help Mr Davies has given me but the problems just seem endless.'

'Well this Mr Davies doesn't appear to be all that effective judging from the state of the premises,' growled Lord

Marrick. 'It seems to me that the whole place wants pulling down and re-building. I'll give Dr Gore a ring to see if we can't do something about it. I mean, this thing wants sorting out once and for all.'

In the Headteacher's room later, during the morning break, we discussed the school curriculum, looked together at the various policies and guidelines, and studied the reading and mathematics test results. Mrs Callaghan's smile was now rather a nervous one as she asked, 'I hope everything is in order?'

'Most certainly. I think this is a cracking good school, Mrs Callaghan,' I said, choosing Lord Marrick's earlier phrase. 'The teachers work hard, the children are well-behaved and achieve good results and you manage the school extremely well.'

The broad smile returned and she sighed in satisfaction.

Lord Marrick nodded in agreement, his eyes twinkling: 'Couldn't have put it better myself.' Then he added with a louring look at me: 'And I take it you are going to mention the flat roof, the rising damp, the condensation, the cracks and the leak!'

Following a knock on the door and the Headteacher's call to 'Come in,' the school secretary entered pushing a trolley on which were china cups and saucers, a large teapot and an array of biscuits. Behind her was Bernadette, clutching a sheet of paper.

'I have my poem about the horse,' she said. 'I've printed it out and done a little drawing.' She passed it to Lord Marrick who read it, nodding and smiling.

'Splendid! Splendid! Thank you very much, my dear, I shall treasure it. Now just you sign your name at the bottom.'

As she did so, Mrs Callaghan poured the tea and passed the cups around.

'Now this is what I call a cup of tea, Mrs Callaghan,' remarked Lord Marrick staring at the rich, dark-brown liquid. 'I cannot abide weak tea. You know my grandmother, the old dowager, lived until her one hundred and first birthday she did. She always insisted the tea was good and strong. She would shout out in fury if it wasn't. She used to say it had to be so strong that she could stand a spoon up in it.'

The Headteacher was just on the point of replying when Bernadette, passing the signed poem to Lord Marrick, piped up, 'My mother's just the same, so she is,' she nodded folding her arms across her chest, 'but not quite as old. She likes her tea so strong you could trot a mouse across it.'

That evening, at home in my small, dark, dank flat, and with a glass of Irish whiskey in my hand, I thought about Bernadette. Her facility with language was much more than an ability 'to talk the hind legs off a donkey'. She had a real and natural gift for oral language, a rich, persuasive, entertaining way of speaking so typical of the Irish. Hers was the language of Jonathan Swift and Oliver Goldsmith, W. B. Yeats and George Bernard Shaw, Oscar Wilde and James Joyce.

Some weeks later I met Lord Marrick again when we literally bumped into each other in a corridor at County Hall. He was striding along lustily in my direction as I, trying to balance two large box files full of papers, was not looking where I was going. We collided.

'Hello, Mr Phinn,' he said cheerily. His face was brown and the great walrus moustache and shock of hair looked bleached.

'Hello, Lord Marrick,' I replied. 'You look as if you've been on holiday.'

'Rome!' he snapped. 'I've been to the "eternal city" and we had lovely weather. I went to receive a knighthood from the Pope for services to education. Now then, young man, what do you think about that?' Before I could answer he continued. 'You are now looking at a Knight of the Order of St Sylvester, a rare honour, particularly for a non-Catholic.' He lowered his voice before confiding, 'The uniform's a bit over the top for me, mind you – bright red and black with a big cocked hat and ceremonial sword. I'm a lot happier in my tweeds, to be honest. But, as you can see, I am as pleased as Punch.'

'Many congratulations,' I said and shook his hand. 'Mrs Callaghan and the children will be celebrating, I'm sure. I bet they'd like to see you in the cocked hat.'

'Yes, it was a memorable occasion, truly memorable. I shall never forget the moment when the Pope entered. His Holiness walked very slowly towards me and gently took my hand, shook it lightly and gave a slight smile and then, in perfect English, he asked me.'

'Asked you what?' I enquired when Lord Marrick stopped speaking.

'He asked me if they'd fixed the leaking roof at Pope Pius X Roman Catholic Primary School, Ribsdyke yet.'

24

'Oh no!' cried Harold looking up from the memorandum he was reading. 'It's the Fettlesham Show in a month. That is something I could well do without.'

'Why?' I asked innocently. 'It sounds really interesting. I've seen it advertised in every shop and post office in the county so it must be a pretty big affair. I thought I might spend a Saturday –'

'Dear, oh dear,' sighed Harold, clearly not listening to a word I was saying. 'It completely slipped my mind. The Fettlesham Show! Next month! Dear, oh dear!'

'Harold!' I said in a loud voice. 'What is so terribly upsetting about the Fettlesham Show?'

'What is so terribly upsetting about the Fettlesham Show?' replied my colleague repeating my words with slow deliberation, 'is that I have to spend all day Saturday manning the County Education Tent, answering numerous questions, sorting out intractable problems, giving advice on all manner of things and listening to interminable descriptions about little Johnny who can't read very well and little Janet who has difficulties with her number work. It's an endless, exhausting, frustrating and thoroughly tiresome business – that is what is so terribly upsetting about the Fettlesham Show, or, as the posters say, the Fine Fettlesham Show.'

'Oh,' I mumbled.

Harold, now getting into his stride, pushed out his chin and gripped the edge of his desk. 'There is usually a heated altercation outside the Education Tent, which inevitably involves me, between the supporters of comprehensive education who berate me about the grammar schools and those who are in favour of grammar schools who berate me about the comprehensives. Last year the public school lobby got in on the act. It was a nightmare. It is something I could well do without.' He rested his large head in his great cupped hands and sighed sadly.

'From the posters, I thought it was an agricultural show – horses, hounds, show jumping, dog competitions – that sort of thing? How does education come into it?'

'It is, it is an agricultural show but there are all sorts of other things – displays and exhibitions, trade stands and information tents, arts and crafts demonstrations.'

'It sounds really interesting. I might just go.'

Harold looked up, pushed a wad of papers across the desk, thought for a moment and then took a deep breath. 'The word "might" does not come into it, Gervase. You *will* be going.'

'Pardon?'

'You'll be attending the Fettlesham Show, along with the other inspectors.'

'I will?'

'You will. You have been assigned your own little job.'

'I have?' I exclaimed.

'Yes, indeed. Sidney will be adjudicating the Art Competition, David organizing the children's sports and you will be judging the Poetry Competition. Dr Gore, in his wisdom, has volunteered our services. Hard luck. For the last few years they have had some local poet, Philomena Phillpots or somebody or other, and very popular by all accounts. She writes about the countryside and the birds and animals. She's into trees and daffodils and little frisking lambs. Wordsworth sort of thing. Anyway, this year she says she can't do it for some reason or another, so you have been dragooned into judging. I gather hundreds and hundreds of children submit their poems, just about now if I'm not mistaken, and it will be your job to select the best five to go forward to the final judging.'

'I'm surely not expected to read hundreds and hundreds of children's poems, am I?' I exclaimed, horrified at the prospect.

'But I thought you liked poetry, Gervase,' simpered Harold with a twinkle in his large eyes and a wry smile on his wide generous mouth. 'You are forever quoting verse and going into raptures about the wonderful poems the children write.'

'I do like poetry, but I just haven't the time to read hundreds of poems. Not in the next few weeks, anyway.'

'Don't worry, Gervase,' Harold reassured me. 'You judge the final shortlist of poems. The organizers do all the preliminary reading and come up with the best ten. The poems, if my memory serves me right, are always about rabbits caught in traps, sheep giving birth, faithful collie dogs, haymaking, the thrill of foxhunting, and cows – lots and lots of poems about cows, so you don't need to worry about the themes. You just turn up on the Saturday of the show, judge the poems, say a few words, smile pleasantly and present the book tokens and rosettes to the five prizewinners. It's a job with minimal duties and a very pleasant and uneventful day out, I should imagine. It is yours truly who has all the hassle and harassment, trouble and vexation in the Education Tent!'

The Saturday of the show was sunny and windless. Beneath the cloudless blue sky, large white marquees and coloured tents were scattered across the wide open field. The showground was a hive of activity. People were preening dogs, grooming horses, brushing sheep and washing cattle. Others were arranging cakes and plates of biscuits on long trestle tables, or putting the final touches to amazing floral creations. In one corner of the field, potters, artists, farriers, saddlers, blacksmiths, cordwainers and a host of other crafts-people were showing how to weave baskets, mould clay figures, build dry-stone walls, shoe horses, make corn dollies and fashion leather. It was a mass of colour and activity.

'I'll see you at the Refreshment Tent at two o'clock,' said Harold, 'and I will treat you to lunch. You should be finished judging by then – it's pretty straightforward. Then, in the afternoon, you can join me in the Education Tent.'

POETRY COMPETITION THIS WAY announced the large printed notice. Some wit had scrawled underneath, 'So come on in and have a nice day!' Inside, the tent was crowded, stuffy and noisy. I peered in every direction until I spotted a dumpy, vigorous, red-faced woman with a bay window of a bust and a powerful stare. She wore thick spectacles and a flowerpot hat and sported a large badge with 'steward' written in gold across it.

'I'm the judge,' I said to her.

'You're the what?' she snapped.

'Gervase Phinn, the judge of the Poetry Competition.'

'Oh, the adjudicator, 'bout time too. Given you up for lost. I've got Mrs Williams searching the showground for you. We were going to put you on the loudspeakers.'

'I was told to report at ten o'clock –' I began.

'Never mind, you're here now,' she retorted. 'I'm Joan Pickersgill. The final ten poems have been selected. We've got some really, really lovely efforts this year so your task won't be easy. Now I've mounted the ones you have to look at on the large boards around the edge of the marquee. You need to pick five out of the ten and then place them in reverse order.' I glanced at the boards. Some of the poems were handwritten in a thin spidery style, others printed in bold capitals. Some were word-processed and several were decorated with little coloured drawings and patterns.

'Is this him?' barked a lean, middle-aged woman with dark, narrow eyes, as she pushed her way through the crowd. She was dressed in a dark green waxed jacket and thick tartan headscarf and carried a vicious-looking shooting-stick with a spike at the end.

'He arrived just after you went looking for him, Myra,' replied Mrs Pickersgill.

'Are you Mr Chinn?' yapped the lean woman.

'Phinn,' I corrected.

'What?' she snapped.

'Phinn. My name is Phinn.'

'Is it? I was told your name was Gerald Chinn. I thought you must be some Eastern poet. I was looking all over for a Chinaman.'

'It's Gervase Phinn,' I said. 'And I'm the County School Inspector for English and Drama, and I was told to report at ten o'clock –'

'School inspector, are you? I thought you were a poet?'

'I am a poet but my –'

'Well, we are looking for the best poem not the best handwriting or spellings, you know.'

'Yes, I appreciate that,' I replied.

'I didn't know he was an inspector, did you, Joan?'

'I didn't,' replied her companion. 'I thought he was a poet.' She turned in my direction. 'You won't frighten the children, will you?'

'No,' I sighed, 'I won't frighten the children.'

'We usually have Philomena Phillpots, the Dales poetess,' said Mrs Pickersgill. 'Wonderful, wonderful writer. Have you come across her?'

'No, I can't say that I have.'

'Well, she's very popular, very popular indeed, and has published poems, you know,' added Mrs Williams. 'Proper published poems. You can't open a woman's magazine without seeing one of Philomena Phillpot's poems, can you, Myra? And she does the insides of birthday cards as well.'

'Does she really?' I replied, wishing I was in the Education Tent with Harold. Anything was better than this.

'She writes poems people can understand,' said the lean woman. 'None of these airy-fairy poems without any rhyme nor reason. Lots of lovely descriptions.'

'Really.' I was getting a sinking feeling in the pit of my stomach. Things, I thought to myself, might not be quite as straightforward as I had anticipated.

'Now, this is the way we do it, Mr Phinn,' said Mrs Pickersgill, referring to her clipboard. 'It goes like clockwork if we stick to the proper agreed routine. Any deviation from the proper agreed routine, Mr Phinn,' she warned, staring through the thick lenses of her glasses, 'will result in the sort of chaos we had a few years ago when some journalist or other presented the prizes. He *would* do things in his own way and as a result there was mayhem. I have an idea he had spent quite a time prior to the judging in the Beer Tent. I could certainly smell alcohol on his breath but that's beside the point.'

'That was one of the reasons why we moved the judging from the afternoon to the morning,' added Myra. I continued to listen to the martinet barking out her orders of the day and explaining in great detail the programme of events. The children would assemble at ten-thirty – all ten finalists – and stand next to their poems. I would then move from one to another, read the poem and have a little chat with the young poet ('not too long or it will take all day'). Then I would say a few words to the children and parents about the high standard of entry and the lovely poems that I had read. Finally I would announce the winners in reverse order and present the rosettes and the book tokens. 'Is that clear?' she snapped.

'Crystal,' I replied bluntly.

'Jolly good, then you can tootle off and browse around the poems, have a quick preliminary read and I will collect you when the judging is about to commence.'

The ten poems ranged from the exceptional to the pretty ordinary so I satisfied myself that this would be an easy task after all. I had already selected the five I considered to be the best; the final judging was merely a formality. Or so I thought. When the time came for me to do the circuit of the tent, Mrs Pickersgill's booming voice came through the loudspeakers.

'Attention! Attention everybody! The poetry judging is about to commence!' The atmosphere changed. The noise subsided, there was a hushed silence and I could feel all eyes upon me. The first poem was of inferior quality and extended over three pages in the same rhyming doggerel. It started:

> All over the land it began to snow,
> Up on the hills and way down below,
> Away from the town where the lights did glow,
> Away from the wood where there lived a crow.
> I did not like the crow, oh no,
> But I liked playing in the snow.

'You have obviously put a great deal of time and effort into this poem,' I told the tall, serious-looking girl who stood next to her composition. She peered at me, solemn and unsmiling and without answering. 'And do you like writing poetry?' She continued to stare impassively.

'She made up all the rhymes herself,' said a red-faced little woman with very dark button eyes. 'Every one.' I smiled and moved on.

The next poem was clearly lifted from 'The Lake Isle of Innisfree'. It began:

> I will arise and go now,
> And go to Fettlesham,
> And a small house I'll build there
> Of stone and of cement.
> And I will have a pond there
> And a hive for the honey bees
> And live alone in the Yorkshire Dales.

'Did you write this poem yourself?' I asked a cheerful-looking youngster with a tangle of ginger curls and a freckled face.

'Oh yes, mester,' he replied firmly. 'Definitely wrote it myself.'

'It's just that it reminds me of a poem I have read before – a poem by W. B. Yeats. Do you know it?'

'Never heard of it,' replied the youngster smiling innocently.

'It is very like a poem called "The Lake Isle of Innisfree",' I persisted.

'This Yeats must have got the idea from our Sam,' interposed an angry-looking man with a face the colour and texture of a walnut. I moved on.

I thought of Marianne, the little farming girl I had met

at Hawksrill School, and our conversation about her sheep when I read the third trite little verse. I wondered what that daughter of the Dales, that expert on sheep and lambing, would have made of the mawkish piece mounted on the board and surrounded by little jumping, cartoon lambs and fluffy white sheep:

> On their fresh, green grassy banks
> The little lambs are at their pranks,
> Here the little lambkins bleat,
> See them jump on woolly feet.
> Oh what joy those lambkins bring
> To the world when it is Spring.

If these poems were considered the best, what on earth were the others like, I thought.

Next to the poem stood a tall woman with waist-length, sandy-coloured hair and wearing a long flowered print dress. She stared fixedly at me as if waiting for some kind of recognition. Next to her was a miniature version of her: a tall, gaunt-looking girl of about eleven with waist-length sandy-coloured hair and also attired in a long flowered print dress.

'Do you live on a farm?' I asked the little poet.

'No,' she replied sullenly.

'What made you write a poem about lambs?'

'Don't know,' she answered in the same tone of voice.

'Are they your favourite animals?'

'No.'

I persevered. 'Did you see some lambs in a field perhaps and that gave you the idea for your poem?'

'No.'

I was getting nowhere so, having smiled weakly at mother

and daughter, and receiving a pair of cold glances in return, moved on. As I read the poems and asked questions of the little poets, I was conscious of the onlookers watching, listening, hanging on my every word. I finally came to the very last of the ten. It was written in the bold, confident handwriting of a small child and was quite clearly the best – the most truthful and the most arresting:

> I love my grannie.
> She has hair like silver,
> And skin like gold,
> Eyes like emeralds,
> And teeth like pearls.
> She is a very precious person.
> My grannie calls me
> Her little treasure,
> But she is mine.
> And I love her very much.

'What did your grannie say when you showed her your poem?' I asked the small girl who stood in front of her writing.

She smiled. 'She said I wouldn't get much for her if I tried to sell her.'

I chuckled and proceeded to ask the little girl a series of questions about her poem. She answered all my enquiries easily and I had no misgivings that this was her own, unaided work.

I had now completed the circuit and had the five winners fixed in my mind beyond any question of doubt. I stepped out confidently into the middle of the throng, referred to my notes and took a deep breath to announce the results. Before I could utter a word, however, Mrs Pickersgill trotted towards me in short jerky movements as if powered by a faulty battery and guided, or rather propelled me, towards a small dais.

'Mr Phinn, the Chief Inspector, will now announce the winners of the Poetry Competition – in reverse order!' she boomed.

'Ladies and gentlemen, boys and girls,' I began, 'it gives me great pleasure to announce the winners of the Poetry Competition. I must say that it has been an extremely difficult task to select just five from the many excellent poems which I have read and enjoyed this morning. All the children have tried extremely hard and produced some very high quality verse. I know you will want to join me in giving them a hearty round of applause.' There was a ripple of lukewarm hand-clapping.

'I wish he'd get on with it!' said the red-faced little woman with the dark button eyes in a loud whisper.

'And so, without further ado, these are the winning poems. In reverse order: the fifth prize goes to Simon Wilmot for his poem, "Shep, my Faithful Collie".' There was a slight ripple of applause. 'Fourth prize goes to Jenny Butterfield for her lovely verse "Harvest Time". Third prize to Debbie Smith for her poem "Milking the Cow" and the second prize to Andrew Baxter for "Forest Flowers".' There was a series of light clapping. 'And the first prize, for a really gentle and carefully written piece of verse, goes to Amy Tunnicliffe for her delightful poem about her grannie.'

The announcement was greeted with one or two slow measured claps and an assortment of grunts, whispers and tut-tutting. By the time I had presented the rosettes, the book tokens and shaken the prize-winners' hands, the crowd had dispersed. A few people, mainly parents of the competitors, remained behind mumbling and shaking their heads.

'Not a popular choice,' announced Mrs Pickersgill,

peering through her thick lenses. I had had just about enough of Mrs Pickersgill.

'It may not be the most popular choice, Mrs Pickersgill,' I retorted, 'but in my considered opinion the poem is far and away the best.'

'It doesn't rhyme though, and is on the short side,' she growled.

'The quality of a poem doesn't depend on its length any more than on its rhymes.'

'Philomena Phillpots, the Dales poetess, felt that a piece of writing wasn't a poem unless it rhymed.'

'Well, I would beg to differ with Philomena Phillpots, the Dales poetess.'

'But she has had her poems published,' persisted Mrs Pickersgill, clearly unimpressed and unconvinced by my argument. 'She has poems on the inside of birthday cards!'

'Yes, well, perhaps next year, Mrs Pickersgill, you might feel it more appropriate to ask Philomena Phillpots, the Dales poetess, to judge the competition. To be honest, listening to your obvious admiration for her I would have thought she would have been here this year.'

'Oh, but she is,' cried Mrs Pickersgill quite undaunted by the sharpness in my voice. 'It's just that she couldn't judge the poems because her daughter Pollyanna submitted an entry. She had to declare an interest.' She gestured with a sweep of the hand to two figures with waist-length sandy-coloured hair and both wearing long flowered print dresses. They glared across the tent at me. 'It was Pollyanna's poem about the lovely little lambkins.'

For the remainder of the afternoon I tried to enjoy myself but as I moved from stall to stall, event to event, I kept hearing mention of the result of the Poetry Competition wherever I went.

'You tell me what a policeman knows about poetry. They had a chief inspector judging this year! They should be out catching criminals not judging poetry!'

'He must know the mother, that's all I can think. I mean, it didn't even rhyme.'

'He wasn't a patch on Philomena Phillpots. Now she's a *proper* poet.'

'This is supposed to be an agricultural show and what poem wins – one about a grannie! I ask you!'

'That poem about the cow brought tears to my eyes. That should have won.'

As I headed for the Education Tent to seek out Harold, I caught sight of Lord Marrick, sporting a large straw fedora hat. He had seen me too, and was striding towards me.

'Now then, Gervase!' he boomed. 'Come and let me buy you a drink, then I'll show you Caesar, my prize Belgian blue. He's just won the silver cup for best bull at the show. I'm as pleased as Punch.' Before I could argue, his arm was through mine and we were heading for the Beer Tent. When I emerged a good hour later, feeling much more at peace with the world, I bumped into Harold who was just making his way into the tent. He was looking extremely hot and flustered, and was clearly ready for some cooling refreshment.

'Ah, Gervase!' he gasped, taking my arm. 'I'm panting for a stiff drink. You will not believe the time I've had.'

'But, Harold—' I tried to explain, but to no avail.

It was nearly three o'clock when I finally extracted myself from the Beer Tent and as I left, somewhat unsteady on my feet, who should I walk slap into but Mrs Pickersgill and her lean companion. They stood observing me with displeasure. I smiled warmly as I passed them, and caught a snippet of their conversation.

'I just knew he'd been drinking,' snorted Mrs Pickersgill. 'No better than that newspaperman last time.'

'I thought he smelt like a brewery when he came into the tent,' replied her companion. 'Probably had difficulty reading the poems through that cloud of alcohol, never mind judging them.'

25

It was July, and I was staring out of the window of Back-watersthwaite Primary School, remembering my very first visit. As a newly-appointed county inspector, I was unused to the small rural schools, hidden from the world, and had searched for hours for that elusive place. Since I had arrived so late, all the children had gone home and I had only met the remarkable headteacher, Mr Lapping. He had courteously invited me to return soon after so I could meet the children.

The big window drew me like a magnet because the view from it was so stunning. A great rolling expanse stretched along the yawning valley to the far away purple moors. The peaty waters of the beck raced and spurned, glistening in the bright sunlight. A grey snake of a road twisted and turned through dark green fields full of grazing sheep. Birdsong joined the honeyed hum of summer. As I stood there now, gazing at the wonderful landscape, a small boy, his round polished face peppered with freckles, joined me.

'Does tha know owt abaat silage then, mester?' he asked. I admitted my ignorance and the child departed shaking his head and, almost as an aside, remarked to an equally healthy-looking companion, 'Off-comed-un!'

I have been called this a number of times on my visits to schools – off-comed-un – someone from out of the dale, a foreigner, and I always smile when I hear the phrase.

Later that morning I came upon the same boy, Andrew. He was sitting by the window poring over his book, his brow furrowed in concentration. As I approached he closed the book and placed a hand firmly on top.

'May I look at your work?' I asked, smiling.

'No,' came the blunt reply.

'Why not?' I asked.

'Because it's not any good, that's why. When Mr Lapping says, "Today, we are doing writing", I don't feel all that well. I have problems with me writing, you see. Me spelling's not up to much and me handwriting's all over t'place.'

'I'd still like to see,' I said.

'Well, tha not.' He kept a firm hand over his book so I could not verify his comments. 'Can't read reight well, either,' he added. 'I have trouble wi' words.'

'I see,' I replied gently.

'I've got what's called special educational needs, tha knows.'

'And what does that mean?' I asked.

'Not much good at owt.'

'Everyone's good at something,' I said.

He just shook his head in a resigned sort of way and stared out of the window to the distant hills.

'Tha not from round 'ere then?' he asked.

'No, I'm from the other side of the dale.'

'Aye, I thowt you were an off-comed-un.'

'Yes, an off-comed-un,' I repeated.

'Are tha married?' He was nothing if not forthright.

'No.'

'Cooartin'?'

'Yes,' I replied, thinking about my dinner date with Christine that very evening. 'I'm cooartin'.' I hoped, by changing the subject, I might eventually prevail upon him to show me his work and answer a few questions so I asked, 'Where do you live?'

'Reight up theer.' He pointed through the window to the far off hills. 'I live on a farm up theer – at t'top of t'dale.'

'What a lucky boy you are,' I murmured. 'You must have one of the finest views in the world.'

'It's all reight,' he said in a matter-of-fact voice. 'What time were you up this mornin' then, mester?'

'Early,' I replied. 'Half past six.'

'I was up at six helpin' me dad deliver a calf.'

'Really?'

'And it were dead. It would've been a good milker an' all, wide solid rear and good udder texture. We got ratchet on –'

'Ratchet?' I interrupted.

'Aye, you put yer ratchet up against cow, it's a sort of metal gadget like. Yer tie yer ropes round yer calf's back legs and yer turn yer ratchet every time there's a contraction. Helping cow along a bit.' He paused. 'Does tha know what a contraction is?'

'I do,' I replied.

'Aye, it were dead all reight. So we've 'ad a month of it, I can tell thee,' continued Andrew, fixing his eyes on a flock of sheep meandering between the grey limestone walls. He sighed and was quiet for a moment. 'Them's ours,' he then remarked casually, 'them sheep. We've got an 'undred yows and two jocks.'

'Jocks?' I asked. 'Are they Scottish sheep?'

He shook his head and dusty mop of hair. 'No, no, jocks are rams, moor sheep. Does tha know why we has all them yows and only the two jocks?'

'Yes,' I replied smiling, 'I think so.'

'Bought another from Fettlesham t'market last week. It'd

only been wi' us three days and it dropped down dead – even before it had done any tuppin',' he continued. 'Me dad were none too pleased.' He paused fractionally and gave a low whistle between his teeth. 'Does tha know what tuppin' means?'

'Yes,' I replied.

'We'd trouble week afore wi' oggits.'

'Hoggits? Little pigs?' I ventured.

He shook his head again. 'No, no, your 'oggits are sheep of an age between your lamb and your ewe. Sort of teenage sheep. Does tha know what a drape is?'

'No, I don't,' I replied. Then added in a whisper, 'When it comes to sheep, I have special educational needs, tha knows.'

He looked at me thoughtfully and a smile formed on his lips for the first time that morning. 'I don't know owt abaat that but tha're an off-comed-un and no mistake.'

'I am,' I admitted. Then, like a sensitive and patient teacher, the child who was 'nowt much good at owt', who 'had trouble wi' words' invited the off-comed-un, the school inspector who had his own 'special educational needs', into his world of hoggits and shearlings, stots and stirks, wethers and tups, tegs and hogs, becoming animated as he realized the extent of his companion's ignorance, surprised that there were people who couldn't tell a Blue-faced Leicester from a Texel or a Masham from a Swaledale.

'We've a sheepdog what's going blind and t'last straw were this calf. It would've been a reight good milker an' all.'

'I'm sorry to hear about all your troubles.' My reply sounded feeble.

'Me dad's got a word for it.' At that point I felt it wise to move on but he reassured me. 'Oh it's not rude. It's a word which describes a yow when she's heavy pregnant, so heavy you see, she falls over on her back and just can't move, she's helpless. Sticks her legs in t'air and just can't shift. It's called "rigged", proper word is "riggwelted". Me dad comes in from t'fields and flops on t'settee and says, "I'm fair riggwelted." '

At the end of a busy morning inspecting Backwaters-thwaite school, I went and found Mr Lapping to bid him farewell and a restful summer holiday.

'Thank you indeed,' he replied, 'and I hope you have a pleasant break yourself. Now tell me, has your first year as a school inspector been as you expected?'

'In many ways, yes,' I replied, 'but I've still got a lot to learn and there's been a good few surprises for me over the year – most of them very pleasant surprises. And it's been exhausting. I don't think I've ever worked so hard. I'm really looking forward to the long summer break because I have to admit to being somewhat "riggwelted".'

'Ah-ha!' laughed Mr Lapping. 'Something tells me you've been talking to young Andrew.'

Although, as is the way of the Dales folk, I expect I will always be considered an 'off-comed-un', I do feel such a part of the great county and have learnt so much about it from the many children and teachers, parents and colleagues that I have met on my travels. I know about the birds and wild animals (the unstuffed variety), the farming methods and the weather, the dialect and folklore, the history and geography and the people who inhabit a county the size of Israel. In that short time I have come to regard the Yorkshire Dales with that same deep sense of wonder and reverence as Lord Marrick does, and have come to love the warmth of spirit, kindness and courage of the Dales folk and their shrewd, down-to-earth insight into human nature.

On that bright summer day close to the end of term, I looked across the fresh flowing green of the fells, beyond the old stone farmhouses crouching against the lower slopes to the hazy blue of the sky, and sighed with contentment. The profession of school inspector is not a glamorous or particularly well-paid one, but I knew in my heart it was the job for me. I thought of the dedicated teachers it had been my privilege to advise and encourage over the past months. I thought of the delightful, unpredictable and ever-friendly children it had been my pleasure to meet. I thought of the talented and supportive colleagues who had such a deep interest in the needs of children however damaged, ill-favoured or deprived those children might be. And I thought of one very special Yorkshire lass who I intended to get to know a whole lot better in the coming months.

A Child of the Dales

From the classroom window rolled the great expanse of
    the Dale.
The sad child in the corner stared out like a rabbit in a
    trap.
'He has special needs,' explained the teacher, in a hushed,
    maternal voice.
'Real problems with his reading, and his number work is
    weak.
Spelling non-existent, writing poor. He rarely speaks.
He's one of the less able in the school.'

The lad could not describe the beauty that surrounded him,
The soft green dale and craggy hills.
He could not spell the names
Of those mysterious places which he knew so well.
But he could tickle a trout, ride a horse,
Repair a fence and dig a dyke,
Drive a tractor, plough a field,
Milk a cow and lamb a ewe,
Name a bird by a faded feather,
Smell the seasons and predict the weather.
Yes, that less able child could do all those things.

GERVASE PHINN

OVER HILL AND DALE

'Miss, who's that funny man at the back of the classroom?'

So begins school inspector Gervase Phinn's second year among the frankly spoken pupils of North Yorkshire. He finds himself confronting Mr Swan, whose hunger for his lunch exceeds his appetite for English; unwittingly plays the stooge to Mrs Peterson's class of juniors, and is alarmingly disarmed by a pupil unsure whether he is learning French or German.

But Gervase is far from daunted. He is still in pursuit of the lovely headteacher of Winnery Nook School, Christine Bentley; he is ready to brave the steely glare of the officious Mrs Savage, and even feels up to helping Dr Gore organize a gathering of the Feofees – just as soon as someone tells him what they are.

This is a delectable second helping of hilarious tales from the man who has been dubbed 'the James Herriot of schools'. It will have you laughing out loud.

HEAD OVER HEELS IN THE DALES

'Could you tell me how to spell sex, please?'

Gervase Phinn thought he'd heard just about everything in his two years as a schools inspector, but a surprising enquiry from an angelic six-year-old reminds him never to take children for granted.

This year, however, he has more important things on his mind besides schools. His impending marriage to Christine Bentley, the prettiest headteacher for miles around, finding themselves somewhere to live in the idyllic Yorkshire Dales, and the chance of promotion, all generate their fair share of excitement, aided and abetted as usual by his colleagues in the Inspectors' office. But it's in the classroom where Gervase faces his greatest challenge – keeping a straight face as teachers and children alike conspire to have him – and us – laughing out loud.

GERVASE PHINN

UP AND DOWN IN THE DALES

Now in his fourth year as an Inspector for English in the Yorkshire Dales, Gervase Phinn still relishes visiting the schools – whether an inner-city comprehensive fraught with difficulties or a small Dales primary school where the main danger is one of closure. With endless good humour, he copes with the little surprises that occur round every corner.

Some things never change, however: Mrs Savage roars, Connie rants, and Gervase's colleagues in the office play verbal ping-pong. But all this can be put behind him each day when he returns home to his lovely wife Christine, who is expecting their first baby. One day, their child will surely take the limelight in the local primary school where the children's contrived innocence never fails to win over even the hardest heart.

THE HEART OF THE DALES

Awkward teachers, pompous school governors and fearsome lollipop ladies might make Gervase Phinn's job as a Yorkshire school inspector difficult – but, as always, the frankly spoken children prove his real challenge.

However, the new school year doesn't get off to the best start when a teacher suggests that Gervase has let him and his school down. Called up in front of his new boss, the formidable Miss de la Mare, Gervase fears he's in hot water. To add to his woes, he is given a 'little job', which means liaising with the infuriating Mrs Savage – the bane of the inspectors' lives.

Meanwhile, away from schools, Gervase's family life is blissful – until some noises in the attic start to disturb his nights...

He just wanted a decent book to read ...

Not too much to ask, is it? It was in 1935 when Allen Lane, Managing Director of Bodley Head Publishers, stood on a platform at Exeter railway station looking for something good to read on his journey back to London. His choice was limited to popular magazines and poor-quality paperbacks – the same choice faced every day by the vast majority of readers, few of whom could afford hardbacks. Lane's disappointment and subsequent anger at the range of books generally available led him to found a company – and change the world.

'We believed in the existence in this country of a vast reading public for intelligent books at a low price, and staked everything on it'
Sir Allen Lane, 1902–1970, founder of Penguin Books

The quality paperback had arrived – and not just in bookshops. Lane was adamant that his Penguins should appear in chain stores and tobacconists, and should cost no more than a packet of cigarettes.

Reading habits (and cigarette prices) have changed since 1935, but Penguin still believes in publishing the best books for everybody to enjoy. We still believe that good design costs no more than bad design, and we still believe that quality books published passionately and responsibly make the world a better place.

So wherever you see the little bird – whether it's on a piece of prize-winning literary fiction or a celebrity autobiography, political tour de force or historical masterpiece, a serial-killer thriller, reference book, world classic or a piece of pure escapism – you can bet that it represents the very best that the genre has to offer.

Whatever you like to read – trust Penguin.